THE ECONOMIES OF SOUTHEAST ASIA

THE CONQUEST OF THE ATLANTIC

The Economies of Southeast Asia

The Growth and Development of ASEAN Economies

Jose L. Tongzon

Senior Lecturer in Economics, National University of Singapore, Singapore

Edward Elgar

Cheltenham, UK · Northampton, MA, USA

Published by
Edward Elgar Publishing Limited
8 Lansdown Place
Cheltenham
Glos GL50 2HU
UK

Edward Elgar Publishing, Inc.
6 Market Street
Northampton
Massachusetts 01060
USA

A catalogue record for this book
is available from the British Library

Library of Congress Cataloguing in Publication Data
Tongzon, Jose L., 1951–
    The economies of Southeast Asia : the growth and development of
ASEAN economies / Jose L. Tongzon.
    Includes bibliographical references.
    1. Asia, Southeastern—Economic conditions. 2. Asia.
Southeastern—Economic integration. I. Title.
HC441. T663   1998
330.959—dc21   97–38250
                                                                        CIP

ISBN 1 85898 264 2

Printed and bound in Great Britain by
MPG Books Ltd, Bodmin, Cornwall

Contents

v

Figures

Tables

Preface and acknowledgements

The main objective of this book is to analyse the economic development experiences of the member countries of the Association of Southeast Asian Nations (ASEAN) in the context of ASEAN economic cooperation. It also discusses other issues of concern to ASEAN such as corporate development, ASEAN growing economic interdependence, prospects for and challenges associated with the establishment of an ASEAN Free Trade Area, economic implications of ASEAN membership enlargement and environmental implications of ASEAN continued industrialization and growth.

To my knowledge, no single book deals with all of the above issues. These issues are usually discussed in various articles and sources. Thus, those who wish to understand the process of ASEAN economic development and the role of ASEAN economic cooperation in a comprehensive and systematic manner have to consult a number of references scattered in the chapters of numerous books and professional journals.

This book emerges out of the need to provide a textbook or a main reference for a course on ASEAN economies or for similar courses offered in other universities. However, this book must also be of interest to anyone interested in development economics in general and in the ASEAN economies in particular. To keep pace with current developments in ASEAN economic performance and cooperation, this book must be updated regularly, or whenever necessary, to reflect new developments and issues affecting the ASEAN economies.

I wish to express my gratitude to the National University of Singapore for the resources made available to me while writing this book and to my colleagues, in particular Dr Peter Wilson, who made very valuable comments on Chapter 2 of this book. Last, but not least, I would like to dedicate this work to the very important persons in my life who are my great source of inspiration and encouragement: my loving wife, Mai, whose understanding has lightened the burden of writing this manuscript, my lovable and sweet daughter, Joy Victoria, who has brought joy and meaning into my life and of course my dear parents, Tatay and Nanay, who have given me life and without whose love and guidance I would not have been where I am.

Overview

The Association of Southeast Asian Nations (ASEAN) has been one of the fastest growing regional groupings in the world.[1] For instance, for the period of 1987 to 1992 the growth rates of the ASEAN5 (Indonesia, Malaysia, the Philippines, Singapore and Thailand) had averaged 7.3 percent. This average growth rate was well above that posted by the developed market economies (2.8 percent) as a group; above that achieved by North America (2.5 percent) and generally above the world growth rate (2.2 percent).

As a result of their high growth rates, their standards of living, as measured by their per capita incomes and other quality of life indicators, have vastly improved. Over the same period the per capita income of the ASEAN5 countries grew on average by 5.1 percent, although the individual country experiences varied with Thailand posting a remarkable growth of 8.3 percent, followed by Singapore (6.4 percent). The Philippines, because of its numerous economic and political problems in the 1980s, only managed to grow in per capita terms by less than 1 percent during the same period. But overall they have graduated from the ranks of low income countries, as classified by the World Bank, to the ranks of middle and in some cases upper-middle income countries. Singapore in particular has the highest per capita income among the five ASEAN countries and had attained the advanced developing country status by 1996. Malaysia is well on its way to becoming one, while Indonesia and Thailand are deemed to be on the threshold of significant economic transformation, and the Philippines is experiencing a robust economic recovery. Accompanying this spectacular growth is a significant structural change, poverty alleviation and improved level of income distribution. This economic success and dynamism is expected to continue into the rest of the 1990s.

What did the ASEAN countries do to achieve this remarkable growth and economic development? What factors account for their differences in economic development experiences? Explaining their economic growth and development has been the subject of many empirical studies. All these studies point to a number of factors such as high saving rates, massive inflow of foreign capital, export-oriented industrialization policies, political and economic stability and others. How are these factors interrelated? What are the underlying factors behind their economic success?

To what extent has this economic success been attributable to ASEAN economic cooperation? If so, what kind of cooperation? The issue of ASEAN cooperation requires formal analysis in the light of many years of attempts to forge regional cooperation among the ASEAN countries. It has been argued that, although intra-ASEAN trade has not been particularly significant, there has been peace and security in the ASEAN region largely due to the growing mutual trust, understanding and cooperative efforts of these countries. This socio-political environment has allowed the market forces to work effectively and, with the export-oriented development strategies adopted, has contributed to the spectacular economic performances of these countries. Despite their varied stages of economic development and differences in development priorities, they were successful in forging economic cooperation not only in various productive sectors but also in their dealings with their traditional trading partners. By developing common positions and a united stance in their negotiations with the US, Japan, the European Union (EU), Australia and other developing countries on matters of market access, investments and security, they have strengthened their bargaining power and have made the ASEAN countries a significant force in international fora.

In the midst of a rapidly changing international environment what future challenges and opportunities are the ASEAN countries likely to face? Will the ASEAN cooperation and solidarity evolve into a higher level? What opportunities and challenges do Vietnam and Myanmar's admission into ASEAN present? How can the ASEAN countries achieve sustainable growth and development?

In the process of deregulation and trade cooperation among themselves, have the ASEAN economies become more integrated? Are they becoming less integrated with their traditional trade and investment partners such as the US and Japan?

This book attempts to answer all these questions while tracing the economic development experiences of the ASEAN5 (the founding members of ASEAN) in the context of their economic development aspirations. As a useful background to the formation of this regional grouping, Chapter 1 explains the evolution of regional cooperation in Southeast Asia and ASEAN'S institutional structure. Chapter 2 proceeds with a review of the structural changes occurring in the ASEAN economies during the period of high economic growth. After a general assessment of their remarkable economic success, Chapter 3 examines the extent to which their economic development experience has been attributable to ASEAN cooperation. Four major sectors are selected for more detailed analysis: trade, manufacturing, agriculture, and services.

Chapter 4 takes a closer look at sub-regional cooperation within ASEAN in the form of economic growth triangles. Chapter 5 discusses in detail the role of government in ASEAN. Chapter 6 examines ASEAN external economic relations, particularly with their major export markets in the US, Japan and the EU, and their newly emerging markets of China and Vietnam in bilateral contexts. Chapter 7 evaluates the implications of other regional trading arrangements (RTAs) for ASEAN. Chapter 8 looks at the issue of regionalism as an approach to achieve a global free trade and the role of the World Trade Organization. Chapter 9 examines further the role of foreign investments in ASEAN economic development. Chapter 10 evaluates the prospects and future of ASEAN economic cooperation. Chapter 11 explores the economic and political implications of Vietnam and Myanmar's admission into ASEAN. Chapter 12 investigates the issue of ASEAN economic interdependence and Chapter 13 looks at the role of domestic capital in ASEAN economic growth and explores the impact of growth on their environment and the various measures to deal with it.

Notes

1. ASEAN in this study consists of Indonesia, Malaysia, the Philippines, Singapore, Thailand, Brunei (which has joined the grouping since 1984) and Vietnam, the most recent member which joined the grouping in July, 1995. Due to insufficient data on Brunei and Vietnam, the focus is on the five original members of ASEAN (ASEAN5). However, an attempt is made to give the most comprehensive coverage as data availability permits.

   The spectacular growth of ASEAN is part of the overall phenomenal rise of the East Asian economies. Today, the nominal share of East Asia in world output is comparable with North America and Europe (EU-15), when in 1980 its nominal share was only about half of North America or Europe (*The Straits Times*, 9 October 1996, p. 38).

PART ONE

ASEAN ECONOMIC DEVELOPMENT AND COOPERATION

1 Evolution of ASEAN cooperation and institutional structure

On August 8, 1967 in Bangkok, the Association of Southeast Asian Nations (ASEAN) was born. Its formation, however, and the level of commitment it requires of its members did not occur without any difficulties. It went through a painful process of transcending differences (in linguistic, religious, historical and economic backgrounds) and of working towards compromises. Reflecting the evolution of ASEAN cooperation is its concomitant institutional structure. Its present institutional machinery is a product, to a large extent, of the ASEAN determination to enhance ASEAN political and economic cooperation, reflecting its changing vision and objectives. Since 1967 it has gone through some modifications in an attempt to provide an institutional environment supportive of greater ASEAN cooperation.

1.1 Pre-ASEAN organizations

Before the formation of the Association of Southeast Asian Nations (ASEAN) in 1967, there were few attempts at developing forms of regional cooperation in response to certain political and economic events. These pre-ASEAN organizations have a pronounced bearing on ASEAN's formation and development.

1.1.1 SEATO (1954–1977)

The Southeast Asian Treaty Organization (SEATO) emerged out of a conference in Manila in 1954 which was held shortly after the Geneva Conference on Indochina following the victory of the Viet Minh over the French colonizers. Initiated by the US and dominated by Western powers (only the Philippines and Thailand were full members from Southeast Asia), this was part of the worldwide US-led system of anti-communist military alliances or security arrangements. SEATO elicited criticisms not only from the Soviet Union and China, but also from the non-communist countries of Southeast Asia including Indonesia. With the military withdrawal of the US military forces from Vietnam, SEATO came to an end in 1977.

1.1.2   ASPAC (1966–1973)

Organized in 1966 at the initiative of South Korea, Asian and Pacific Council (ASPAC) was another major example of a multi-regional organization designed to bring together most of the leading non-communist nations of the Western Pacific to deal with external threats and to provide a framework for more widespread cooperation. Only four of its members were Southeast Asian states – Malaysia, the Philippines, South Vietnam and Thailand. Indonesia refused to join. ASPAC was dissolved in 1973.

1.1.3   ASA (30.07.61–16.09.63)

As a first attempt by countries of Southeast Asia to form a regional cooperation, Association of Southeast Asia (ASA) was formed on 30 July 1961 at the instigation by the former Prime Minister of Malaya, Tunku Abdul Rahman in 1959, with very limited membership (Malaya, the Philippines and Thailand) and a set of economic objectives (that is, to promote cooperation in economic and cultural areas). This was later dissolved on 16 September 1963 with the formation of the Federation of Malaysia comprising Malaya, Sabah, Sarawak and Singapore. The Philippines, which had a long-standing claim on Sabah, did not recognize the enlarged Federation. Further, it did not get any support from Indonesia under the regime of the late President Sukarno who was against the formation of the Federation of Malaysia.

1.1.4   MAPHILINDO (31.07.63–16.09.63)

As a rival organization to ASA, this organization, consisting of Malaya, the Philippines and Indonesia, was established at a conference held in Manila on 31 July 1963 to promote cooperation in economic, military, cultural and social fields and primarily designed for the welfare of the Melayu region in Southeast Asia. It was shortlived, being just over a month old when the Federation of Malaysia came into being. Neither the Philippines nor Indonesia recognized the new Federation, and Sukarno soon launched a guerilla war against Malaysia which led to a bitter and sometimes bloody confrontation. This lasted until Sukarno's fall in 1967. MAPHILINDO did not get support from non-Malay members of the region as it was perceived to be for the promotion of the Melayu region.

Thus, the early attempts failed due to nationalism, lack of mutual trust and regional identity, territorial claims and conflicting perceptions of the regional political order.

1.2 Formation of ASEAN

The formation of ASEAN was officially opened at the signing of the Bangkok Declaration on August 8, 1967 by five countries: Indonesia, Malaysia, the Philippines, Singapore and Thailand. Brunei later joined the grouping in 1984. Political and economic considerations have influenced these countries to form a regional cooperation. All the signatory countries saw the need to foster their economic development and promote regional security in the face of a growing communist threat in Southeast Asia, precipitated by the fall of Indo-China to communism and the declared intention of the West to withdraw their military forces from the region. Their common objectives could be best achieved through mutual cooperation in the economic, social and cultural areas.

1.2.1 Overcoming obstacles

A number of obstacles were in the way of the formation of ASEAN and during the initial stages of development of the ASEAN cooperation. The countries had diverse colonial traditions and influences. The American colonization of the Philippines and the Dutch colonization of Indonesia produced legal and political systems in their respective economies quite diverse from those in Malaysia and Singapore which were colonized by the British. Only Thailand was not colonized by a foreign power. Further, their pre-independence and post-independence problems such as ethnic pluralism, communist insurgency and irredentism (for example, the Philippine claim on Sabah) have called for nationalism rather than regionalism.

There are also different economic priorities arising from their different stages of economic development and differences in factor endowments. Singapore was striving for full employment, and due to its small domestic market has been pursuing an export-oriented strategy with heavy reliance on foreign investments since its separation from the Federation of Malaysia. The other ASEAN countries, particularly Indonesia, the Philippines and Thailand, were slow in adopting an export-oriented strategy due to their relatively large domestic markets and inefficient agricultural sector.

Despite these obstacles, there were common grounds for regional cooperation. First, there was a realization that regional cooperation would confer economic benefits on member countries. Second, they realized that a common bargaining position and unified stance in their negotiations with the outside countries would make them a significant force in the international sphere and thus enable them to influence the outcome of multilateral negotiations. Third, the threat of growing protectionism and regionalization, as manifested in the formation of regional economic trade blocs and diminishing flows of capital to the developing countries, had made them more committed to regional cooperation. Fourth, from the political perspective the growing threat of communism, vulnerability to external powers and the need for physical security have bound the ASEAN countries under one group. Fifth, their geographical proximity and the importance of maritime trade, and finally the existence of quasi-authoritarian regimes and similarities in approach to development, have facilitated cooperation and coordination.

1.3　ASEAN institutional structure (1967–76)

During the first ten years of ASEAN existence (1967–76), the ASEAN organizational structure was based on the Bangkok Declaration of 1967 where the highest decision making body was the Annual Meeting of Foreign Ministers which met on a rotational basis in each of the ASEAN capitals. This grouping was responsible for policy formulation, coordination of activities and reviewing of recommendations from lower-level committees (see Figure 1.1).

The ongoing work of the Association between ministerial meetings was conducted by the Standing Committee, comprising the Foreign Minister of the host country as chairman, and the resident ambassadors of the other four ASEAN countries in that country. The seat of this committee, which was also on a rotational basis, conformed with the site of the next Annual Ministerial Meeting. This committee met several times a year and its Annual Report was submitted to the meeting of Foreign Ministers for adoption. It also reviewed recommendations from other lower-level committees before they were submitted for ministerial consideration.

The Standing Committee was an overseer of the three special committees created to handle the external relations of ASEAN. These were the Special Coordinating Committee of ASEAN Nations (SCCAN) created in 1972 to coordinate links with the European Community. This was reinforced by the establishment of the Joint Study Group in 1975 charged with the task of examining the substance and mechanism of cooperation between the two regional organizations. The other two committees handling external relations and coming under the purview of the Standing Committee were the ASEAN Brussels Committee (ABC) and the ASEAN Geneva Committee, made up of ASEAN representatives in Brussels and Geneva, respectively.

Preserving an element of continuity was a more permanent group of officials who were involved in the actual supervision of ASEAN's activities and the preparatory work of the Standing Committee including the

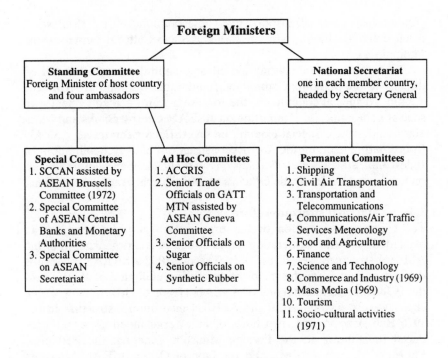

Foreign Ministers		

| **Standing Committee** Foreign Minister of host country and four ambassadors | | **National Secretariat** one in each member country, headed by Secretary General |

Special Committees	**Ad Hoc Committees**	**Permanent Committees**
1. SCCAN assisted by ASEAN Brussels Committee (1972) 2. Special Committee of ASEAN Central Banks and Monetary Authorities 3. Special Committee on ASEAN Secretariat	1. ACCRIS 2. Senior Trade Officials on GATT MTN assisted by ASEAN Geneva Committee 3. Senior Officials on Sugar 4. Senior Officials on Synthetic Rubber	1. Shipping 2. Civil Air Transportation 3. Transportation and Telecommunications 4. Communications/Air Traffic Services Meteorology 5. Food and Agriculture 6. Finance 7. Science and Technology 8. Commerce and Industry (1969) 9. Mass Media (1969) 10. Tourism 11. Socio-cultural activities (1971)

Source: ASEAN Secretariat (1978), *Ten years of ASEAN*, pp. 17–20.

Figure 1.1   Organization of ASEAN, 1967

screening of recommendations submitted by the various permanent and ad hoc committees. This group of officials were the Secretaries-General of the five ASEAN National Secretariats.

One important group that was invisible within the formal institutional structure of ASEAN was the Senior Officials Meeting. This committee of senior Foreign Ministry Officials (at Permanent Secretary level or its equivalent) was established by the ASEAN Ministerial Meeting in 1971 to discuss the implementation of the Zone of Peace, Freedom and Neutrality (ZOPFAN), and has now become a regular forum for intra-ASEAN political consultation.

There were 11 permanent committees of officials and experts in the pre-Bali summit years which worked on a range of ASEAN pro-grammes with their respective sites in brackets: Civil Air Transport (Singapore), Communications Air Traffic (Malaysia), Food and Agri-culture (Indonesia), Shipping (Thailand), Commerce and Industry (the Philippines), Finance (Malaysia), Mass Media (Malaysia), Tourism

(Indonesia), Land Transport and Telecommunications (Malaysia), Science and Technology (Indonesia), and Socio-Cultural Activities (the Philippines).

There were several special and ad hoc committees, which reported directly to the Standing Committee. In addition to the three previously mentioned special committees, the following were created to deal with special issues: Special Committee on ASEAN Central Banks and Monetary Authorities, Special Committee on ASEAN Secretariat, ASEAN Coordinating Committee for Reconstruction and Rehabilitation of Indo-China States, Senior Officials on Synthetic Rubber, Senior Officials on Sugar, and Senior Trade Officials on Multilateral Trade Negotiations.

1.4 Institutional structure before 1992
The changing orientation of the organization and the need for an expanded ASEAN cooperation led to attempts at reorganization of the ASEAN structure (see Figure 1.2). The pre-1992 ASEAN structure is derived mainly from the major restructuring endorsed at the time of the 1976 Bali summit meeting of ASEAN Heads of Government. Three changes were introduced in the ASEAN institutional structure in the 1976 Bali summit: first, two blocs of ministerial meetings were introduced in addition to the Foreign Ministers Meeting: the Economic Ministers Meeting (AEM), and the bloc of Other ASEAN Ministers (OAM), a general rubric which covers separate meetings of ASEAN Ministers of Labour, Social Welfare, Education, Information, Health, Environment, Energy, Science and Technology; second, the permanent and ad hoc committees of the pre-Bali period were regrouped into five economic and three non-economic committees; third, the establishment of an ASEAN Secretariat based in Jakarta and headed by its own Secretary General.

The ASEAN Economic Ministers were charged with the task of accelerating economic cooperation, and met annually to review various areas of economic cooperation and to consider the reports and recommendations. Among the ASEAN projects and areas of cooperation were the ASEAN Industrial Projects (AIP), industrial joint venture schemes (AIJV), industrial complementation schemes (AIC) and the Preferential Trading Arrangements (PTA). The ASEAN Economic Ministers were serviced by Senior Economic Officials Meeting (SEOM).

The Annual Meeting of ASEAN Foreign Ministers (AMM) formulated policy guidelines and coordinated all ASEAN activities. It also provided for the convening of the ASEAN Heads of Government Meeting, 'as and when necessary' to give overall directions to ASEAN. The Bali Conference was the first ASEAN Heads of Government

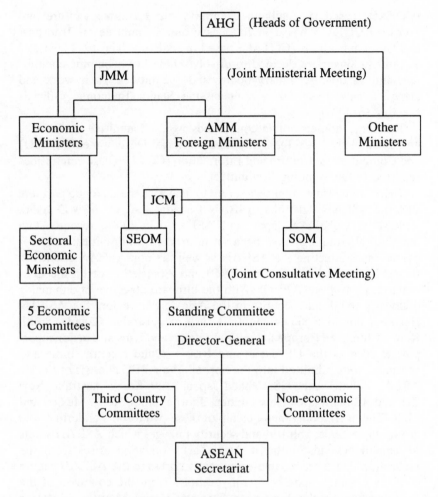

Source: Chng (1992) ASEAN Economic Cooperation for the 1990s, p. 92.

Figure 1.2   Pre-1992 ASEAN organizational structure

Meeting or Summit (1976), followed by the Second Summit in 1977. It took ten years before the Third Summit was held (1987). The fourth Summit was in 1992, and the fifth Summit was held in December, 1995.

The five economic committees, serviced by the interim technical secretariat, were: Committee on Trade and Tourism (COTT) based in Singapore; Committee on Industry, Minerals and Energy (COIME) based in the Philippines; Committee on Finance and Banking

(COFAB) based in Thailand; Committee on Food, Agriculture and Forestry (COFAF) based in Indonesia; and Committee on Transport and Communications (COTAC) based in Malaysia. The 1992 ASEAN Summit in Singapore decided to dissolve these five economic committees and all their subsidiary bodies and committees. Their work and activities have been taken over by the Senior Economic Officials Meeting (SEOM).

The three non-economic committees were: Committee on Science and Technology (COST), Committee on Social Development (COSD) and Committee on Culture and Information (COCI). These committees reported to the Standing Committee.

There were also committees set up to deal with the dialogue partners such the ASEAN–Australia, ASEAN–Canada, ASEAN–New Zealand, ASEAN–EU, ASEAN–Japan and ASEAN–US. Quite recently, two multilateral groupings have been set up to deal with political and economic issues affecting the ASEAN as well the non-ASEAN countries: the ASEAN Regional Forum (ARF) and Association of Pacific Economic Cooperation (APEC). With the ultimate objective of enhancing political stability and security in the Asia–Pacific region, the ASEAN Regional Forum includes countries such as Australia, Canada, South Korea, China, the European Union, Vietnam and Laos and major superpowers such as the US, Japan and Russia. Quite recently, India and Myanmar were admitted into the Forum. The APEC consists of the six ASEAN countries, the US, Canada, Japan, South Korea, Australia, New Zealand, China, Papua New Guinea, Taiwan, Hong Kong, Mexico and Chile. The overlapping membership of these two forums underlines the growing economic, political and security linkages which ASEAN wants to expand beyond Southeast Asia. This motivation arises from the realization that a sustainable economic progress in the ASEAN region crucially depends upon cooperative efforts from the countries of the Asia–Pacific. As the Singapore Foreign Affairs Minister Professor Jayakumar put it,

> while ASEAN can continue to play an instrumental role in forging predictability, it can not do so alone. The need for stability in the region is not just an ASEAN or even Asian concern. An unstable Asia–Pacific will have wide global repercussions.[1]

1.5 Existing institutional structure

The basic features of the pre-1992 ASEAN institutional structure are retained in the current structure, except for some reforms introduced since 1992 to streamline its organization, reduce the overlapping of functions and to make it more supportive of the ASEAN organization's new vision and objectives, as follows. First, the institutionalization of the ASEAN Heads of Government meeting, the ASEAN Summit. In 1992 the Fourth ASEAN Summit in Singapore decided that the ASEAN Heads of Government would meet formally every three years and informally at least once in between to lay down directions and initiatives for ASEAN activities. Second, the establishment of the AFTA Council to supervise, coordinate and review the implementation of the Common Effective Preferential Tariff (CEPT) scheme for ASEAN Free Trade Area (AFTA). Third, the five economic committees have been dissolved since 1992 and their functions taken over by the Senior Economic Officials Meeting.[2] Fourth, the ASEAN Secretariat's role has recently been strengthened to support the Summit's initiatives. The Protocol Amending the Agreement on the Establishment of the ASEAN Secretariat, signed at the 25th Annual Ministers Meeting in Manila in 1992, vested the Secretariat with an expanded set of functions and responsibilities to initiate, advise, coordinate and implement ASEAN activities. The Secretariat has been expanded from three to five Bureaus – General Affairs, Economic Cooperation, Functional Cooperation, ASEAN Cooperation Unit and Dialogue Relations, and the AFTA Unit – the last one established to support the Secretariat's role in assisting the implementation of AFTA.

The current ASEAN institutional structure reflects to some extent the nature and objectives of ASEAN. With more emphasis given to economic cooperation since the Bali Summit of 1976 and to meet the need for expanded ASEAN cooperative activities, the introduction of a separate ASEAN Economic Ministers structure, the establishment of a central ASEAN Secretariat and other changes were added to the original institutional structure. However, despite its changes, ASEAN's institutional structure is still based on a loosely-structured decentralized committee system geared to political consultation and consensus building. A policy of consensus based on a constructive, cautious and confidence-building approach is reflected in the absence of a supranational body that demands an all-embracing commitment from the member countries.

Suggestions for further reading
For a historical account of previous attempts at regional cooperation and the evolution of ASEAN institutional structure, read Sandhu et al. (eds) (1992), pp. xvii–xxii, 3–49, 50–82; and Saw Swee-Hock (1980, pp. 322–36). For more recent evaluation and prospects, read Chng (1992, pp. 91–105) and Tan (1996, pp. 4–22).

Notes

1. Taken from *The Straits Times*, 9 August 1994, p. 23.
2. The 1992 ASEAN Summit in Singapore decided to dissolve the five Economic Committees on Food, Agriculture and Forestry (COFAF), Finance and Banking (COFAB), Industry, Minerals and Energy (COIME), Transport and Communications (COTAC), and Trade and Tourism (COTT) and all their subsidiary bodies and committees. The work and activities of the five defunct economic committees and their subsidiary bodies have been taken over by the Senior Economic Officials Meeting (SEOM). SEOM reports to the AEM which meets at least once a year.

   The AEM oversees and provides policy guidance in the implementation of economic cooperation programmes and activities. The policy decisions of the Ministers are carried out, implemented and monitored by the SEOM, which are required to meet at least four times a year. In carrying out its functions and responsibilities, SEOM is supported by the strengthened ASEAN Secretariat which assists, among others, in coordinating, monitoring and implementing economic cooperation activities.

2 ASEAN economic development: an overview

Economic development in the current literature refers to a consistent rise in real per capita income accompanied by structural transformation, poverty alleviation and improved distribution of income. It is, therefore, more than just about economic growth. There are other equally important aspects to economic development such as high life expectancy, better educated workforce, quality of housing and health care, lower incidence of poverty and so on. It is, therefore, a multidimensional process involving physical and social transformation with the fruits of economic growth being widely shared.

This chapter attempts to explain the economic development performance of the ASEAN group of countries, focussing on the ASEAN5 (particularly the remarkable economic success achieved by Indonesia, Malaysia, Singapore and Thailand and the recent economic recovery of the Philippines).[1] Before doing so, however, it is useful to present first an overview of the ASEAN6 economies (that is, the ASEAN5 and Brunei) in terms of their common characteristics, economic strengths and weaknesses.

2.1 Overview of the ASEAN6 economies

2.1.1 Common characteristics
The ASEAN6 economies are highly diverse economically and socially (that is, in terms of size, historical background, resource endowments, stages of economic development, and culture). However, they have a number of common economic characteristics that can define ASEAN as an economic region. First, although the extent of government intervention varies among the ASEAN economies, they are all market-based economies. Second, they are all export-oriented with a high degree of export dependence. Third, they have common economic aspirations with a lot of emphasis placed on economic growth as they had generally a long history of underdevelopment, poverty and high unemployment. Fourth, except for Brunei and Singapore, their economies are dualistic where more than 50 percent of their population live in the agricultural and rural sector. These commonalities have bound them together in

their pursuit of greater economic development and improvement of the life of their respective constituents.

2.1.2 Economic strengths and weaknesses

The ASEAN economies differ in terms of economic strengths and weaknesses. Brunei has enjoyed political stability and is blessed with abundant oil and gas resources free from the problems associated with high population density and urban congestion. But Brunei, having the smallest population size and the second highest per capita income in ASEAN, relies heavily on its oil and natural gas reserves for export revenue. Although these resources have provided Brunei with a high and consistent flow of income for many years, they are exhaustible. Once these depletable resources run out, the economy will have to face a very uncertain future. Diversification of its economy with reduced dependence on the two products has long been recognized as the only long-term path to a sustainable development. However, the diversification policy has so far been unsuccessful. The volume of investments in the manufacturing sector has been inadequate due to high operating costs, shortage of skilled and unskilled labour, very limited domestic market and inadequate support services sector.[2]

Indonesia is rich in agricultural and mineral resources, not to mention its abundant supply of human resources. Due to its large domestic market, relatively low-cost labour and political stability under the Suharto regime, Indonesia has for some time been attracting foreign and domestic investments into its manufacturing sector, resulting in a more diversified economy. There are, however, weaknesses and potential sources of problems if not handled effectively. Its level of bureaucratic efficiency and quality of rural infrastructure are still inferior to some of its ASEAN neighbours such as Singapore and Malaysia. Moreover, the matter of political succession after Suharto remains unresolved. Although the Indonesian constitution has a clear order of political succession, the question of who will eventually assume the political leadership after Suharto and the manner of succession remain unclear due to the absence of sufficient political opposition and alternative leadership.

Malaysia is also well endowed with mineral and agricultural resources, without problems associated with high population density.[3] It has good infrastructure in the urban as well as in the rural sector. It has also enjoyed political and economic stability, and unlike in Indonesia, there is a transparent smooth mechanism for the transfer of political power in Malaysia.[4] However, currently Malaysia is facing an unskilled and skilled labour shortage. Malaysia's short-term solution to this labour shortage has so far been to import foreign labour. Apart from its negative social implications, it does not provide a long-term solution. Malaysia has experienced infrastructural bottlenecks and a large current account deficit mainly due to its excessive imports of shipping and insurance services.[5]

The Philippines is well endowed with natural and human resources (an area of 300,080 square km and a population of 68.70 million, as of May, 1995) and has shown some signs of economic recovery resulting from greater confidence in its economic and political future, as manifested in the increased inflow of foreign capital.[6] On the other hand, the sustainability of its economic recovery greatly depends on how successful it can resolve its long-standing problems of inadequate infrastructure, bureaucratic inefficiency, high rates of underemployment and unemployment and social instability.[7]

Singapore's economic strength is based on its superior infrastructure, efficient bureaucracy, political stability and sound macroeconomic fundamentals. But, due to its limited domestic market, high labour and land costs and lack of natural resources including water, Singapore constantly has to depend on foreign trade. It is, therefore, highly vulnerable to changes in external conditions.

Thailand is well endowed with agricultural resources and abundant labour. It has an area of 514,000 square km and a population of 60.25 million, as of May, 1995. Thailand's high growth rate has been largely driven by exports of labour-intensive manufactures such as textiles, footwear and electronics and a significant inflow of foreign direct investment. But its urban-biased development policy has resulted in poor infrastructure in the rural areas and greater economic opportunities in the urban sector, contributing to greater income inequality. Thailand has a persistent current account problem due to its heavy dependence on oil imports. Thailand is now trying to move up the production ladder from highly labour-intensive manufacturing to more capital-intensive and technology-intensive ones as it faces increasing competition from the low-wage newly-emerging economies of India, China and Vietnam.[8] But its effort to restructure its industry is hampered by the shortage of skilled labour.[9] Its urban traffic congestion problem has further constrained its ability to move ahead.

2.2 Economic performance of the ASEAN5

A remarkable record of consistently high economic growth for the ASEAN countries in the past three decades is well-known.[10] The group's four 'growth economies' (that is, Singapore, Malaysia, Thailand and Indonesia) have consistently outperformed most other regions over the

Table 2.1   ASEAN real GDP growth (%)

	87–92	1993	1994	1995	1996	1997*
Brunei	1.2	–4.1	–	–	1.8	–
Indonesia	6.3	6.5	7.3	7.3	7.0	7.5
Malaysia	8.3	8.3	9.2	9.6	8.0	8.5
Philippines	3.2	2.2	4.3	5.0	6.5	7.5
Singapore	8.4	9.9	10.1	8.3	6.5	7.5
Thailand	10.1	7.8	8.6	8.5	6.7	7.0

Notes:
*Forecasts by Yamachi Institute of Research
–: not available.

Sources: Asian Development Bank, *Asian Development Outlook* (1993); *Asiaweek*, 12 January 1996, pp. 46–7.

past 25 years. On the other hand, the Philippines has shown a remarkable recovery since 1993. Table 2.1 illustrates this economic dynamism particularly from the year 1987 after their mid-1980s recession. The growth rates of the ASEAN5 had averaged around 7 percent, well above that posted by the developed market economies (around 3 percent) and significantly above the world average growth rate (around 2 percent). Despite the economic recession in the late 1980s, they continued to post high growth rates. Most recent indications suggest that this dynamism would continue into the rest of the 1990s.

High economic growth rates experienced by the ASEAN countries have been accompanied by significant improvements in the quality of life, as measured by such standard indicators as infant mortality, literacy rates and life expectancy. As illustrated in Tables 2.2a and 2.2b, the ASEAN6 (that is, Brunei, Indonesia, Malaysia, the Philippines, Singapore, and Thailand) have performed better in improving life expectancy, infant mortality and literacy than the South Asian economies and the Southeast Asian transitional economies (SATEs). There is a strong positive correlation between per capita income and quality of life indicators, except in the case of the Philippines with respect to literacy rates. Singapore, which has the highest per capita income in nominal as well as in purchasing power parity (PPP) terms, also has the longest life expectancy, lowest mortality rate, highest calorie intake and literacy rate (excluding the Philippines and Thailand). However, the correlation is not very close. Vietnam, which has the lowest per capita income among the ASEAN7 countries (that is, Brunei, Indonesia, Malaysia, the Philippines, Singapore, Thailand and Vietnam), has performed

Table 2.2a ASEAN major development indicators, 1996

ASEAN10	Per capita GNP, nominal (US$)	Per capita GDP (PPP)	Life expectancy 1996	Life expectancy 1990	Infant mortality (per 1000)	Literacy rate (%)	Calorie intake (ave per person/day)
Brunei	20 000	20 589	74	–	8	89.2	2837
Indonesia	780	3 388	63	62	60	84.4	2750
Malaysia	3 530	8 763	72	70	12	89.3	2884
Philippines	1 010	2 660	67	64	40	93.5	2452
Singapore	22 520	21 493	76	74	5	91.6	3198
Thailand	2 315	6 816	69	69	26	93.8	2443
Vietnam	220	1 263	67	–	34	88.6	2250
Myanmar	890	676	59	61	79	81.5	2598
Laos	325	2 071	52	–	94	83.9	2630
Cambodia	215	1 266	52	–	110	37.8	2021

Note: –: not available.

Source: *Asiaweek,* 19 January 1996, p. 60.

Table 2.2b *Major development indicators: selected countries, 1996*

Countries	Per capita GNP, nominal (US$)	Per capita GDP (PPP)	Life expectancy 1996	Life expectancy 1990	Infant mortality (per 1000)	Literacy rate (%)	Calorie intake (ave per person/day)
South Asia							
Bangladesh	245	1 350	56	52	90	36.6	2100
India	335	1 280	61	59	75	52.1	2243
Nepal	180	1 165	54	52	84	27.0	2246
Pakistan	465	2 235	62	56	88	35.0	2377
Developed							
US	26 620	25 900	77		8	95.5	3671
Japan	36 315	21 350	80		4	100.0	2956
Australia	19 100	19 007	78		7	99.5	3216
Canada	18 900	21 268	78		6	99.0	3482
France	25 860	19 774	77		6	98.8	3465
Germany	24 905	20 165	76		6	100.0	3522

Source: Asiaweek, 12 July 1996, p. 53; Asiaweek, 19 January 1996, p. 60; World Bank, 1992, pp. 218–9, 274–5.

better than Indonesia and the Philippines in terms of infant mortality rates, and better than Indonesia in terms of life expectancy.

Compared to the selected developed countries, it is quite clear that Singapore has performed better in terms of per capita income except the US and Japan, and in terms of infant mortality except Japan, as Table 2.2b shows.

2.3 Structural changes in ASEAN5

2.3.1 Transformation from low income to middle and upper-middle income

Reflecting this rapid growth, the rate of improvement in living standards has been significant for the ASEAN5 countries. As Table 2.3 shows, although their standards of living, as measured by their per capita income, differ considerably, the ASEAN5 countries have consistently enjoyed an increasing living standard during the period. They have graduated from the ranks of low income countries, as classified by the World Bank, to the ranks of middle and in some cases upper-middle income countries. Singapore in particular has the highest per capita income among ASEAN.

Table 2.3   ASEAN'S per capita GNP for selected years

	Population (1994) million	Per capita GNP (US$)			
		1985 $	1992 $	1994 $	1995ᵈ
Brunei	0.285	15 878	14 276ᵃ	15 918	20 589
Indonesia	190.00	400	570	888	3 388
Malaysia	19.25ᶜ	1 848	2 320	3 495ᵇ	8 763
Philippines	65.65	575	730	1 010	2 660
Singapore	2.70	7 160	13 057	20 380	21 493
Thailand	60.00	710	1 420	–	6 816

Notes:
ᵃBased on available 1990 data.
ᵇBased on Malaysia's 1993 population count.
ᶜBased on 1993 population count.
ᵈIn terms of per capita GDP (PPP).
–: not available.

Sources: IMF, *International Financial Statistics* (various issues); Singapore's Department of Statistics, *Economic Survey of Singapore* (1995); Brunei Statistics Division, Ministry of Finance, *Brunei Darussalam Key Indicators* (1994).

The World Bank has classified Indonesia, the Philippines and Thailand as lower-middle income; Malaysia as upper-middle income; Brunei as high income, and Singapore as an advanced developing country since 1996. The Philippines, due to political crisis and power shortage in the early 1990s, did not perform well, as expected. However, since 1993 the Philippine economy is recovering. It posted a growth rate of about 5 percent in 1994, 6 percent in 1995 and it is projected to grow by at least 6 percent in 1996 (*Far Eastern Economic Review*, 16 June 1994, pp. 48–50).

2.3.2   Diminishing role of agriculture and growing importance of manufacturing and service sectors

Although the primary exports still acccount for a significant proportion of ASEAN exports, the share of manufactured exports has been increasing distinctly, as a result of their deliberate policy to diversify their exports and to reduce their dependence on the exports of agricultural and mining products. As can be gleaned from Table 2.4, in 1970 the share of manufactures in total merchandise exports was marginal, ranging from 1.2 percent to 7.5 percent among the ASEAN4 (Indonesia, Malaysia, the Philippines and Thailand). This was largely due to their reliance on their natural resource endowments. But since

Table 2.4   Shares of manufactures (SITC 5–8) in total merchandise export (%)

	1970	1980	1990	1993
Japan	92.5	94.5	95.9	95.8
Hong Kong	95.7	91.1	91.8	93.5
South Korea	76.5	89.5	93.5	93.1
Taiwan	75.8	87.9	92.5	92.9[a]
Brunei	0.1	–	12.6	2.4[a]
Indonesia	1.2	2.3	35.5	53.1
Malaysia	6.5	18.8	54.2	69.7
Philippines	7.5	21.1	39.0	41.6
Singapore	27.5	43.1	71.7	78.5
Thailand	4.7	25.2	63.1	71.1

Notes:
[a]Based on 1992 data since 1993 data are not yet available at the time of writing.
–: not available.

Source: UNCTAD, *Handbook of International Trade and Development Statistics* Table 4.1 (1994).

the beginning of 1980 the share of manufactured exports has started to rise.[11]

2.4 Explaining economic growth in ASEAN5 countries

There is a strong correlation between per capita income and other standard indicators of the quality of life in the ASEAN economies, as shown in the previous section. Their remarkable economic growth has largely contributed to the achievement of other equally important development objectives. For this reason, explaining ASEAN economic growth is crucial to understanding ASEAN economic development experience.

Explaining the growth performances of the ASEAN5 countries has been the subject of many empirical studies.[12] However, not one of the explanations is totally satisfactory because not one explanation by itself has covered all the facets of the phenomenon in a logical and consistent framework. The spectacular growth of the ASEAN countries can only be explained to a certain extent by traditional economic growth theories which consider input accumulation and technological improvements as sources of economic growth. Apart from these, other important factors have also accounted for their economic success such as their openness, high quality of government intervention, high degree of political stability, pragmatic economic policies and social values.

In this section an attempt is made to explain the phenomenon in a consistent, logical and comprehensive framework. To do this, a new analytical framework proposed by Lim (1996) is appropriate. This is a four-step backtracking analytical approach which: (i) identifies the sources of output growth; (ii) identifies the factors behind these sources; (iii) identifies the economic policies adopted to produce the factors and to ensure their efficient use; and (iv) then examines the social values that facilitate the introduction of such economic policies.

2.4.1 Sources of output growth

To identify the sources of output growth of the ASEAN countries and quantify the contribution of each of these to the measured growth rate of output requires the use of the production function framework. This framework is based on the theory of the firm. If a production function can be written for a firm, so one can also be done for the economy as a whole. The output of the economy is thus a function of the factor inputs available for the economy as a whole and the technology prevailing:

$$Q = f(L, N, K, T)$$

where Q is aggregate output, and L, N, and K the total supply of labour, land and capital, respectively, and T is the prevailing technology. All are expressed over a period of time.

The above aggregate production function shows that there are three broad sources of economic growth: first is input accumulation; second is increasing returns to scale and third is technological progress which increases the productivity of the productive inputs.

2.4.1.1   *Prominence of capital accumulation*   Tongzon and Loh (1995) attempted to identify the influences of these sources of growth on four ASEAN countries, namely Indonesia, Malaysia, the Philippines and Thailand by fitting unconstrained production functions to their individual annual data on output, labour and capital for the period 1962–91. In addition, possible influences of trade liberalization and investment in human capital were taken into account in light of the current debate between endogenous and exogenous theories of economic development and controversy on the influence of trade liberalization on economic growth.

These countries were chosen because they had initially adopted an import-substitution strategy in their industrialization efforts and have subsequently undergone various stages of trade liberalization. Singapore has always pursued an export-oriented industrialization strategy since its political separation from the Federation of Malaysia largely due to its small domestic market. Brunei is also left out in this study due to insufficient data.

The production function estimated for the individual ASEAN four countries is written in log form as:

$$Y_t = b_0 + b_1 L_t + b_2 K_t + b_3 E_t + b_4 X_t + \sum_{i=1}^{x} b_5 D_i + \sum_{j=1}^{y} b_6 D_{j,k} X_t$$

where

Y = growth in real GDP per capita (net of exports);
L = labour force growth;
K = gross fixed capital accumulation growth;
E = educational expenditure growth;
X = growth of real exports;
D_i = intercept dummy variable for each liberalization period;
$D_{j,k}$ = slope or interaction dummy variables.

The dependent variable (Y) is netted out of exports to remove the simultaneity problem between exports and GDP since exports is a component of domestic output. By using per capita GDP, effects of population growth on GDP growth are factored out of consideration. This variable is deflated by its corresponding consumer price indexes due to the unavailability of data for GDP deflators for the entire period of study.

Labour (L) and capital (K) are measured by the number of persons in the labour force and gross capital expenditure, respectively. Real exports (X) are obtained by deflating nominal exports by the corresponding export price indexes. Investment in human capital is proxied by expenditures on education (E) by respective ASEAN four governments.

Trade liberalization effects are represented by the dummy variables. The intercept dummy (D_i) is supposed to capture the externality effect which leads to an improvement in total factor productivity. The slope dummy $(D_{j,k})$ is supposed to capture the productivity differential effect of trade liberalization that will alter the sensitivity of one of the parameters of the model, in this case exports.

The empirical results show the lack of a significant effect trade liberalization has on all the ASEAN four countries. But the most salient feature of the results is the high significance of the capital variable (K) in all the ASEAN four countries (except for Thailand where K is significant at the 10 percent level). But the labour force variable did not come out statistically significant. This suggests that capital accumulation has played the most significant role in the output growth of the ASEAN four countries.

The above finding about capital is consistent with previous studies for other developing countries. In Maddison's (1970) study of 22 developing countries (including the Philippines, Malaya and Thailand) for the 1950–65 period, capital accumulation was the most important source of output growth for all countries covered. For most countries, additions to the effective labour force came next with technical progress a very distant third.

The same conclusion was reached in a recent study by the World Bank (1993b). Using cross-country data and regression analysis, the World Bank in its report on *The East Asian Miracle: Economic Growth and Public Policy* found that the rapid growth of the four fastest growing ASEAN economies (Thailand, Singapore, Malaysia and Indonesia) has been primarily driven by the rapid capital accumulation both in human and physical terms. The role of technological progress was found to have a secondary role. The above findings were further confirmed by Abimanyu (1995) for Indonesia, Kawai (1994) for

Malaysia, Austria and Martin (1995) for the Philippines, and Limskul (1995) for Thailand.

Studies to quantify the relative influences of the sources of output growth for Singapore have also supported the prominence of capital accumulation. Tsao's study (1986), which examined the period 1966–80 for Singapore using the growth accounting framework, found no role for technological progress (TFP growth), a marginal role for labour force and a very important role for capital accumulation, behind Singapore's high growth rates in its early years of industrialization. Young (1992, 1994a) also produced the same results for the period 1970–90.

Young's studies have generated some debate and further work on explaining output growth in Singapore. In addition to informal reactions, three technical papers attempted to challenge the findings of Young. One was by Toh and Low (1994) whose estimates implied a virtually zero contribution of technological progress (TPF growth) over the entire period 1971–92, but whose estimates for the specific period 1982–92 registered some positive contribution (contributing either 0.51 or 1.87 percentage points to the observed 7 percent output growth after 1981) of technological progress.

The other paper by Wong and Gan (1994) accounted for Singapore's output growth in manufacturing in the 1980s. They examined the role of technological progress (TFP growth) in 27 manufacturing industries in the 1980s and found that from 1981–90 overall TFP growth contributed 24 percent of the observed 6.7 percent average growth in gross manufacturing output. However, going by industry for the entire decade of the 1980s, the results showed 16 industries with negative TFP growth offset by positive growth in 11 industries. After 1986 TFP growth was negative in 12 industries offset by large positive estimates in few sectors.

The most recent paper by Rao and Lee (1995) broke up the time period into three sub-periods: 1966–73, 1976–84 and 1986–94, and adjusted the labour input for hours and changing educational composition. Using the growth accounting framework, they estimated a TFP growth of 1.3 percent for 1966–73, 0.6 percent for 1976–84 and 2.6 percent for 1986–94. The 2.6 percent growth in TFP implied that technological progress alone accounted for 30 percent of output for 1986–94. Structural shifts in manufacturing from less efficient to more efficient sectors were considered a major factor.

The three studies have come up with different estimates of the relative contributions of the sources of growth due to differences in data used and assumptions, but all found a positive role of technological progress in Singapore's output growth particularly from the second half of the 1980s. Further, they have not ruled out the prominence of capital accumulation in Singapore's output growth.

2.4.1.2 Sustained increase in exports   Another major source of output growth for the ASEAN5 countries is their sustained increase in exports. There is a link between economic growth and export growth, as supported by a number of cross-sectional empirical studies (see, for example, Michalopolous and Jay (1973), Michaely (1977), Balassa (1978, 1985), Tyler (1981), Feder (1983), Kavoussi (1984), Esfahani (1991) and the World Bank (1993b)). The link is both direct and indirect. Since exports is a component of national output in a national accounting sense, an increase in exports means an increase in GDP, assuming no offsetting fall in any one of the other components.

The indirect link is through the impact on productivity. Productivity increases due to the resource allocation effect, externalities and greater import capacity. The resource allocation effect refers to the greater capacity utilization driven by the external markets and to the more rapid shift of resources from low productive sectors to high productive sectors. Externalities include the economies of scale associated with a larger market and better access to information and technology. Exports also increase their capacity to import the required capital for industrialization and economic development.

The finding of no positive impact of trade liberalization on growth by Tongzon and Loh (1995) is consistent with previous time-series studies, for example, Greenaway and Sapsford (1994), Greenaway (1993) and Jung and Marshall (1985). It, however, contradicts the findings based on cross-sectional studies. This result could be due to two possible factors: first, the approach adopted in dealing with the problem of double-counting was to net out the export element from the output growth variable. Thus, the regression analysis was run for the non-export GDP against a set of explanatory variables. It is highly possible that the effects of trade liberalization have not yet been reflected in the non-export GDP variable for the period of study (1962–91). Second, the effects of trade liberalization are more subtle and complicated than those captured by the econometric model. In particular, the dummy variable technique could not fully quantify the effects of trade liberalization. The interaction with other policy variables and the role of other nonquantifiable factors are likely to be more important. This casts doubt on the sufficiency of the production function framework to deal with other nonquantifiable factors such as the indirect effects of export growth on output growth.

2.4.2   Factors behind the sources

In the previous section it was argued that to have a consistent increase in national output requires a sustained increase in exports. This section will describe the factors behind the sustained increase in exports experienced by ASEAN5 countries.

2.4.2.1   Diversification of exports
The ASEAN5 export expansion was largely a result of their success to diversify their export base and markets. Their export diversification consisted of enlarging their primary export base, promoting manufactures and shifting their emphasis from labour-intensive manufactures to capital-intensive ones at a later stage of industrialization.[13]

As mentioned in Section 2.3.2, since 1980 the reliance by ASEAN4 resource-rich countries (that is, Indonesia, Malaysia, the Philippines and Thailand) on primary exports has declined. Since the 1980s they have also diversified their primary commodity exports to include other primary products such as liquefied natural gas, palm oil, wood, marine products and copper in addition to oil, natural rubber and tin (in the case of Indonesia and Malaysia), and fruits, corn, coffee, tapioca, cassava, cacao, natural fibres and marine products (in the case of the Philippines and Thailand) in addition to sugar, copra, coconut and rice.

Singapore and Malaysia in particular started with exporting labour-intensive manufactures and later on shifted their emphasis to capital-intensive manufactures as their comparative advantage in labour-intensive production diminished.[14] Singapore was pursuing with remarkable success an export-oriented labour-intensive industrialization since its separation from the Federation of Malaysia in 1965. But since the 1970s Singapore has begun to experience an increasingly tight domestic labour market and a threat of competition from lower-wage competing countries. By 1979 a restructuring programme, together with a 'high wage' policy and fiscal incentives for research and development, were introduced to promote capital-intensive, skill-intensive and higher value-added exports of goods and services (Peebles and Wilson, 1996, p. 168).

Malaysia started to emphasize on capital-intensive and technology-intensive exports in its Seventh Malaysian Plan (1996–2000) after experiencing a shortage of labour constraint for the last five years. The adoption of an export-oriented labour-intensive industrialization strategy by Malaysia from 1970 was so successful that more than 50 percent of Malaysia's total manufactured exports were accounted for by its labour-intensive electronics, clothing and textile industries in the early 1980s (Osman-Rani, 1985, p. 22). After the recession of the mid-1980s its labour-intensive exports continued to perform well in the late 1980s. However, due to labour constraints aggravated by infrastructure bottlenecks in the early 1990s, Malaysia saw the need to make the policy shift towards higher value-added exports.

Market diversification to reduce their dependence on the markets of the US and Western Europe has also helped the ASEAN5 countries maintain their strong export growth, particularly in the late 1980s when the Western markets experienced a prolonged recession. This issue will be discussed further in Chapter 6.

2.4.2.2 Rapid expansion of foreign direct investment (FDI) One important contributing factor behind the strong capital accumulation as a prime source of ASEAN output growth is the massive inflow of foreign capital in the form of export-oriented and manufacturing-based foreign direct investments, especially from Japan and the newly industrialized countries of Taiwan, South Korea and Hong Kong.[15] Table 2.5 shows the respective shares of the ASEAN5 countries in overall foreign direct investment inflows to developing countries over the 1983–95 period based on the latest available UNCTAD data. Malaysia and Singapore's shares were consistently increasing until 1992 after which a decline in their shares was noticeable. Thailand experienced a declining share from 1991 while the Philippines, which had the lowest share, started to attract more FDI from 1993. No evident pattern can be seen from Indonesia's shares. The general deceleration in the inflow of FDI into ASEAN in the first half of the 1990s must be due to the emerging competition from China and Vietnam. The importance of FDI to Malaysia and Singapore cannot be overemphasized in the context of their massive capital requirements for a sustainable growth and export orientation due to their limited domestic markets. By bringing in capital, technology, export market linkages, managerial skills and an in-built capacity to respond to changes in comparative advantage, FDI has been an important catalyst in their sustained rapid growth and industrial development. To a lesser extent, but still significant, FDI has also been behind the economic performance of Indonesia and Thailand.

2.4.3 Economic policies

2.4.3.1 Foreign direct investment The ASEAN5 countries, with the exception of the Philippines, had attracted a significant amount of foreign direct investment particularly during the 1987–92 period. A number of push factors were responsible for this significant inflow including the appreciation of the yen since the 1985 Plaza Accord, rising costs of labour in Japan and other newly industrializing countries,

Table 2.5 *FDI flows to developing countries: ASEAN shares (US$million)*

	1983–88	1989	1990	1991	1992	1993	1994	1995
Developing countries	19 757	28 622	34 689	40 889	54 750	73 350	84 441	99 670
Indonesia	341	682	1 093	1 482	1 777	2 004	3 000	4 500
	(1.7)	(2.4)	(3.6)	(3.6)	(3.3)	(2.7)	(3.6)	(4.5)
Malaysia	731	1 668	2 332	3 998	5 183	5 206	4 500	5 800
	(3.7)	(5.8)	(6.7)	(9.8)	(9.5)	(7.1)	(5.3)	(5.8)
Philippines	249	563	530	544	228	763	1 500	1 500
	(1.3)	(2.0)	(1.5)	(1.3)	(0.4)	(1.0)	(1.8)	(1.5)
Singapore	1 947	2 887	5 575	4 888	6 730	6 829	7 900	5 302
	(9.9)	(10.1)	(16.1)	(12.0)	(12.3)	(9.3)	(9.4)	(5.3)
Thailand	439	1 775	2 444	2 014	2 116	1 715	2 700	2 300
	(2.2)	(6.2)	(7.1)	(4.9)	(3.9)	(2.3)	(3.2)	(2.3)

Note: Figures in brackets are percentage shares.

Source: UNCTAD, *World Investment Report 1995*. Transnational Corporations & Competitiveness Annex Table 1 (1995); *World Investment Report 1996*. Investment, Trade and International Policy Arrangements, Annex Table 1 (1996).

increasing lack of security in Taiwan and the 1997 reversion of Hong Kong to China (Lee, 1990).

In terms of the pull factors, three major factors have made ASEAN attractive to foreign investors: stable macroeconomic environment, liberal economic regimes, and secure competitive rates of return on investments.[16]

(a) *Stable macroeconomic environment.* Economic and political stability ranks high in the list of factors influencing the portfolio decisions of capital-exporting countries. On these counts the ASEAN5 countries have done well, although individually their performances varied.[17] As suggested by the indicators of long-term economic stability in Table 2.6, from 1987 onward (when FDI inflows accelerated) all the ASEAN5 countries have achieved lower inflation, reduced their debt–service ratios and accumulated more international reserves, with the exception of Indonesia and the Philippines, but individually have recorded differently on these indicators. They have improved their current account balance, with the exception of Thailand, and maintained relatively stable exchange rates, with the exception of the Philippines and Indonesia.[18] These country differences must have accounted for their different performances in attracting foreign investments.

Generally, continuity in political leadership has played an important role in maintaining political stability in all the ASEAN5 countries but the Philippines. Frequent changes in Thailand's political leadership is well-known, but the unifying presence and public admiration for Thailand's King have given Thailand some sense of continuity in leadership. Thus, frequent changes in political leadership have been stabilised by the presence of Thailand's well-respected royalty which has enjoyed the support of all Thais, including the opposing political parties. Although their political systems have often been criticized for being autocratic and undemocratic, the ruling parties have enjoyed popular public support based on their remarkable record of economic performance.

(b) *Liberal economic regimes.* All of the ASEAN5 countries have embraced a free-market philosophy. Although in their initial years of political independence the respective ASEAN governments had intervened in the markets by regulation and direct participation in some sectors, over time they have gradually dismantled regulatory controls and deregulated particularly the financial and trade sectors of their economies.

Table 2.6 ASEAN indicators of macroeconomic stability

	Indonesia		Malaysia		Philippines		Singapore		Thailand		Vietnam	
	1980–86	1987–96	1980–86	1987–96	1980–86	1987–96	1980–86	1987–96	1980–86	1987–96	1980–86	1987–96
Inflation rate	10.4	8.3	4.4	3.7	18.0	8.7	3.4	2.8	6.7	5.1	211.9	44.4
Current account balance[a]	-4.0	-3.3	-7.0	-5.7	-3.7	-2.8	-3.6	12.6	-4.2	-6.7	-17.6	-7.9
Debt–service ratio[b]	28.1	26.9	21.2	7.7	36.0	19.5	2.0	0.57	27.5	14.5	–	17.2
International reserves[c]	5.6	2.8	6.2	8.6	0.30	0.25	25.3	39.3	2.0	4.1	–	–
Exchange rate[d]	892.67	2209.70	2.36	2.54	12.97	25.65	2.15	1.49	23.63	23.6	–	9,560

Notes:
[a] As a percentage of gross domestic product.
[b] Total debt service as a percentage of exports of goods and services, except for Vietnam where it is a percentage of its GDP. Due to data limitation, the years 1993 and 1994 are not covered for the ASEAN countries, except for Vietnam.
[c] Quoted in millions of SDRs as a proportion of their respective gross national product quoted in national currency units. Except for Malaysia and Singapore, all the GNPs are in billions of their national currencies.
[d] With respect to the US dollar.
–: not available.

Source: Asian Development Bank, *Asian Development Outlook* (various issues); International Monetary Fund, *International Financial Statistics* (various issues); World Bank, *World Debt Tables* 1992/93.

Apart from a few remaining restrictions, virtually all foreign exchange markets in ASEAN are already liberalized. In Thailand, for example, commercial banks are subject to limits on their net foreign exchange positions. Public sector borrowings are subject to an annual ceiling set in line with the government policy on public debt management. Because of international reputation and credit rating, only top companies in Thailand have direct access to foreign funds. Residents are not allowed to hold foreign exchange-denominated deposits, except for exporters. Certain outbound investment such as property and portfolio investment continues to require approval from the authorities. Despite these limitations, the financial markets in ASEAN exhibit many characteristics common to those of a highly open economy. The most important is that domestic interest rates have been increasingly influenced by foreign interest rates (Nijathaworn, 1993).

The Philippines, which used to have the most protected banking sector, has recently opened up its banking system to more foreign competition by admitting more foreign banks into the country.

(c) *Competitive rates of return on investment.* The ASEAN5 countries have deliberately enticed foreign investments by offering a guarantee scheme and elaborate tax incentives.[19] It is guaranteed that assets will not be appropriated and earnings can be repatriated. There is a guarantee against competition from new state enterprises, state monopolization, competing imports by government agencies and price controls, permission to own land and to bring in foreign technicians. Tax exemptions on imported capital goods, raw materials and on income from companies granted a pioneer status are a common feature of their tax incentive scheme. They allow, however, different periods of tax relief, different rates of deduction from taxable corporate income with respect to depreciation allowance during the relief period, and company expenses. They also have different foreign equity guidelines (a maximum of 95 percent in the case of Indonesia), although they all allow for 100 percent foreign ownership in areas where no local partners can be found, in export-oriented projects and designated investment promotional zones. In the case of Thailand, for example, up to 100 percent foreign ownership is allowed for export-oriented projects and a maximum of 49 percent is permitted for industries supplying mainly the domestic market. Bureaucratic procedures and tariff systems have been simplified as part of the overall trade reform.

(d) *Quality of government intervention.* It is beyond any doubt that the government sector has played a significant role in ASEAN's remarkable growth and structural change. But it should be pointed out that the high quality of government intervention, rather than quantity, has been the factor behind ASEAN5's economic success story. A good example is the contrasting development approach adopted by Singapore and Thailand. The Singapore government is by far more interventionist than Thailand's, but both economies are highly successful.[20]

It is argued that not only are their bureaucracies less corrupt than those in other developing countries, but they are also effective in raising productivity, in generating employment and developing their human resources. In addition, they have supplied the necessary infrastructures, physical as well as legal, for the efficient conduct of free enterprise.

2.4.3.2 Policies on exports   The ASEAN countries have successfully promoted their manufactured exports by shifting from an import-substituting (IS) to an export-oriented (EOI) industrialization strategy.

The ASEAN5 countries, with the exception of Singapore, from the time they obtained their political independence, had adopted an import-substitution strategy for the development of their manufacturing industry.[21] This strategy was designed to save on foreign exchange and to reduce their reliance on their previous colonial masters for imports of manufactures. However, this approach resulted instead in foreign exchange crisis, deterioration in their external trade position and an inefficient manufacturing sector.[22] The accelerated industrialization plan through import substitution required heavy importation of capital, technology and industrial materials under a highly capital-intensive Western technology. It meant provision of protection for their import-substituting industries sheltering from foreign competition to the detriment of their export-oriented primary sector. Further, the limited size of their modern sector ran counter to the economies of scale principle, and the protection afforded to the import substituting industries encouraged inefficiency in the absence of foreign competition.

On the other hand, their traditional primary exports (their major source of foreign exchange at that time) had experienced secular deterioration in terms of trade and instability due to the vagaries of the weather, low income and price elasticities for these commodities. Further, the import substitution policies encouraged the maintenance of overvalued currencies and a consequent discrimination against traditional and potential new exports.

Hence, due to the failure of their import-substitution policies, the

ASEAN (particularly Indonesia, Malaysia, the Philippines and Thailand) countries have shifted to an export-oriented industrialization strategy from the 1980s.[23] Apart from the success stories of their Asian neighbours which had earlier adopted an outward-looking strategy, this shift was necessary for other reasons: for Indonesia this was considered a means of offsetting the anticipated slowdown in oil exports and of generating more employment opportunities for its large pool of labour;[24] the Malaysian government recognized the importance of manufactured exports in the light of its depleting tin reserves and uncertain long-term prospects for its natural rubber exports; the Philippines expected a substantial reduction in dependence on primary exports, significant increases in foreign exchange earnings and expansion of employment opportunities; and for Thailand this export promotion was part of its overall industrial development programme. Measures to promote both manufactured exports and to assist its import-substituting industries were adopted as early as in 1972.

It is now a well-known fact that the ASEAN export-oriented policies have partly been responsible for the significant growth of their manufacturing sector and, thus, contributed to the rapid expansion and diversification of their exports. See, for example, Abimanyu, 1995; Limskul, 1995; Tham Siew Yean, 1995; World Bank, 1993b.

The rapid growth of their manufactured exports has made the ASEAN export–GDP ratios grow. Reflecting their different degrees of export orientation and openness, the performance of their manufactured exports (as indicated by their export–GDP ratios) has varied within ASEAN. Indonesia, who has had the least outward-looking (most inward-looking) policy, has the lowest export–GDP ratio among ASEAN, whereas Malaysia and Singapore, who are the most outward-looking (least inward-looking) of them, have the highest ratios. Singapore has, since its political separation from Malaysia, been the most outward-looking with almost all its items being import duty-free, and it is no surprise that it has the highest export–GDP ratio. Malaysia's overall simple average tariff rate is quite low, and effective protection rates for manufactured goods are also low (Naya and Imada, 1990). Malaysia has had few non-tariff trade restrictions. The Philippines and Thailand, which are intermediate cases, have resorted to non-tariff barriers with fairly high nominal tariff rates for manufactures. Effective rates of protection are also relatively high, particularly for capital-intensive import-competing industries.

2.4.4   *The role of social values*

The economic policies required to bring about the factors responsible for output growth are not easy to implement because they involve a great deal of sacrifice on present consumption and often are politically unpalatable. The ASEAN5 countries, particularly the high performing ones, were able to implement the required economic policies due to their competent and honest bureaucracy and appropriate social values.

The role of social values in economic development has been recognized in a number of studies such as Weber (1904), Rostow (1952), Lewis (1955), McClelland (1961), Inkeles and Smith (1974), and Triandis (1971, 1973). Although some of these studies are not without their limitations, they do bring out the point that social values can impinge on economic growth.

The values of hard work, diligence, loyalty and reverence for education are some of the values that can facilitate the implementation of the required economic policies. In the case of the ASEAN countries, their varied economic performance in terms of savings and fiscal prudence can be partly explained by their social values of hard work and diligence. Loyalty increases labour productivity and the reverence for education reinforces the willingness to acquire education and skills, formally or on the job.

2.5   Poverty and income distribution

Except for some government efforts to assist indigenous groups, the ASEAN countries have emphasized the importance of promoting economic growth, rather than income redistribution.[25] It is, therefore, interesting to consider the poverty and distribution implications of their economic growth experience.

2.5.1   *Poverty*

The acid test for economic development is not just the economic growth numbers, but equally important, it is also whether human lives are improving and whether the fight against poverty is achieving success. Measuring poverty incidence and its trend for the purpose of inter-country comparison is fraught with conceptual and statistical difficulties. Data availability dictates the use of a headcount index representing the proportion of the population that falls below (but ignoring how far below) a given poverty line.[26] The choice of the poverty line itself is necessarily subjective. The most commonly used definition of poverty line pertains to the *income level sufficient to purchase a certain amount of calorie intake per person.*[27]

The World Bank (1993b), Balisacan (1996) and Wolfensohn (1996)

Table 2.7   Changes in poverty incidence

	Year	% of population below the poverty line	
		First year	Last year
Indonesia	1972–90	58	15
Malaysia	1973–90	37	10
Philippines	1971–94	49	36
Singapore	1972–82	31	10
Thailand	1962–86	59	26

Note: These years are chosen based on data availability.

Sources: World Bank (1993b); Balisacan (1996, p. 448); Wolfensohn (1996).

revealed that all ASEAN5 countries have reduced poverty incidence for the periods under consideration, as dictated by data availability. Their estimates of poverty incidence are shown in Table 2.7. It is likely that poverty alleviation in these countries was partly attributable to the rapid economic growth. Bautista (1992, pp. 11–16) has shown that there is a systematic relationship between poverty incidence and economic growth. Rapid output growth accompanied by growth in productivity and wages have led to more employment opportunities for the unemployed and low skilled, and increased overall per capita income. Other factors include their success in slowing down population growth, improvements in agricultural productivity resulting from the adoption of modern technology and the provision of welfare-enhancing public goods such as subsidies to education, housing and healthcare.

Singapore had the lowest poverty incidence with only 10 percent of the population living in poverty by 1982. This trend continued into the 1980s so that for Singapore absolute poverty is now an issue of the past. The other remarkable achievements were made by Indonesia and Malaysia. The Indonesian and Malaysian fight against poverty has been so successful that in 1990 the percentage of their people living in absolute poverty dropped to 15 percent and 10 percent, respectively (Wolfensohn, 1996).

2.5.2   Poverty in the Philippines
Although poverty alleviation was achieved between 1971 and 1994, the Philippines has got the highest poverty incidence in ASEAN. Bautista (1992, p. 15) attributed this to the 15 percent decline in per capita

income that accompanied the adoption of stabilization measures prescribed by the International Monetary Fund in 1984–85.

However, there are other long-standing structural factors behind the severe poverty incidence in the Philippines compared to other ASEAN countries. Balisacan (1996) attributed this to its historically feudal system with one of the highest tenancy rates in Asia, lack of off-farm job opportunities and to the failure of the land reform programmes.

The Philippines has a very large agricultural sector where land ownership is highly concentrated, especially in areas dominated by sugar. The landless agricultural workers (the poorest of the poor) are unskilled and less educated and, thus, face little prospect of obtaining employment in the industrial sector. The lack of off-farm employment opportunities in the rural sector has locked them in poverty.

Various attempts have been made to institute land reform virtually throughout the entire Philippine post-colonial history. The objective of the land reform before 1986 was basically to abolish share tenancy in lands primarily devoted to rice and corn and to transfer to tenants the ownership of the land which they were tilling, with the exemptions given to less than seven hectares of tenanted rice and corn lands. The exclusion of farms and plantations planted to export crops meant that the scope of the programme missed the larger source of land inequality. The impact was further eroded by misdeclarations by many landowners, conversion of rice and corn lands into residential enclaves, or planting crops not covered by the land reform programme, evicting tenants and replacing them with hired workers (Otsuka, 1991) and by the exclusion of landless agricultural workers (Balisacan, 1996, p. 489).[28]

The new land reform programme during the Aquino government, dubbed as the Comprehensive Agrarian Reform Programme (CARP), has included all agricultural lands and gone beyond tenancy arrangements to also include other alternative production arrangements such as production or profit-sharing, labour administration and distribution of shares of stock. The progress of this ambitious programme, however, has been very slow due to strong political opposition, administrative weakness and financial constraints (Hayami, Quisumbing and Adriano, 1990).

The Green Revolution, which resulted in greater agricultural productivity through the introduction of high-yieding varieties, mechanization and input subsidies, have favoured the large farm owners and reduced the demand for labour in the early implementation of the Green Revolution.

The Philippine government's pricing policies and overvalued currencies, resulting from industrial protection, have indirectly discriminated the agricultural sector. The Philippines, like Indonesia, has had programmes to stabilize prices, especially for rice, which is a sensitive political issue. Through the operation of marketing authorities, explicit export taxes and direct price controls, producer prices of many farm products are suppressed to the detriment of the poor rural workers. Low agricultural prices have penalized landless workers via the reduced demand for their labour. This is especially true for the landless sugar workers where the food-price effect is marginal. High levels of protection for the manufacturing sector has biased against the primary export sector.

The agricultural sector in the Philippines has been less productive than its urban counterpart due to an inadequate rural infrastructure (such as irrigation, electricity, transport and credit) and due to the lack of work incentives. Since a number of farmers are tenants, the lack of land ownership has produced uncertainties.

2.5.3 Income distribution
This issue may not present a problem as serious as poverty for some policy makers, but it has been argued that the extent of poverty depends on the country's per capita income and the degree of inequality. Thus, for a given per capita income, it is most likely that the higher the degree of inequality, the higher is the level of poverty incidence. Maintaining fairly equitable income distribution is also beneficial as it could lead to increased national productivity, more foreign exchange available to purchase capital, increased national spending on wage goods and other necessities, and social stability. It is, therefore, important that we now consider the degree of income inequality in the ASEAN5 countries.

2.5.3.1 Measures of income inequality Income inequality can be measured in many ways. Here the Gini ratio, an index of income inequality representing the Lorenz curve, is used mainly due to easy inter-country comparison and data availability. Using this measure, Table 2.8 describes their relative performances in this area for selected years.

2.5.3.2 Declining levels of income inequality Based on the available data, all ASEAN countries have experienced declining levels of income inequality, except for Thailand. Krongkaew (1994) attributed the fall in inequality in Indonesia to the following factors: improvements in the real earnings for most workers in lower-income groups resulting from the strong pace and pattern of economic growth; the reduced burden of adjustment during the period 1983–88 on the agricultural sector

Table 2.8   ASEAN income inequality for selected years (Gini ratios)

	1976	1984	1987	1990	1993
Indonesia	0.34	0.33	0.32	–	0.34
Malaysia	–	0.48	0.45	–	–
Philippines	0.48	0.45	0.45	–	–
Singapore	0.44	0.47	0.46	0.43	–
Thailand	0.43	0.50	0.48	0.50	–

Note: –: not available.

Sources: Krongkaew (1994); Oshima (1993), pp. 201–2.

resulting from the exchange rate depreciation, agricultural pricing policies and some diversification from rice to profitable non-rice crops; and a surge in the non-oil exports and the maintenance of public consumption particularly with respect to human resource development.

The 1971 launching of the New Economic Policy (NEP) in the Second Malaysian Plan 1971–75 after the racial riots of 1969 was the key factor that reduced the level of inequality in Malaysia. In an effort to raise the income of the poor Malays (most of whom live in the agricultural sector), several rural development programmes were launched including the land rehabilitation programme, irrigation and land distribution schemes. Increase in educational attainment among the Malays relative to other ethnic groups has resulted from universal primary education and highly subsidized tertiary education. Higher education brought greater employment opportunities and higher income, reducing the ethnic income gap and thus improving income equality. The shift to labour-intensive industrialization policy with the dispersal of industries in the rural sector by way of export zones and industrial states, and the rapid expansion of the public sector in the 1970s and early 1980s benefited the poor. Finally, the asset ownership restructuring in favour of the Malays has reduced the concentration of wealth among the non-Malays.

The declining level of income inequality in the Philippines from 0.48 in 1976 to 0.45 in 1984 and 1987 is not surprising. If the data are accurate, the following factors could have explained this declining trend. Although the land reform programme was fraught with deficiencies, it was, however, a partial success particularly in the conversion of tenancy to leasehold arrangements, and the protection of tenants' rights against unlawful eviction by landlords has boosted the tenants' sense of security, resulting in greater productivity. The benefits of the Green Revolution which used to be concentrated among the large farms have gradually benefited the small farmers. The increased farm incomes resulting from the adoption of the new technology expanded the demands for non-farm goods and services and generated off-farm employment opportunities.[29]

Singapore's strong economic growth with the achievement of full employment and the expansion of employment opportunities in the manufacturing and services sectors were mainly responsible for its declining income inequality during the period under consideration. The government's policy of granting substantial subsidies to education, housing and health care has also contributed to this trend.

Thailand's poor performance in this area was unstable. The commercialization of agriculture in the 1960s and 1970s had benefited only large farms near Bangkok and large rivers, but had not affected most farms away from the cities and large rivers. With agricultural prices falling and unemployment rising in the first half of the 1980s, income inequality rose to 0.50 in 1984 from 0.43 in 1976. With prices improving and unemployment falling, the Gini ratio fell slightly to 0.48 in 1987. But income inequality rose again to 0.50 in 1990. The main feature underlying the Thai trend is the strong concentration of industrial activities and services in Bangkok. The emphasis has been on industrial development promotion favouring capital-intensive activities.

One can discern some general trends in the pattern of income distribution for the ASEAN5 countries. There is a tendency for income inequality, with the exception of Singapore, to rise to a peak and then fall much earlier in the development stage than it does in the West, which is not consistent with Kuznets' hypothesis. Agriculture has led the way, in contrast to the industrial revolution in the West. The ASEAN5 experiences have provided further evidence that the neglect of agricultural development enables economic development to proceed without any long-term stability. The experiences of the Philippines and Thailand which had initially focussed on industrial development to the neglect of agriculture could attest to this.

2.6 Conclusion

Inter-country differences in poverty and income inequality reduction are largely due to the differences in economic policies pursued, differences in history, style of economic development and differences in the extent and quality of government intervention. Countries whose governments are more involved in providing welfare-enhancing public goods such as subsidized education, health care, housing and sanitation and implement them more effectively are better off. With the partial exception of the Philippines and Malaysia, ASEAN5's food crop economy is not historically characterized by marked inequalities in the distribution of landholdings and wealth. Since agrarian holdings were invariably the precursor of large commercial-industrial empires and political power, the initial conditions in most of ASEAN5 have favoured relatively even distribution of income. Pro-urban policies of development have resulted in rural poverty and greater income inequality.

Rapid growth in ASEAN5, except for Thailand, has not prevented the achievement of a more egalitarian income distribution and a wider participation of the poor in that growth. The foregoing discussion has shown that rapid economic growth can be accompanied by rapid progress in various aspects of social development. This economic development experience is not consistent with Kuznets' hypothesis which says that during the initial stages of economic development income inequality gets worse as economies grow. The ASEAN5 experience has also demonstrated that reduction in income inquality is not automatically achieved with rising economic growth. This is particularly true for Thailand. This means that effective appropriate policies are needed in order to distribute the fruits of economic growth more widely.

Redistribution from growth remains a challenge for all ASEAN countries today and in the future. In the process of promoting high growth, the equity aspect of development could easily be overlooked. Unless this is taken seriously, there is the danger that their economic growth may not be sustainable. Growth must not be pursued for its own sake. It is only a means to achieve a better quality of life. The social aspects of development (for example, poverty alleviation, respect for human rights, and the like) must be given equal importance in the overall economic planning, rather than just as a by-product of economic growth.

Suggestions for further reading

Lim (1996) is recommended for a systematic and rigorous examination of the growth experiences of the newly industrializing economies of East Asia, using his new analytical framework. For a comprehensive account of the East Asian miracle and of the role of capital accumulation (physical and human), read the World Bank (1993b). Perkins (1994) shows that there is no single model of East Asian development.

For a more detailed appraisal of poverty and income distribution in

Indonesia, the Philippines and Thailand, read Krongkaew (1994) and Quibria (1996).

Notes

1. Vietnam, due to its special case and its very recent membership of ASEAN, is not included in this discussion and will be treated separately. Vietnam, the newest and only member with a different political ideology, is on its way towards a market-based economy. Brunei will be included only when data availability permits.
2. The government in Brunei still remains a major source of production, investment and employment, although its role has declined (Hashim, 1996).
3. Malaysia has an area of 329,758 square km and a population of 20.26 million, as of May, 1995.
4. Malaysia was classified as a very low risk country for investments based on International Country Risk Guide (ICRG) Composite Index, with a high rating for its political and economic environment, higher than those obtained by the Philippines, Thailand and Indonesia (*ICRG*, vol. 27(5), May 1996).
5. Malaysia together with Thailand and Indonesia have larger foreign debts as a share of GDP than did Mexico in 1994. Forecast for Malaysia's current account deficit as a proportion of GDP in 1996 is almost 10 percent. As a rule of thumb, any deficit greater than 5 percent of GDP is dangerous (*The Straits Times*, 31 August 1996, p. 37).
6. The Asian Development Bank in its country economic review predicted that the Philippines is capable of growing at an annual rate of 6 to 7 percent over the next few years. Other economists are also optimistic about the Philippine economic future in the context of the growing peace and political stability in the country (*The Straits Times*, 12 September 1996, p. 41).
7. Based on the International Country Risk Guide composite index the Philippines was ranked 76th, well behind Singapore, Brunei, Malaysia, Thailand and Indonesia, as of May, 1996.
8. For example, footwear exports, which had been growing an average of 40 percent a year between 1992 and 1995 as Korean and Taiwan industry relocated factories to Thailand, experienced a decline by nearly half over 1995.
9. Thailand is short of trained engineers, in contrast to South Korea and Taiwan which have ten times as many per capita (*Asiaweek*, 4 October 1996, p. 27).
10. Rapid growth rates of Indonesia, Malaysia, Singapore and Thailand between 1960 and 1985 have been observed and analysed by Naya (1987) and by Lee (1990) for the period of 1971 to 1989. Both studies attempted to explain the continued rapid growth of the ASEAN4 countries.
11. Singapore has experienced an increasing importance of manufactured exports since 1970. Due to its lack of natural resources, Singapore has been promoting the export of manufactures. In the 1970s they were largely labour-intensive exports until the economy was faced with labour cost constraints. Since the 1980s the policy has been to promote high value-added and capital-intensive exports in line with changing comparative advantage.
12. For example, the World Bank's *East Asian Miracle* (1993b), Lee (1990) and Naya (1987).
13. There has been a significant shift in the composition of ASEAN5 manufactured exports towards more capital-intensive products since the 1980s such as office and telecommunications equipment, computer parts, chemicals, electronic goods, semi-conductors, consumer durables, machinery and equipment. As well as ASEAN5's policy of export diversification, the relocation of production and outsourcing of parts, components and intermediaries in the ASEAN5 countries by major companies from Japan and newly industrializing countries have contributed to this trend.
14. The ASEAN industrialization experience will be discussed further in Chapter 3.

15. High domestic savings rates experienced by the ASEAN5 countries, especially Singapore, Malaysia, Thailand and Indonesia, was also cited in the literature as a major factor behind the massive accumulation of capital. The following were their domestic savings rates in 1994: Indonesia (38.7 percent), Malaysia (35.6 percent), Philippines (15.4 percent), Singapore (51.3 percent) and Thailand (37.2 percent), (Asian Development Bank, 1995).

16. Other desirable pull factors are efficient and adequate infrastructure and relatively cheap but educated labour force (Chia, 1985, 1986, 1993).

17. In the 1970s to 1980s, the Philippines and Thailand underwent political instability which led to adverse effects on the inflow of FDI (Idem, 1974). For example, between 1982 and 1985 when there was political crisis and uncertainty engendered by the political assassination of Aquino, FDI from the US and Japan dropped from 10 to −82 US$million and from 62 to 21 US$million, respectively (Alburo and Gochoco, 1992).

     In the period of 1972 to 1975, public discontent over the Japanese domination of the Thai economy caused the inflow of FDI from Japan to drop significantly from 707.7 million baht in 1973 to 423 million baht in 1975 (Chinwanno and Tambunlertchai, 1983).

18. The significant depreciation of the Philippine peso was largely due to the massive capital outflow engendered by economic and political instability starting from the political assassination of the late Benigno Aquino.

19. For a description of the various tax incentives offered in ASEAN for promotion of foreign investments, see Pussarangsri and Chamnivickorn (1995). This will be discussed in greater detail in Chapter 9.

20. It is quite evident from the smooth traffic flow in Singapore and the long traffic jams in Thailand that both governments have adopted different degrees of intervention.

21. Singapore, since its political separation from Malaysia in 1965, has discarded the import-substitution policy due to its small domestic market resulting from the associated collapse of the Malaysian common market proposal and the British military withdrawal. An import-substituting strategy is an attempt to replace imports, usually manufactured products, with domestic production and supply. The idea is to develop certain domestic industries by protecting them against foreign competition. It generally involves the cooperation of foreign firms behind the walls of protection.

22. Except for Indonesia and Malaysia, which were substantial oil producers, the ASEAN5 countries experienced deteriorating trade balances throughout the 1960s and 1970s. The IS strategy failed due to the limited domestic market and concentration of benefits among the few foreign firms and local partners, adoption of capital-intensive technology, overvalued currency and inefficient forward and backward linkages.

23. Indonesia was the last ASEAN country to adopt an export-oriented industrialization (EOI) strategy starting in 1986. Malaysia attempted to adopt EOI in the 1970s, but slipped into a second round of an import-substitution industrialization (ISI) strategy in the early 1980s due to Malaysia's heavy industrialization plans (Jomo, 1994). Thailand started to initiate an export-oriented scheme in the third plan (1972–76) and followed it up with further trade liberalization in the fifth plan (1982–86). But Thailand experienced a rising and persistent balance of payment deficit during the fifth plan so that the ISI was implemented together with EOI. Thailand's trade regime underwent a drastic change in the beginning of the 1990s (Pussarangsri and Chamnivickorn, 1995, p. 14).

24. Hence, special emphasis was initially given to small-scale and cottage industries.

25. The ASEAN5 countries do not have welfare assistance programmes to assist the poor and the underprivileged to an extent similar to the West. Nor do they have substantial measures to redistribute income in the form of high marginal tax rates.

26. Another problem is the lack of up-to-date data on poverty due to the lack of frequent income and expenditure surveys in the ASEAN countries.

27. Chenery (1979, p. 459) defined this poverty line as the income level accruing to the

46th percentile of the Indian population in 1975 – roughly equal to the total consumption expenditure needed to ensure a daily supply of 2150 calories per person.
28. Evidence of eviction is also provided by Ledesma (1982) and Mangahas (1985).
29. For a review of the literature on the adoption of the new rice technology in Asia, issues and empirical evidence on technology adoption, see Herdt and Capule (1983), Feder et al. (1985) and Balisacan (1989).

3 ASEAN development and economic cooperation

The previous chapter has provided an overview of the economic development experiences of individual ASEAN countries, focussing on its five founding members and highlighting the major sources and factors behind their varied economic performances.

This chapter will review the role and progress of ASEAN economic cooperation in four important sectors of ASEAN such as international trade, agriculture, manufacturing or industry and services. As discussed in Chapter 1, one major objective in the formation of ASEAN was to foster regional economic cooperation. Since 1976 this objective has grown in importance as economic development has become their main priority in view of, among other things, the increasing need to maintain their international competitiveness in the midst of growing international competition and sustain their pace of economic development in light of rising expectations.

There have been two types of economic cooperation in ASEAN: market sharing and resource pooling. These types of economic cooperation have developed since the Bali Summit of 1976. At this summit the ASEAN5 leaders signed a Declaration of ASEAN Concord which laid out a programme of action for regional cooperation in political, economic, social, cultural and security matters.

3.1 Development and cooperation in international trade

The most important form of market-sharing cooperation envisaged in the Bali Summit was the establishment of preferential trading arrangements to promote intra-ASEAN trade. The agreement on ASEAN Preferential Trading Arrangement (PTA), signed in February, 1977, was the first attempt by ASEAN member countries to promote a higher level of intra-ASEAN trade.

Five measures have been identified to achieve the objective of greater intra-ASEAN trade: exchange of tariff preferences; purchase finance support at preferential rates for selected products of ASEAN domestic origin; long-term (3–5 years) quantity contracts for basic commodities such as fuels and agricultural products;[1] preference in procurement by government agencies; and liberalization of non-tariff barriers on a preferential basis.

3.1.1 Theory of preferential trading arrangements (PTAs) and intra-ASEAN trade

The basic concepts of trade creation and diversion, as developed by Viner (1950), Meade (1955), Lipsey (1957, 1960) and other international economists, in their analysis of economic implications of a formation of a customs union provide a relevant framework for evaluating the role of ASEAN preferential trading arrangements in promoting intra-ASEAN trade. However, more relevant to the issue of trade preferences among developing countries are the works by Cooper and Massell (1965), Johnson (1965), Bhagwati (1968) and Krishna and Bhagwati (1994) which provide an economic justification for such trade preferences.[2]

The standard (Vinerian) theory of customs union stresses the short-run static effects of preferential trading arrangements. Under constant cost technology, perfect elasticity of substitution between alternative sources of supply, static market size and exclusion of the most efficient supplier from the customs union, the theory predicts two major consequences for the member country joining the preferential trading club: the welfare-enhancing trade creation effect (resulting from the replacement of the home country's high-cost industries by low-cost industries in the preferred country) and the welfare-reducing trade diversion effect (which results from the replacement of lowest cost non-preferred suppliers by preferred suppliers). The trade creation effects are caused by changes in both production and consumption – the replacement of the domestic by the preferred country's production (production effect) and the increased consumption of the preferred country's substitutes for the home country's goods (consumption effect). Thus, trade creation produces an economic gain of two types: savings on the real cost of goods previously produced domestically and now imported from the preferred country, and gain in consumer surplus from a substitution of lower-cost for higher-cost means of satisfying economic needs. The overall impact for member countries, therefore, depends on the size of the trade creation and trade diversion effects.

The standard (Vinerian) theory can be modified and extended to allow for the fact that similar commodities from alternative sources are imperfect substitutes and that industries are subject to increasing costs. To illustrate the trade impact of preferential trading arrangements under assumptions of increasing costs and imperfect substitutability of products, refer to Figure 3.1.

S_f represents the nonpreferred export supply curve before the imposition of trade barriers. S_f' represents the nonpreferred export supply curve inclusive of tariffs and price effects of other trade barriers. D_m

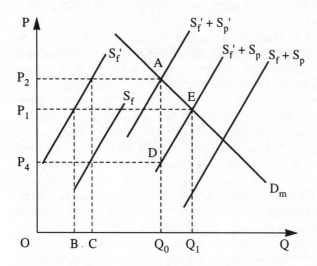

Figure 3.1   Trade effects of preferential trading arrangements

represents the preference-granting country's import demand curve. S_f' + S_p' represents the combined export supply curve of the non-preferred and preference-receiving countries inclusive of tariffs and other price-inflating trade barriers. S_f' + S_p represents the combined supply curve after the trade preferences have been granted. As can be gleaned from the graph, the volume of exports from the nonpreferred country reduces from C to B, but unlike the perfect elasticity of substitution case, the trade preferences do not lead to a complete replacement of the nonpreferred imports with similar imports from the preferred country. Moreover, due to the increasing cost assumption, domestic prices fall only by less than the amount of trade preferences, and part of the reduction in prices is reaped by the preference-receiving country in terms of higher export prices. See Appendix for estimation models based on Figure 3.1.

The above partial equilibrium model does not take into account the dynamic and long-run economic benefits associated with the growth of the internal market brought about by the reduction or removal of trade barriers. The enlargement of internal markets has important effects on productive efficiency within firms and on the rate of growth by way of its impact on the inducement to invest and the opportunities to exploit the economies of scale. Firms of member countries will be subject to more competition, and competition enforces efficiency and leads to greater specialization of production. In this process of interpenetration of markets, as producers can enjoy the savings arising from longer runs in production, consumers will benefit from lowered prices and improved quality of goods and services traded. But the greatest long-run implication is that more competition will lead to increasing average growth of member countries since the enlargement of markets creates special incentives for firms to invest their resources and efforts in the introduction of innovation and expansion.

The extent to which members and nonmembers can gain or lose by the establishment of PTAs will depend largely on the following factors: elasticities of domestic demand and supply, production patterns and costs, size and initial level of protection. A country is more likely to gain from trade creation, the more elastic the domestic demand and supply of goods which the member country is capable of producing. Further it is more likely to gain on its terms of trade with outside countries, the more inelastic is the foreign supply of imports relative to its domestic supply of exports. On the other hand, a country is also less likely to lose from trade diversion, the smaller are the initial differences in costs between the member and the outside countries.

For trade creation to dominate, the economies of the member countries must be competitive before the integration, but potentially complementary after the integration, because the possibility of relocation of resources will be greater.

The larger the economic area of the integration, the greater is the chance that the world's most efficient producer is a member, and hence all other members could enjoy the advantage of being able to buy from the most efficient producer.

The extent of an unfavourable redistributive effect on a member country is determined by the degree of preferential access it gives to the partner country in relation to the preferential access it receives from the latter. The greater the margin of preference the country gives the more it stands to lose. This means that when a country with a high degree of protection forms a preferential trading arrangement with a country with relatively open markets, the former may well be faced with a net welfare loss (Bhagwati, 1996).

3.1.2 ASEAN PTA and intra-ASEAN trade

Whether or not the ASEAN Preferential Trading Arrangements (PTA) was effective in promoting intra-ASEAN trade can be ascertained by investigating whether the value of intra-ASEAN trade as a proportion of ASEAN total trade has grown over time. In 1977, the year of signing the ASEAN PTA, intra-ASEAN trade as a proportion of total ASEAN trade was roughly 15 percent (Naya and Barretto, 1994, p. 3). This share increased considerably to about 20 percent in 1984 (when Brunei joined the grouping), but dropped in 1992 to about 18 percent. It then recovered in 1994 to slightly over 20 percent and remained roughly at the same level in 1995.

Based on this pattern one can say that intra-ASEAN trade cooperation via the PTA has not been a significant contributor to ASEAN trade growth. Although intra-ASEAN trade as a share of ASEAN's total trade increased generally in the 1980s, the increase has not been persistent in the 1990s.

The ASEAN PTA has clearly failed to increase the share of intra-ASEAN imports which dropped slightly from 20.8 percent (of total ASEAN imports) in 1984 to 19.0 percent in 1992 and which dropped again to 18.4 percent and 16.9 percent in 1994 and 1995, respectively. The trend in intra-ASEAN exports is a little bit encouraging. Its share dropped from 20.0 percent in 1984 to 16.5 percent in 1992, before it went up to 22.7 percent in 1994 and 22.8 percent in 1995.

Singapore–Malaysia–Indonesia trade continues to dominate intra-ASEAN trade. Four major trade flows, in order of magnitude, have dominated trade within ASEAN: Singapore's exports to Malaysia, Malaysia's exports to Singapore, Indonesia's exports to Singapore and Singapore's exports to Indonesia. To investigate further the importance of one ASEAN country in another ASEAN country's foreign trade, the trade intensity approach is adopted. The trade intensity indexes for each of the ASEAN6 countries are presented for selected years in Table 3.1. In 1977 when the ASEAN PTA was signed, the highest trade intensity indexes were between Singapore, Malaysia and Indonesia (Tan, 1996). The trade intensity index between Singapore and Brunei has also been quite high, but Brunei did not join ASEAN until 1984.

These flows (Singapore–Malaysia–Indonesia trade) accounted for 61 percent of all intra-ASEAN trade in 1992 (inclusive of Brunei).[3] In 1995 these flows accounted for 79 percent of all intra-ASEAN trade flows. The increase in trade flows between these three countries occurred together with increases in trade activity in Thailand, the Philippines and Brunei. Singapore remains the most important component of these trade flows, accounting for more than half of total intra-ASEAN trade in 1995 (see Table 3.2).

Trade between Malaysia and Thailand and between Malaysia and Indonesia has been relatively little, but since 1989 this trade has risen strongly reflecting mainly the robust growth in exports (ESCAP, 1994) and growth in intra-industry trade.[4]

It is, however, interesting to note the diminishing importance of Singapore–Malaysia–Indonesia trade to total ASEAN trade as reflected

Table 3.1 *ASEAN trade intensity indexes: 1977, 1987, 1995*

Countries		Brunei	Indonesia	Malaysia	Philippines	Singapore	Thailand
Brunei	1977		0.00	6.93	0.00	4.04	1.68
	1987		0.06	2.64	2.91	5.40	18.27
	1995		0.06	0.13	1.18	3.92	8.51
Indonesia	1977	0.00		0.45	2.91	9.45	0.08
	1987	0.37		1.05	2.89	16.09	1.26
	1995	1.57		1.67	2.30	1.75	0.97
Malaysia	1977	15.60	0.53		3.13	16.29	2.27
	1987	7.91	0.74		7.00	13.69	5.81
	1995	5.71	1.69		1.63	8.22	2.67
Philippines	1977	1.33	1.23	1.65		2.09	0.65
	1987	0.39	0.19	3.84		2.38	3.12
	1995	0.29	0.91	1.36		2.13	3.08
Singapore	1977	55.31	10.91	33.73	3.59		6.49
	1987	44.09	3.48	11.96	4.36		8.21
	1995	17.71	0.75	12.29	2.86		3.91
Thailand	1977	7.31	10.33	12.45	0.66	6.47	
	1987	5.27	1.21	0.60	1.29	7.18	
	1995	1.57	1.83	1.78	1.30	5.66	

Sources: Tan (1996), Table 8.3; International Monetary Fund, *Direction of Trade Statistics Yearbook* (1996).

Table 3.2 *Intra-ASEAN trade matrix, 1995 (%)*

Countries	Brunei	Indonesia	Malaysia	Philippines	Singapore	Thailand	ASEAN
Brunei		2.2	12.9	0.60	71.2	13.1	44.9
Indonesia	0.70		31.3	10.0	36.5	21.5	8.4
Malaysia	0.90	6.6		3.4	74.2	14.9	21.9
Philippines	0.4	14.7	20.5		40.5	23.9	11.0
Singapore	2.7	4.1*	67.2	4.9		21.2	25.7
Thailand	1.8	7.5	24.3	5.1	61.3		15.1
Total							19.7

Notes: Columns 2–7 show trade of individual ASEAN countries as a proportion of total trade with ASEAN. Column 8 shows intra-ASEAN trade as a proportion of total trade. * Singapore's trade with Indonesia is not reported, and has been estimated from Indonesia's trade with Singapore. 1994 figures are used as 1995 figures are unavailable.

Source: IMF, *Direction of Trade Statistics Yearbook* (1996).

in their declining trade intensity indexes, particularly in the case of Malaysia's exports to Singapore, Indonesia's exports to Singapore and Singapore's exports to Indonesia between 1987 and 1995, as Table 3.1 shows.

3.1.3 The declining role of petroleum in intra-ASEAN trade

Petroleum had predominated in intra-ASEAN trade in the last three decades, that is, the 1960s, 1970s and 1980s. In 1989 exports, for example, of mineral fuels accounted for about 23 percent of Malaysia's total exports, and about 20 percent of Singapore's total exports. However, since 1992 machinery and transport equipment have become the dominant items in intra-ASEAN trade. For example, in 1992 Malaysia's main exports to Singapore were manufactured products comprising mainly of telecom equipment, electronic component parts, electrical machinery, transport equipment and office equipment. Manufactures, together with mineral fuels (mainly crude petroleum) and food items, accounted for more than 90 percent of Malaysia's total exports to Singapore. The share of manufactures in total exports to Singapore rose dramatically and consistently from 45 percent in 1987 to 65 percent in 1990 and 74 percent in 1992. Malaysia's imports from Singapore are now dominated by manufactured goods (especially electrical machinery, electronic component parts, telecom equipment, chemicals, office equipment and metal products) and mineral fuels, with the shares of manufactures in total imports from Singapore rising from 58 percent in 1987 to 65 percent in 1990 and 75 percent in 1992 (ESCAP, 1994).

Until 1991 Malaysia's exports to Thailand were dominated by crude petroleum, but in 1992 exports of manufactured goods (mainly machinery and transport equipment) became Malaysia's leading export to Thailand.

3.1.4 Factors hindering the growth of intra-ASEAN trade

A number of factors could explain the insignificant role of ASEAN PTA in promoting intra-ASEAN trade. First, in the early phase of tariff liberalization, the voluntary and open-ended (no time frame) tariff reduction resulted in the offer of irrelevant items. For example, Thailand offered a 40–50 percent margin of preference for more than 100 log items, most of which other ASEAN countries could not produce, while the Philippines included snow ploughs in its list of preference items. Indonesia offered a 20 percent margin of preference to imports of pure-bred cows and day-old chicks for which the existing tariff rate was zero. Second, the product-by-product and consensus approach to tariff reduction was time consuming as each product had to be discussed and examined closely before tariff preferences could be agreed upon. Third, the across-the-board tariff reduction approach adopted in 1980 was undermined by the exclusion (sensitive) list provision. Since each member country decided its own list of sensitive items, the impact was minimized to the extent that the ASEAN countries made use of this rule. Further, most of the preference items were low-valued. For example, Thailand's 1978 trade statistics listed 1512 items of an import value below US$50,000. Of these only 813 or just under 54 per cent were included in Thailand's list of preference items. Fourth, while there has been an attempt to reduce the tariff barriers, the non-tariff barriers have been largely ignored. Quotas, varied customs procedures and technical norms have been the most widely encountered barriers in intra-ASEAN trade. Finally, there has been a general trend within the region towards lower tariffs for goods imported from outside ASEAN. This has eroded any advantage gained in ASEAN tariff preferential agreement. Indonesia, as part of the economic restructuring programme advised by the World Bank, has reduced tariffs on some 94 products to 5 percent from a range of 10–40 percent, and abolished import duties on 59 products. The Philippines and Thailand have been moving in the same direction. Malaysia's tariff rates on average are low, and Singapore's trade regime is virtually free (Ooi, 1987, p. 59).

Underlying the poor performance of ASEAN PTA are the structural problems inherent in the ASEAN economies. (a) Different stages of economic development: these countries have different levels of development, structure and pace of industrialization which have led to different national policies and priorities. Indonesia, Thailand and the Philippines with relatively less efficient export sectors and with sizeable domestic markets tend to be inward-looking, while Singapore and Malaysia with limited domestic markets and relatively more efficient export sectors tend to be outward-looking. (b) Dependence on extra-ASEAN trade: Northeast Asia is the most important trading partner for Brunei and Malaysia while the USA is the most important trading partner for the Philippines, Singapore and Thailand; Japan is Indonesia's most important trading partner. (c) Competitive rather than complementary economies: similar factor endowments in their early stages of economic development have made the ASEAN economies less complementary relative to their major trading partners. These have made them more competitive and thus made it difficult to arrive at agreements that result in mutually beneficial trade.

Due to the above structural problems, the growth of intra-ASEAN trade has not been as remarkable as the growth of total ASEAN trade. However, it should be recognized that ASEAN economic cooperation, particularly in formulating a common stance and forming a united bloc in dealing with their extra-regional trading partners, has significantly contributed to enhancing their clout and bargaining power in inter-national trade negotiations and other fora, especially on matters of market access for their exports.

3.1.5 Conclusion

The ASEAN Preferential Trading Arrangements (PTA) has been the main instrument of intra-ASEAN trade cooperation to enhance greater intra-ASEAN trade. However, it has contributed only marginally to the promotion of intra-ASEAN trade due to factors including their conflict of interests resulting from their different stages of economic develop-ment, weak complementarities and their dependence on extra-ASEAN trade.

3.2 Industrialization and industrial cooperation

The preceding chapter has outlined the rationale for the switch from an import-substituting industrialization (ISI) strategy to an export-oriented one (EOI) in ASEAN. It has argued that this switch is one major factor behind the ASEAN economic success. This section will discuss in more detail the ASEAN industrial development experiences under an export-oriented industrialization strategy. Under this strategy, they have achieved a significant economic transformation, as reflected in the increasing importance of manufactured products in their national output. But it must be noted that the adoption has been a matter of emphasis, rather than a mutually exclusive one, in terms of government policy and outcome. The ASEAN experience with industrialization is generally best described as an emphasis on an import-substituting industrialization (ISI) in the initial stages, particularly in the 1960s and the 1970s, and a gradual shift towards an export-oriented industriali-zation (EOI) since the 1980s.

3.2.1 ASEAN experience with export-oriented industrialization policy

Growth performance and industrialization are intricately related in ASEAN, where manufacturing has emerged as an engine of growth and bell-wether of the state of the economy. Thus, for instance, manufac-turing growth of 13.3 percent per annum in Singapore from 1965 to 1980 led to an average GDP growth of 10.4 percent, but when manufacturing growth fell to 2.2 percent per annum from 1980 to 1986, Singapore's average GDP growth fell to only 5.3 percent (Chng, 1991).

Industrialization has been seen by the ASEAN countries as the key to economic independence and progress ever since they attained their political independence. Hence, though varying in degrees and duration, they have embarked on a programme of industrialization.

The Philippines was the first ASEAN country to embark on industrialization in the early 1950s, followed by Malaysia in the late 1950s, Singapore and Thailand in the early 1960s, and Indonesia in the late 1960s. Though late starters, Brunei and Vietnam are also intensifying their efforts to diversify their economies through industrialization. For Brunei its over-reliance on oil and gas makes it imperative to industrialize. A break from central planning and the adoption of a market-based economic system was necessary for Vietnam's complete integration with the world economy.

Indonesia   Prior to 1986 Indonesia's industrialization strategy was generally inward-looking due to its enormous natural resources and large domestic market. As pointed out earlier, there were liberalization attempts in the late 1960s in terms of tariff reduction, removal of import licensing and foreign exchange controls, but from 1974 to 1985 there was a general reversal to economic nationalism of the early 1960s with the re-introduction of protection and regulations aided by the windfall gains in oil exports, especially from the 1973 and 1979 oil price hikes.

The oil crisis in 1986 with a resultant BOP deficit and foreign debt crisis had prompted Indonesia to re-embark on trade liberalization. Tax reforms, export incentives and subsidies were introduced to boost its non-oil exports.

Malaysia   The launching of the Second Malaysian Plan in 1979 marked the start of Malaysia's adoption of an export-oriented industrialization strategy. The strategy was more of an increase in assistance to exports, rather than as a substantial reduction in protection levels. Malaysia, compared to other ASEAN countries, had traditionally low protection levels. The import-substitution policy in Malaysia only resulted in low protection levels due to the perception that the protectionist policy would only benefit the Chinese industrialists to the detriment of the rural indigenous population.

Philippines   The enactment of the Export Incentives Act of 1970, followed by devaluation of the peso, marked the Philippine adoption of an export-oriented approach to industrialization. The Act involved the provision of subsidies and tax exemptions to companies exporting more than 50 percent of their production. The establishment of export processing zones, such as the Bataan Export Processing Zone, depreciation of the peso and simplification of its tariff structure were other instruments used to boost its manufacturing exports in the 1970s.

However, the unfavourable external conditions, aggravated by political instability, led to an exchange rate crisis which prompted the Philippine government to re-impose quantitative restrictions and foreign exchange rationing during the first half of the 1980s. It was only in 1985 that there was a final reversal of policy towards export orientation.

Thailand   Thailand adopted the EOI strategy with the launching of its Third Plan (1972–76) and its Investment Promotion Act of 1971. This was followed by a series of currency devaluations in 1984 and 1986 as part of its export promotion drive in response to its foreign debt crisis.

3.2.2   Results of EOI strategy

One prominent consequence of the ASEAN export promotion policy is the industrial transformation from being producers and exporters of low value-added primary products to those of high value-added manufactures. The rapid growth of their manufactured exports since the 1970s has led to a restructuring of their manufacturing sector towards higher value-added production, as Table 3.3 shows.

In all the ASEAN5 countries, as shown in Table 3.3, the share of machinery in total manufacturing output increased substantially during the period, especially for Malaysia, Singapore and Thailand. In all cases the share of food declined significantly. Except for Indonesia, the share of other industries dropped substantially as the ASEAN countries shifted away from predominantly extractive activities to more capital and technology-intensive production.

Malaysia's major manufactured products for exports are mainly electronic components and electrical appliances. Thailand's major manufactured products are textiles and clothing, electronics and processed food while Indonesia's are textiles and clothing, footwear and processed wood products. However, the fast-growing sectors are electrical appliances, telecom equipment, electronic components and processed food. Singapore's main manufactures are electronic products, computers, hard disk drives and printers.

However, Brunei and the Philippines did not experience the kind of industrial transformation experienced by the above-mentioned ASEAN countries. Brunei's economy is still very much dependent on oil and natural gas, although its dependence is declining. In 1990, for example, oil and gas accounted for more than 60 percent of Brunei's GDP, down from its 88 percent share in Brunei's GDP in 1974. This was of course

Table 3.3 *ASEAN structure of manufacturing (% of manufacturing value added)*

	Indonesia		Malaysia		Philippines		Singapore		Thailand	
	1970	1992	1970	1992	1970	1992	1970	1992	1970	1992
VA (million $)	994	27854	500	–	1665	12811	379	13568	1130	31185
Food	65	23	26	10	39	37	12	4	23	16
Textile	14	16	3	6	8	13	5	3	14	16
Machinery	2	14	8	34	8	11	28	54	4	40
Chemicals	6	7	9	11	13	12	4	9	25	5
Others	13	40	54	39	32	27	51	30	34	23

Notes:
Food = food, beverages and tobacco (ISIC division 31); Textile = textiles and clothing (division 32); Machinery = machinery and transport equipment (major groups 382–84); Chemicals = chemicals (major groups 351 and 352); Other = wood and related products (division 33), paper and related products (division 34), petroleum and related products (major groups 353–56), basic metals and mineral products (division 36 and 37), fabricated metal products and professional goods (major groups 381 and 385), other industries (major group 390).
–: not available

Source: The World Bank, *World Development Report 1995*, Table 6.

accompanied by an increasing share of the non-oil sector from 12 percent in 1974 to 40 percent in 1991 (31 percent in 1993). A greater part of this increase, however, was due to increases in government sector activities which registered a percentage share of about 22 percent in 1991 (30 percent in 1993) from only 4 percent in 1974. This is not a commendable structural transformation simply because it did not bring about the desired impact of its diversification drive.[5]

In the case of the Philippines, manufactured exports are small in absolute value and its manufacturing value-added is dominated by food processing industries.

3.2.3 Prospects and challenges
The prospect for continued industrialization among the ASEAN5 countries largely depends on how they can successfully deal with the following problems and constraints:

Indonesia As a latecomer in the EOI strategy, Indonesia has performed well in labour-intensive manufactures, but with the emergence of labour-surplus historically-planned economies such as China and Indo-China, Indonesia is most likely to face more competition in the textile and footwear industry.

Malaysia and Thailand Their main problem is the shortage of skilled labour and available labour to work in the agricultural sector. In some parts of Malaysia and Thailand, infrastructure is still not adequate to cope with fast increasing demand. Malaysia is too dependent on electronic components and electrical appliances while Thailand is on exports of textiles and footwear. They are also facing inflationary pressures and persistent current account deficits resulting from the massive inflow of foreign capital.

Philippines The presence of vested interests remains a major obstacle in the current government's deregulation and microeconomic reform. Further, the basic requirement of establishing law and order is still a slippery area and has been from time to time challenged. Inefficient infrastructure, bureaucracy and growing income inequality are other major constraints (*The Sunday Times*, 5 January 1997, p. 15).

Singapore Although Singapore has the most superior infrastructure in Southeast Asia, it is increasingly plagued with rising wages and land costs due to its limited size and shortage of skilled labour.

3.2.4   *ASEAN industrial cooperation*

The individual ASEAN experiences with industrialization vary in terms of timing, emphasis and impact, although there are elements common to them. One common element is the ASEAN resolution that industrialization and economic development of their members can be largely facilitated through industrial cooperation. There is also a common realization that a significant increase in intra-ASEAN trade can only occur if the supply side of the market is also increased. Thus, since 1976 three major schemes of ASEAN industrial cooperation, that is, ASEAN Industrial Projects (AIP) Scheme, ASEAN Industrial Complementation (AIC) Scheme and ASEAN Industrial Joint Venture (AIJV) Scheme, have been established to create a new industrial capacity jointly owned by member countries serving the regional market. Unlike the trade liberalization which raises apprehensions of uncontrolled trade flows and market disruption, industrial cooperation is linked to the creation of specific new production facilities giving rise to much more predictable trade flows.

3.2.4.1   *Rationale for industrial cooperation*

(a) *Larger combined market and economies of scale.* The various schemes are based on the concepts of resource pooling and market sharing. Most of the ASEAN countries have relatively small domestic markets because of their small population. But taken as a whole, ASEAN has a combined population of roughly 350 million (excluding Vietnam, Laos, and Myanmar), larger than the US. Moreover, the ASEAN market is expected to increase and its per capita income to grow over the next two decades. Given such a large and expanding market, ASEAN can sustain high volume manufacturing industries which are not presently viable in any of the individual ASEAN countries. Regional projects require less investment and less labour per unit of output than similar national projects and can therefore operate at lower costs. And cooperation allows ASEAN countries not only to reduce, but also to share the capital costs of regional industrial projects and make the maximum use of their limited skilled manpower resources.

(b) *Reorientation of traditional ties.* Industrial cooperation enables the ASEAN countries to reorient their traditional ties, that all these countries except Thailand have, with their former colonial rulers. Due to their past colonial relationships, the ASEAN countries have been more closely integrated with the industrially advanced countries than within the region. The industrialization programmes of ASEAN are, therefore, designed to suit national rather than regional requirements. Industrial cooperation helps to disengage the traditional economic ties of the member countries and reintegrate them by redirecting economic activities towards the region.

(c) *Specialization and enhancement of investment climate.* Most importantly, industrial cooperation is expected to enable each ASEAN country to specialize in the manufacture of selected components. Given the present competitive environment, this may be the only strategy to ensure the development of certain large-scale industries such as motor vehicles and machinery. Such a strategy will not only help to increase intra-ASEAN trade but also enhance the overall investment climate in the region and induce more investors to invest in the ASEAN countries. Hence, industrial cooperation will help ASEAN countries increase their industrial complementarity and promote regional trade in manufactured products.

In the long run, industrial cooperation can lead to coordinated industrial planning on a regional scale which will increase the industrialization potential of the region as a whole. The process of regional industrial cooperation and the region's industrial development can feed on each other and provide an impetus for further industrial growth in the region through the opening up of opportunities for the establishment of new industries to take advantage of the regionally-based division of labour.

3.2.4.2   ASEAN schemes of industrial cooperation: success or failure?

(a) *ASEAN Industrial Projects (AIPs).* Proposed by the UN team in 1973 and officially adopted at the Bali Summit of 1976, these are large-scale joint industrial projects between ASEAN governments designed to utilize the raw materials of member countries and produce for the ASEAN market at preferential rates.

Four industrial projects were initially proposed to be located in the following ASEAN5 countries: urea projects in Indonesia and Malaysia; a natural soda ash project in Thailand; a superphosphate project in the Philippines; and a diesel engine project in Singapore. At the estimated cost of US$300–400 million each, 60 percent of the equity was to come from the host country and 10 percent each from the other four ASEAN countries. The private sector in each country was expected to take up about 40 percent of equity participation, while most of the infrastructure costs of these projects were to be financed through foreign loans.

In 1977 the Japanese government had announced it would

provide US$1 billion in loans (Fukuda soft loan) to help finance the AIPs. This prompted proposals for a further set of AIPs to be considered including the manufacture of heavy-duty rubber tyres in Indonesia, machine tools in Malaysia, newsprint in the Philippines, television picture tubes in Singapore and potash in Thailand (Tan, 1996).

   Limitations. The above proposals under the AIP scheme have met with very limited success. Only the urea projects in Indonesia and Malaysia out of the five proposals got off the ground. All the other ASEAN members have withdrawn from their original AIP projects. The following reasons explain the lack of progress in the AIP scheme:

(i)   Project identification. The most serious limitation with the AIPs was that they were conceived and announced rather hastily. Without the benefit of detailed feasibility studies, most of the proposed projects were subsequently found to be unprofitable due to high production costs found to be much higher than originally thought. The cancellation of Thailand's soda ash project after it was found that a 500-kilometre railway had to be built to transport the raw materials to the plant, and that it needed to export more than half its output, is a good example. Projections of raw material and operating costs indicated that the plant would not be able to compete in world markets.

(ii) Project implementation. There were several weaknesses in the institutional and procedural framework. The need for a consensus in their decision making and need for the participation of all ASEAN countries in the AIPs made agreement difficult to achieve which resulted in the abandonment of some AIPs. Long delays in the implementation resulted in cost escalation, making some AIPs ultimately non-viable.

(iii) Project financing. Government-to-government projects were difficult to negotiate especially in financing the projects. Although the Japanese government had pledged a loan of US$1 billion towards the AIPs, other terms of the loan package were not specified at the time. There were long negotiations and delays when the Japanese government was approached to finance the scheme.

(iv) Lack of private sector participation in the identification, formulation, financing or implementation. It underestimated the role of small industry in ASEAN development. Also since they were large-scale, capital intensive and high-risk investments due to the long gestation period, the AIP did not appeal to the private sector.

Thus, it was left to the ASEAN governments and respective national agencies and corporations to participate in such projects. Of the five AIPs identified, only two (urea projects) have been implemented on a reduced scale.

(v) Lack of commitments by member countries to the market sharing arrangement. The experience of the last two decades has demonstrated the unwillingness of ASEAN national governments to grant others – and therefore deny themselves – exclusive rights of production in specific areas even if these were part of an exchange arrangement. All of them had highly ambitious plans for their countries' industrial future, and for many ASEAN governments receiving a specific AIP often seemed unequal to the apparent sacrifice of industrial ambitions in various areas. Thus, every government had tried to restrict as much as possible the scope of the AIPs hosted by other countries so as to give themselves the greatest freedom for future action, even to the point of rendering such projects non-viable. One good example was the proposal to locate a 200 hp diesel engine in Singapore. But Indonesia wanted the diesel engine project. After unsuccessful attempts to divide the project between the two countries according to the capacity of the diesel engines, Singapore abandoned it completely (Tan, 1996). Another good example was the Indonesian announcement of its decision to proceed with a national soda-ash plant in 1981 despite the apprehension of the other ASEAN countries, especially Thailand, that this would adversely affect the ASEAN soda-ash.

(vi) Complexities and bureaucracy. Given the range of issues to be settled and complexities involved, the implementation of the AIP had not been facilitated by the decentralized ASEAN machinery. Matters had been negotiated and decisions arrived at through a series of meetings at different levels held at different time intervals. The procedures for receiving Japanese soft loans had been long drawn out. For example, in the case of Indonesia's ASEAN urea project, from the feasibility study to the final approval it took 20 months to complete. By the time the project was ready for launching, its cost had escalated by more than 30 percent (from the initial cost of US$300 million to US$400 million). At another level private sector cooperation, frustrated by ASEAN bureaucracy, was moving forward without ASEAN support.

(b) *ASEAN industrial complementation (AIC) and brand-to-brand complementation (BBC).* The AIC (established in 1981) is an improved version of the AIP after facing implementation difficulties. Under this scheme member countries are allocated complementary products in the specific industrial sectors for the production and preferential trade among themselves, that is, the provision of tariff preferences of 50 percent and protection from competition up to three years by disallowing competing projects during this period.[6] By dividing different production stages of vertically integrated industries among themselves, the ASEAN countries hope to increase intra-ASEAN trade and investment and bring about competitive prices and product quality of international standard.

Based on resource pooling and market sharing, the scheme was to be participated in by at least four member countries, and the identification of appropriate products for inclusion in the scheme was to be done by the ASEAN Chambers of Commerce and Industry (CCI), as its key feature, subject to the approval of the ASEAN Committee of Industry, Minerals and Energy (COIME) and by the ASEAN Committee on Trade and Tourism (COTT) for tariff preferences. The ASEAN CCI was supposed to act as an official spokesman of the private sector and as a channel of communication between the government and the private sector for the purpose of industrial complementation (Chee and Jang-Won, 1988, p. 3). This identification and consultation role of the ASEAN CCI was meant to bring out the much needed private sector initiative which was lacking in the AIP programme.

A number of AIC projects have been recommended to the government for consideration, but only one package, involving automobile parts and components, has been approved. This project has proven to be unsuccessful. Similar problems were encountered in the identification and implementation of the AIC projects. The long bureaucratic procedure adopted in the identification and implementation of an AIC project had produced a number of time-consuming extensive consultations, discussions and approvals. Another stumbling block in the area of industrial complementation has been the absence of established goals and guidelines shared by the interested private sector bodies and the respective ASEAN governments. Such shared goals could make negotiations regarding product choice, market access and investment funding less prone to bureaucratic delays. But there was too little private sector participation. The AIC guidelines in terms of planning and implementation were drawn up without private sector participation and have been described as inflexible and impractical by ASEAN businessmen. The exclusivity clause of three years provided in the AIC basic agreement did not offer sufficient incentives. Also, apart from the preferential tariffs, other forms of incentives and assistance were excluded. It did not allow a firm to have a full monopoly by specifying an unfavourable time limit for exclusive privileges of AIC products. The requirement that at least four ASEAN countries participate in an AIC project has made it difficult to identify projects. Existing avenues of AIC procedures did not facilitate easy identification or approval of projects. Even if it was easy to identify the projects, it would have been difficult to allocate them, especially those deemed desirable by most ASEAN countries. In the AIC scheme every country wanted to produce the high value-added rather than the low value-added component. Thus, the allocation of products to participating member countries has proven to be difficult. Further, the proliferation of different models and brands has led to a situation where a country imported a product of one brand from another member country without exporting to that country due to the mismatch of brands.

In view of the above, the AIC project for automotive components was not successful. With the exception of Singapore, all the other ASEAN countries have developed their own automobile industries with participation from multinational automotive companies.

The BBC (established in 1988) is an offshoot of the AIC and is similarly concerned with the production and exchange of automotive parts and components to facilitate horizontal specialization in the production of these products in the region. But unlike the AIC, this scheme encourages automotive brand owners to exploit the economies of scale of production by exchanging approved automotive parts and components for specified automotive brand. There are about 70 approved BBC projects currently being implemented involving more than 10 automotive manufacturers (ASEAN Secretariat, 1995, p. 14).

(c) *ASEAN Industrial Joint Venture (AIJV)*. About the same time that the AIC scheme was announced, the ASEAN–CCI Council, which met in Jakarta at the end of 1980, proposed a new scheme in response to the difficulties encountered in the AIP and AIC schemes. AIJVs are private sector equivalents of AIPs enjoying exclusivity and other privileges similar to the AIC projects, but with added elements of flexibility. They are not required to have total ASEAN ownership. In contrast to the AIP and AIC projects, investors are free to locate their projects in any participating

countries to produce accredited AIJV products. They are open to
non-ASEAN nationals, and ASEAN ownership can be waived
as long as the ASEAN component is at least 51 percent. Any
manufactured products involving investors from at least two
ASEAN countries holding a combined 51 percent minimum equity
would qualify for tariff preferences in all ASEAN countries. Tariff
preferences on AIJV products applied to only participating countries for a four year period (this exclusivity was subsequently
waived). A margin of preferences at 90 percent based on the
prevailing ASEAN PTA rate of the importing country has been
extended to approved AIJV products. While receiving AIJV preferences, they must also extend the same preferences. There is an
emphasis on equity and market sharing, unlike AIC's reciprocity.

There are two types of AIJV projects: single AIJV – single
product produced by two or more ASEAN countries, and complementary AIJV – for example, machinery, textile, automobile.
Most of the AIJV projects proposed in the early 1980s were large
scale and involved heavy industry such as the manufacture of
paper, tractors, ferro-alloys and so on. Of the 21 projects which
have been proposed, very few have been implemented. Most of
the AIJV projects have foreign equity participation and few are
ASEAN-wide in their coverage (Tan, 1996, p. 154). To date, 23
AIJV projects have been approved (ASEAN Secretariat, 1995,
p. 14).

Limitations. The AIJV projects have encountered bureaucratic delays
in identification, formulation and approval. The time and bureaucracy
involved in gaining the acceptance by governments of an AIJV in most
cases far exceed the economic benefits obtainable after the acceptance
within the scheme. For example, it took three years to win the ASEAN
ministers' approval to launch the AIJV agreement.

Dumping actions by non-ASEAN suppliers have also eroded the
tariff preferences provided under the scheme and some in the private
sector have found the tariff preferences insufficient incentives. But the
most serious problem has been the reluctance of member countries to
participate in such joint ventures which could pose a threat to their
own existing domestic industries.

3.2.5   Conclusion

In summary, although progress has been made to make the industrial
cooperation schemes more attractive to the private sector by shifting
away from the government-initiated AIPs to the more private sector-
based AIJV and brand-to-brand complementation, the impact of the

schemes on industrial development has been quite limited due to administrative and implementation problems and lack of private sector involvement.

Having realized the shortcomings of current industrial cooperation schemes, the ASEAN countries have been exploring ways to improve their effectiveness. First, at their informal meeting in Phuket in April, 1995 the ASEAN Economic Ministers agreed to scrap the brand-to-brand complementation and AIJV schemes, and to develop a more effective industrial cooperation scheme with the active participation of the ASEAN private sector. Second, at the Fifth ASEAN Summit in December, 1995 held in Jakarta, the ASEAN Heads of Government approved the establishment of an ASEAN–CCI permanent secretariat at the ASEAN Secretariat in Jakarta.[7] Third, the ASEAN Senior Economic Officials in Jakarta on September 12, 1996 agreed to set in motion another investment liberalization scheme – ASEAN Industrial Cooperation (Aico) Scheme by November, 1996. The main privilege under Aico is that participating companies can enjoy preferential tariff rates of zero to five percent immediately upon approval for the export of their products within the region.

3.3 Development and cooperation in agriculture
This section describes the importance of agriculture to ASEAN; reviews the past developments in agriculture; the transformation and modernization of the food sector, largely under the impetus of the Green Revolution; and cooperative undertakings within ASEAN agriculture.

Although the importance of agriculture as a source of output to the ASEAN countries is diminishing, more than half of the ASEAN population still live in the rural sector and are engaged in agriculture. Agricultural development has, therefore, been given due importance by most of the ASEAN countries. But the ASEAN development experiences in this sector have been varied due to the differences in policies pursued and the different institutions existing in each country. Further, ASEAN cooperation in this sector has been highly technical and developmental in nature, rather than in terms of market sharing arrangements.

3.3.1 *Importance of agriculture*
As can be gleaned from Table 3.4, agriculture has been and still is an important sector in ASEAN. It is a major contributor to the GDP of the ASEAN countries, except for Brunei and the city-state Singapore which have limited land. During the past decade (1980–90), the relative share of agriculture has declined significantly, except in the Philippines,

Table 3.4   ASEAN share of agriculture in GDP (%)

	1980	1985	1990	1993	1994	1995
Brunei	0.6	1.2	1.7	–	–	–
Indonesia	30.7	22.6	19.7	18.0	16.6	15.9
Malaysia	22.9	20.7	19.4	16.0	14.8	13.9
Philippines	25.6	29.2	26.9	22.7	22.3	21.5
Singapore	1.1	0.7	0.3	0.2	0.2	0.2
Thailand	20.6	19.6	14.2	12.2	11.1	10.9
Vietnam	50.0	47.2	37.5	28.8	27.7	–

Note: –: not available.

Sources: ADB, Key Indicators of Developing Asian and Pacific Countries (1991); Asian Development Outlook (1995/1996 and 1996/1997).

as a result of rapid industrialization: from 30.7 percent to 19.7 percent in Indonesia; 22.9 percent to 19.4 percent in Malaysia; 1.1 percent to 0.3 percent in Singapore and 20.6 percent to 14.2 percent in Thailand.[8] This trend continued into the early 1990s so that in 1995 agriculture's share was reduced for all ASEAN (minus Brunei). Although there has been a significant decline in the relative share of agriculture in the total GDP, agriculture still occupies a substantial portion of GDP in ASEAN and will continue to have profound socio-economic implications.

Although the agricultural sector is the backward sector in the ASEAN economies (plagued with problems of high unemployment, underemployment and mass poverty, due to the rural population explosion and low productivity), the number of employed persons found in the agricultural sector is significant. No less than 45 percent of the employed persons in Indonesia, the Philippines, Thailand and Vietnam are found in the agricultural sector in 1995. Thus, it is the main provider of jobs in ASEAN. The share of agricultural employment in Singapore and Brunei has always been negligible as their economies are not agri-based, as Table 3.5 shows.[9] Except for Brunei and Singapore, ASEAN countries are net exporters of food, agriculture and forest products. They are major world exporters of natural rubber (Malaysia), palm oil (Indonesia and Malaysia), copra and coconut oil (the Philippines), and rice (Thailand and Vietnam). Other major agricultural products for each of the four ASEAN countries are: for Indonesia rubber, coffee, tea, tobacco, pepper; for Malaysia sawn logs and sawn timber; for the Philippines sugar, desiccated coconut and lumber; and for Thailand corn, cassava, sugar, molasses and rubber. Agricultural exports represent a

Table 3.5   Number of persons employed by main industry (as % of total number of persons employed)

ASEAN countries	Agriculture					Manufacturing				
	1970	1980	1990	1994	1995	1970	1980	1990	1994	1995
Brunei[a]	–	5.0	2.0	–	–	–	4.0	8.8	–	–
Indonesia[b]	64.0	56.0	55.9	50.8	–	7.0	9.1	10.1	11.4	–
Malaysia[c]	18.0	37.2	26.0	19.9	18.9	13.0	15.5	19.9	24.7	25.5
Philippines	54.0	51.4	45.2	44.7	44.5	12.0	11.0	9.7	10.3	9.8
Singapore	4.0	1.6	0.4	0.3	0.2	22.0	30.1	28.4	25.7	24.0
Thailand[d]	79.0	70.8	64.0	56.7*	–	4.0	7.9	10.2	12.3*	–
Vietnam	–	69.9	71.6	72.5*	68.9	–	10.7	11.2	10.7*	12.1

Notes:
–: not available; * figures for 1993 as 1994 data are unavailable.
[a] Only figures for 1981 and 1991 are available.
[b] Figures for 1970 are based on 1971 figures.
[c] Figures for 1970 are based on 1974 figures. The 1974 figures are for Peninsular Malaysia only.
[d]Figures for 1970 are based on 1971 figures.

Sources: *ASEAN Statistical Yearbook on Food, Agriculture and Forestry, 1980–90*; ADB, *Key Indicators of Developing Asian and Pacific Countries* (1995, 1996); Brunei Ministry of Finance, *Brunei Darussalam Statistical Yearbook* (1993).

substantial source of foreign exchange earnings for the ASEAN4 countries and are thus crucial to their economic growth and stability.

Agriculture has also proven to be a potent engine of growth for the whole economy. In the case of the Philippines, for example, in the 1980s GDP growth had averaged –0.02 percent while agriculture posted a positive growth.

3.3.2   ASEAN agricultural performance
The ASEAN agricultural sector is basically made up of two subsectors: the large landholding subsector which produces cash crops mainly for export markets, and the relatively small landholding subsector which produces mainly rice and corn for domestic consumption and domestic markets.

This dualistic nature has posed as a serious obstacle to achieving a balanced growth and agricultural integration within ASEAN. But despite this, the ASEAN countries on the whole have achieved significant agricultural progress in terms of increased productivity and reduced

income inequality in the rural sector through the effective implementation of appropriate policies and technological improvements.

The most significant development in the ASEAN agriculture has
been the successful transformation and modernization of their food
sector, largely under the impetus of the Green Revolution, that is, the
introduction and diffusion of modern high-yielding varieties (HYVs) of
rice. In the past, expansion of the land area had been the main source
of agricultural output growth, but since the 1970s increase in productivity has become the major source of growth, aided by the
expansion of rural infrastructure and introduction of new technology,
closing the gaps in rice productivity between ASEAN and other East
Asian countries.[10] By 1975, 62 percent of the rice area in the Philippines
was planted with the modern varieties, 41 percent in Indonesia, 36
percent in Malaysia, but only 7 percent in Thailand.[11]

The most notable success stories are Indonesia (which had been the
largest world rice importer due to its large population and partly as a
result of the neglect of agricultural development under Sukarno) and
Malaysia (which had traditionally been a net food importer as cash
crops dominated their agricultural sector). There has been a creditable
growth in rice production over the 1980s, but in the past the growth in
domestic demand had outpaced the growth in domestic production.[12]
The same thing was true with corn. The Philippines has gone through
a number of food production programmes since the mid-1970s, but has
remained as one of the region's biggest food importers until quite
recently. Among the ASEAN countries, Thailand seems to be the only
consistent rice exporter.

Green Revolution   The basis of the ASEAN Green Revolution is a
biological and chemical innovation involving the use of high yielding
varieties of miracle rice, fertilizers, insecticides, pesticides, rodenticides,
herbicides and fungicides. It also requires mechanical innovation, for
example, mechanical farming, requiring heavy capital investment and a
new pattern of farm management and cultivation technology and water
control.

Although there are direct costs and indirect costs such as environmental costs due to rapid use of fertilizers and multiple cropping-
induced erosion, there are substantial benefits including increased rice
production, increase in efficiency (measured by output per unit of
input), diversification of agricultural commodities (multiple cropping
concept), provision of additional rural employment, increased income
at individual level and generation of foreign exchange with spill-over
effects into other economic sectors (forward/backward linkages).[13]

The overall pattern of agricultural development progress in the ASEAN4 since the adoption of the new production technology has been uneven, however, partly due to their differences in capacity to absorb and diffuse improved technology and partly due to their different institutional responses (Wong, 1979, p. 96). Their varied experiences with the Green Revolution is a good reminder that institutions do play a significant role and that productivity increases depend not just on the strength of technological innovations but also on the favourable interaction of the technological change with the institutional environment.

Quality of institutional environment   Institutional environment refers to a country's legal, political and regulatory framework. Indicators often used to measure the quality of the institutional environment are security of land ownership or use, policy environment (right policies and stable/ credible government) and bureaucratic quality.

Security of land ownership   The principal consequence of an inadequate institutional environment is insecure land rights. In the context of ASEAN agriculture, this land right refers to the right of a farmer to the land, to the revenue streams generated by the land, and to any other contractual obligations due to a farmer. These rights are more secure to the extent that political and legal institutions inhibit unilateral private and public decisions that reassign land rights. Well-defined and transparent laws on land ownership and use are examples of an institution that protects individuals from violation of their land rights. Differences in structure of land ownership and in the legal protection of the rights of tenants have given rise to the differences in the agricultural performance among the ASEAN countries. There is a strong link between the benefits of technological progress and secured tenure of land ownership or use. This explains Thailand's more notable performance in agricultural productivity compared to the Philippines where land distribution under the land reform programme failed. Such land reform is essential in the Philippine context where land ownership is highly skewed. Without effective protection of the tenants' rights or guaranteed investment, land use will be unsecured and thus farmers tend to refrain from investment in new agricultural technology.

Policy environment   Appropriate policies conducive to the adoption of a new technology, accompanied by a stable and credible government are necessary. Credit policy is the most important component of these policies. ASEAN agriculture consists of a large proportion of small-scale farmers who usually are short of capital and have difficulty in access to credit financing. Since costly inputs like machineries, fertilizers and pesticides are necessary complements for the adoption of high-yielding varities (HYVs), small-scale farmers are unlikely to benefit from the use of the HYV seeds if they cannot finance the purchase of these inputs. Therefore, credit policies that favour only large-scale farmers and fail to cater for the needs and abilities of the small-scale farmers will hinder the adoption of new technological methods by small-scale farmers.

Policies that emphasize industrialization without equal attention to agricultural development have also acted as barriers to the balanced distribution of the benefits of the Green Revolution. This overemphasis on urban development has led to inadequate provision of the required infrastructure (such as irrigation, harvest facilities, transport, electrification, agricultural research and extension of services) critical to the generation and diffusion of technology in the agricultural sector. Inadequate funds allocated for the rural sector have also contributed to the low literacy rate in the ASEAN rural areas, preventing the farmers from being receptive to new technological methods and to the transfer of relevant skills and knowledge for the proper application and management of new technology. Except for Malaysia, the ASEAN countries had embarked on urban-biased development strategies in the 1960s and 1970s, leading to significant income disparity between the urban and rural sectors. In contrast, Malaysia's impressive agricultural performance in productivity and poverty alleviation in the rural sector were largely due to its less urban-biased policies. Consequently, more resources have been channeled to the agricultural sector in terms of infrastructure provision and subsidies.

Stable and credible government   Governments perceived to be unstable and without credibility create an uncertain atmosphere which is not conducive to agricultural investment in new technological methods. This is because the returns from such a heavy investment are substantially affected by changes in taxing and subsidising policies.

The less notable performances of Indonesia in the 1960s, and the Philippines in the 1970s and early 1980s, could be largely attributed to their political instability resulting in frequent changes in policy and creating an atmosphere of uncertainty for investment in agricultural technology.[14]

Quality of bureaucracy   Policies and projects are only successful if they can be implemented and managed effectively, and the effective implementation of policies and management of projects hinges on the efficiency of bureaucracy. Bureaucratic efficiency is particularly important in the management of an irrigation system. Since success of cropping depends on the adequate and timely supply of water, proper maintenance and operation of an irrigation system is crucial. Hence, bureaucratic inefficiency, which prevents the proper operation and maintenance of an irrigation system, would hinder a broad-based adoption of new cultivation technology.

3.3.3 ASEAN economic cooperation in agriculture

As an important sector in ASEAN, cooperation in agriculture has been numerous. But all the cooperative undertakings in agriculture have so far been technical and developmental in nature. The Committee on Food, Agriculture and Forestry (COFAF) is responsible for the identification and implementation of cooperative undertakings in the agricultural sector. Formed in March 1977, it undertakes the following tasks: (a) to coordinate, review and prepare studies on the prospects of the agricultural sector; (b) to develop efficient methods for the exchange of information on agriculture; (c) to identify areas for cooperation; (d) to maintain close ties with related committees in ASEAN and with other related organizations inside and outside the region; and (e) to report its progress to the ASEAN Economic Ministers (AEM).

Between 1978 and 1988 COFAF had identified 46 cooperative projects – 7 in food, 10 in agriculture, 15 in forestry, 8 in livestock and 6 in fishery. By 1985, 13 of them were ongoing, 4 completed, and 29 not yet implemented. The largest number of projects were located in the Philippines followed by Malaysia, Thailand and Indonesia in descending order. The majority of the fundings for these projects came from sources outside the region. Only a few projects were pursued on a long-term basis. One of them was the ASEAN Food Security Project which established in 1979 an ASEAN Emergency Rice Reserve to be contributed to by each of the member countries. The objective was to create a stockpile of 50,000 tonnes of rice to meet shortfalls in domestic supply. This is currently being reviewed for the purpose of creating a more dynamic food security arrangement to enhance intra-ASEAN trade and promote food production under the principle of comparative advantage. Others included the Food Handling and the Seed Technology project.

ASEAN cooperation in agriculture has also been successful in their dealings with the developed countries on matters of market access for their primary exports, better terms of trade, stabilization of export earnings and other non-sensitive areas of cooperation.

3.3.4   Obstacles to trade liberalization for agriculture

The type of ASEAN cooperation in agriculture has been technical in nature aimed at increasing production and guaranteeing supply, rather than at market sharing. Despite the perceived benefits of integrating agriculture, progress in this area has been slow because of the following reasons:

(i)   Political priorities (for example, national security). The first and foremost justification for trade restrictions in agriculture is the need to safeguard national security. Any country with an agricultural capacity tends rather to be self-sufficient or to hedge and diversify sources of imports, especially of food supplies. Although specialization under free trade could lead to efficient allocation of resources, it could also lead to dependency which is politically risky. This fear was vindicated in 1973 when a rise in the price of Thai rice created some problems in countries importing heavily from Thailand. Agriculture is protected by almost all countries for other political reasons such as to improve the balance of payments and redistribute income in favour of farm groups in the context of high unemployment and inefficiency in the agricultural sector.

(ii)   Structural and technological dualism in agriculture. Another obstacle is the inherent structural and technological dualism of ASEAN agriculture, with its small-landholding subsector producing primarily food (rice) and feed grains (corn) and the large-scale landholders producing cash crops (for example, sugar, bananas, rubber) mostly for export. In the event that complete liberalization takes place, the small-scale subsector could be left behind while increased competition propels the latter to greater efficiency and productivity, thereby exacerbating income disparity and social problems. Thus, trade liberalization may hurt the agro-industries and the livelihood of small farmers. This partly explains the exclusion of rice from immediate tariff reduction under the ASEAN Free Trade Area's (AFTA) Common Effective Preferential Tariff (CEPT) scheme.[15]

(iii)   Competition rather than complementarity. Another problem is the highly competitive nature of agricultural products produced by the ASEAN countries. Due to similarity in factor endowments and climatic conditions, they have produced similar agricultural products. Under integration there will clearly be losers, and thus the public support for intra-regional trade in agriculture is weak.

(iv)   Inadequate infrastructure. Transportation and telecommunication networks within the region are relatively costly and inefficient. ASEAN infrastructure networks have been set up to serve the domestic markets and their traditional extra-regional trading partners like Japan, the US and European Union (EU). This lack of regional orientation is a significant obstacle to trade expansion as the costly and inefficient port and other related transport facilities hinder the trading of agricultural products which are relatively bulky and low-valued.[16]

Other minor obstacles include ASEAN countries' lack of first hand experience in agricultural cooperation relative to other areas like the joint service and industrial projects. Thus, ASEAN is uncertain as to which is the best approach and what effects would result. Moreover, ASEAN countries do not have the capacity to liberalize trade significantly and yet protect farmers from price fluctuations and more efficient regional suppliers.

3.3.5 Prospects for agricultural integration
Given the political sensitivity and low degree of complementarity of agriculture in ASEAN, the type of economic cooperation could only be in terms of resource pooling, rather than market sharing. Trade liberalization can also occur in commodities of a less politically sensitive nature, and in new products that will not affect the original level of employment.

However, the long-term prospect for a complete agricultural integration in ASEAN is far from bleak. Agriculture is already included in the proposed ASEAN Free Trade Area, except for a few obstacles. Most of the above problems have partly been resolved, and thus the ASEAN governments need to merely encourage and consolidate more joint ventures in agriculture and agri-processing to increase productivity and to ensure a constant and stable source of primary commodities and to be selective in its inclusion of the various agricultural products in the integration programme.

Laudable proposals attempted at the recent AFTA council meeting are ambitious yet brave and commendable. Under the proposed Common Effective Preferential Tariff (CEPT) scheme, all ASEAN members are expected to cut tariff rates on most agricultural products by zero to five percent by the year 2003. Given the strong competition posed by China, India and other regional groupings, ASEAN must respond quickly so as not to be left behind. The CEPT scheme is a move in the right, much needed, direction. In view of the trends to explore more ways of speeding up liberalization and noting how the other regions were removing tariffs swiftly, the complete integration of agriculture in ASEAN should not be long. This can be seen in reports from Thailand claiming to be a strong advocate for free trade in agriculture, wanting as much access to other markets as possible and in the Brunei Sultan's persistent call to speed up the trade liberalization process. Thus, the tricky question to ask is how to cut the number of items in the sensitive list, which are shielded from tariff reduction under the CEPT scheme, because of the perceived strategic and security value to the member countries. At present, some products which are considered sensitive – such as rice, maize and soya beans – are excluded from tariff reduction until the year 2010, instead of the proposed 2003, the target date for trimming tariffs to zero to 5 percent. However, with much confidence, this will probably be done in due time, through the greater flexibility and sensitivity of the ASEAN member countries towards one another.

3.3.4   Conclusion

The ASEAN cooperation in agriculture has been successful so far in areas that only require the pooling of resources to guarantee food supply and improve production as well as in their external economic relations to gain more market access and better terms of trade. To the extent that agricultural development implies food security and improved productivity, the ASEAN cooperative undertakings, most notably the ASEAN Food Security Reserve Project and the Seed Technology Project, have played a significant role in ASEAN agricultural development.

3.4   Development and cooperation in services

Another important feature of ASEAN economic development has been the rapid growth of their services sector since the 1960s. In 1994 the services sector contributed roughly 40 percent to 62 percent of Gross Domestic Product (GDP) in ASEAN countries, as Table 3.6 shows, and consistent with the normal pattern of economic development, its share has grown over time. It is now the largest contributor to national output in the ASEAN countries, with the exception of Indonesia and Malaysia. Singapore has the largest and most developed services sector as a proportion of GDP, its activity accounting for 62 percent of its GDP in 1994.

ASEAN cooperation in this sector has been instrumental in the sector's rapid growth, although its contribution has not been as spectacular. ASEAN cooperation in the services sector has been technical in nature and the ASEAN countries have been reluctant to expand

Table 3.6 ASEAN share of services in GDP (%)*

	1970	1980	1993	1994	1995
Brunei	–	12.4	43.8	–	–
		(73.8)	(37.3)		
Indonesia	37.0	34.3	40.3	39.8	41.9
	(28.0)	(41.3)	(42.1)	(43.6)	(42.2)
Malaysia	–	41.3	40.0	39.8	39.0
		(35.8)	(44.2)	(45.4)	(47.1)
Philippines	38.1	36.0	42.9	42.8	43.0
	(33.7)	(40.5)	(34.4)	(34.8)	(35.5)
Singapore	61.4	60.0	63.3	62.4	57.1
	(36.4)	(38.8)	(36.5)	(37.4)	(42.7)
Thailand	44.1	49.7	46.9	46.8	46.9
	(25.7)	(30.1)	(40.9)	(42.1)	(42.2)
Vietnam	–	31.0	–	42.4	38.4
		(26.3)		(25.3)	(27.7)

Notes:
*Figures in brackets are shares of industry in GDP.
–: not available.

Sources: ADB, *Asian Development Outlook* (1994, 1995, 1996 and 1997); Brunei
Ministry of Finance, *Brunei Darussalam Statistical Yearbook* (1993).

their scope of cooperation in trade (trade liberalization) to the services
sector. There is, however, now an attempt to include the trade in
services for trade liberalization within ASEAN. In the last ASEAN
Economic Ministers Meeting held in Brunei, September, 1995 (*The
Straits Times*, 9 September, 1995), the ASEAN officials accepted in
principle an ASEAN Framework Agreement on Services which was
signed at the ASEAN Summit in December, 1995. They identified
four areas in the services sector for specific negotiations for market
concessions: financial services, tourism, infrastructure development,
transport and communications.

This part of the chapter will highlight some of the key characteristics
of the services sector in ASEAN and then outline the role of ASEAN
cooperation in each of the specific subsectors: banking and finance,
transport and tourism.

3.4.1   Key features

Since the 1980s one has seen a rapid technological revolution in ASEAN in almost all services activities. Moreover, considerable variety exists between services sectors of the ASEAN countries, reflecting different stages of economic development, resource endowments and economic orientation. As already shown in Table 3.6, Singapore has the most developed service sector which provides most of the country's output and employment.

Significant variation also exists within their services sector. In finance, for example, the services range from those of the rural money lenders to those from multinational banks; road transport can also range from modern intercity buses to trishaws.

Moreover, in this sector their respective governments have played a key economic role, both as a direct source of employment and indirectly through expenditure programmes designed to improve the quality of physical and social infrastructure. In Singapore the big banks such as the Development Bank of Singapore (DBS) and Post Office Savings Bank (POSBank) are government banks. In Indonesia and Malaysia, banks have been set up not only for economic objectives but also for political reasons.

Finally, there is the internationalization of services. Services were traditionally regarded as non-tradables, an ancillary to the goods sector and rarely traded across national borders. However, reduced barriers to international commerce, increasing personal mobility, and revolution in transport and telecommunications have internationalized the services industries. Banking, professional and personal services, insurance, tourism, data processing and construction services are increasingly traded within and beyond the region.

3.4.2   Subsectors

The rapid growth of the services sectors in ASEAN is to a large extent reflective of the strong performance of the following subsectors: financial services, transport and tourism.

3.4.2.1   Financial services   The financial subsector has grown and evolved into a more sophisticated financial system due to technological innovation, rise of non-traditional modes of service production and delivery, growth of the real sector, greater internationalization, deregulation and greater mobility of financial resources within the region.

Based on standard microeconomic theories, deregulation and greater mobility of financial resources can lead to an efficient allocation of savings and real capital, increase the supply of savings by increasing the rate of return and eliminating the non-price disincentives to savings. These allow individual asset holders to diversify their potfolio investments and enjoy a higher risk-return trade-off. They can also broaden and deepen the financial markets and increase liquidity in secondary markets, lower the cost of borrowing and improve the matching between the borrowers and lenders.[17]

The role of government has been crucial in the ASEAN's financial development by establishing a favourable macroeconomic environment in terms of low inflation. The stable environments of Malaysia, Singapore and Thailand have been particularly important in instilling confidence in holding cash and quasi-money holdings; on the other hand, the less predictable environment of Indonesia and the Philippines had once hindered financial development. Further, their respective governments have taken the lead in deregulating their financial sector. Prior to the 1980s, Indonesia and the Philippines had the most heavily regulated formal banking sectors. They later recognized the self-defeating nature of financial regulation, and in the 1980s started deregulating their financial sector.

They have also directly participated in the financial sector through ownership of banks. Bank ownership has been part of a deliberate strategy of economic development in Singapore and in the more regulated environments of Indonesia and the Philippines. In Indonesia and Malaysia state-owned banks are a key instrument of ethnic redistribution and promotion of indigenous businesses. But over time there has been a trend towards privatization, and the share of state-owned banks in the total financial sector has shrunk, or has grown slower compared to their private competitors.

3.4.2.2 Transport All major forms of transport have expanded quickly due to the ASEAN governments' massive infrastructure programmes, the reduction in costs of transport due to technological advancements in air travel and light commercial transport, and the simplification of government regulations and rising incomes leading to more personal mobility and demand for transport services.

3.4.2.3 Tourism Tourism is now an important ASEAN foreign exchange earner, ranking highly with major manufactured exports such as textiles. It has expanded quickly due to the deregulation and simplification of immigration requirements, rising income and competitive exchange rate regimes, and the decline in the real cost of international travel and effective promotional efforts.

Apart from being a major foreign exchange earner, tourism is important to the ASEAN countries because the ASEAN region has now become one of the fastest growing tourist destinations in the world. Although tourism has made different contributions to individual ASEAN members, intra-ASEAN tourism has become an important and growing fraction of total ASEAN tourism.

3.4.3   ASEAN financial cooperation

The ASEAN cooperation in the area of financial services has contributed to the growth and development of their financial sector by fostering greater mobility of financial resources within the region through the standardization and harmonization of rules and regulations governing the banking and financial practises in ASEAN and the reduction of the 'ability and willingness barriers' to financial integration.[18] Among ASEAN's notable achievements include the ASEAN Swap Arrangement to assist member countries bridge temporary international liquidity problems in times of crisis and the increased use of ASEAN currencies in the settlement of intra-ASEAN trade in recent years.

3.4.3.1   Government   On the governmental level, the Committee of Finance and Banking (COFAB), established in 1976, is in charge of exploring and monitoring the possible area of financial cooperation. The major activity of COFAB is to supervise the meetings of ASEAN insurance commissioners, tax administrators and ASEAN working groups on customs matters. The major accomplishments of COFAB include the agreement on the need for bilateral investment guarantees and avoidance of double taxation and its ability to act as a vehicle for ASEAN–third party dialogue in financial matters.

COFAB is responsible for the creation of the ASEAN swap facility (1977). The ASEAN swap arrangement is intended for short-term liquidity crises. The fund was US$100 million in 1977 and US$200 million in 1979 which members can borrow in times of short-term liquidity crisis. The borrowing limit was up to US$80 million repayable in 3 months, renewable once for 3 months. In 1983, four swap transactions took place. At this time Benigno Aquino was assassinated causing a large outflow of capital from the Philippines.

3.4.3.2   Private sector   On the private sector level, there is the creation of the ASEAN Bankers Association (1976). Membership consists of member countries' banking industry associations. There are three components of the ASEAN Bankers Association: conference (ASEAN Banking Conference), council (ASEAN Banking Council) and secretariat. ASEAN Banking Conference's major accomplishments include the formulation of policy for coordination of ASEAN cooperation among ASEAN bankers, financing of agriculture and agro-based industries, and banking education and cooperation in investment, trade and finance. ASEAN Banking Council's major accomplishment is the establishment of AFC (ASEAN Financial Corporation). As a joint venture among the private banks of the ASEAN member countries, it is intended as a vehicle for the pooling of resources required to finance regional development projects. Its specific objectives are to promote industrial development, intra-regional trade, financial cooperation and mobilization of financial resources.

A number of proposals were proposed in the late 1970s and early 1980s such as the setting up of an ASEAN Trading and Investment Corporation (ATIC) and an ASEAN Bankers Acceptance (ABC), but were not successful due to the lack of interest and financial non-viability.

3.4.4 Prospects for ASEAN financial integration

It is evident from the previous section that ASEAN financial cooperation has played an important and supportive role in the growth and development of their financial sector and in facilitating trade and investment in the region. ASEAN financial cooperation, however, is only one of the many factors responsible for the rapid growth of their financial sector. Individual countries' uncoordinated policies of deregulation, stable macroeconomic environment and growth of their real sector have also played a very important role.

The prospect for greater ASEAN financial cooperation depends on how the ASEAN countries can influence the following factors or determinants affecting the level of financial integration: (i) Comparative levels of financial development. Domestic financial development is a prerequisite for international financial integration; Singapore is the most financially developed among ASEAN. (ii) Level of intra-ASEAN banking linkages. The ASEAN Finance Corporation and ASEAN Banking Council are formal links between ASEAN banking industries. (iii) Level of real economic integration. Intra-ASEAN trade and other forms of economic cooperation lay the essential groundwork for financial integration. As real economic linkages increase, the demand for financial cooperation will increase. (iv) The degree of foreign exchange/capital controls. (v) Exchange rate variability which relies on the adoption of a common unit of account and the strength of the existing forward markets. (vi) Tax treatment neutrality. (vii) Comparative regulatory policies for domestic financial institutions, particularly in relation to the asset and liability structure of banks. (viii) Conformity/nonconformity with acceptable commercial standards. Noncompliance with certain regulations may form a barrier to financial integration if significant loss of confidence results. Financial crises or scandals can undermine both the domestic and international financial systems.

3.4.5   ASEAN cooperation in transport

Cooperation in the area of transport falls under the supervision of the Committee on Transportation and Communications (COTAC). Working to implement and follow up on the decisions of COTAC are subcommittees. Based on the Integrated Work Programme on Transport and Communications (IWPTC) 1982–86, COTAC has identified 59 cooperative projects (mostly in the maritime sector), but only eight had been completed by the end of 1986. Many were withdrawn or deferred and included in the IWPTC 1987–91. Of the 90 projects included, only 20 were completed by the end of 1991. Completion of a project, however, in many cases just meant that the data gathering and technical part of the study had been realized. Nothing happened in terms of closer regional cooperation in the movement of goods and people. Overall, despite the priority accorded to regional cooperation in transport, the record has not been impressive.[19]

It has been argued that the lack of progress in regional cooperation in transport could be attributed to the following: absence of a coherent set of objectives; national priorities superseding regional priorities; lack of regional character in the projects identified aggravated by the lack of expertise on the part of the COTAC members; and over-reliance on external sources for project funding.[20]

3.4.6   ASEAN cooperation in tourism

The ASEAN cooperation in tourism is under the jurisdiction of the Committee of Trade and Tourism (COTT) which has established a Subcommittee on Tourism (SCOT) to deal with tourism matters. Much of the progress in this area is highly concentrated in certain operational areas such as marketing, promotion and research, with little private sector involvement. It has taken the form of establishing: (i) the ASEAN Tourism Information Centre to coordinate and manage marketing programmes and projects approved by SCOT, liaise with other world and regional tourism bodies and the private sector, and conduct public relations and other activities related to the promotion of ASEAN travel; (ii) the ASEAN Tourism Fora, annually organized and funded by ASEAN NTOs, to bring together ASEAN sellers and buyers from government and private sectors. Efforts to get the ASEAN private sector to assume a greater role have not been successful; (iii) ASEAN

Promotional Chapters which are promotional arms in major tourist markets, staffed by government personnel and collective representation to project the 'ASEAN Image'; (iv) ASEAN Travel Films and Brochures which are combined resources to produce a travel film, 'ASEAN Mosaic' and 'ASEAN Welcome' brochure; (v) Research and Manpower Training to foster exchange of information and training of personnel; (vi) Third Party Technical Assistance and Dialogue which are tourism market studies funded by UNDP, ASEAN–EU Cooperation and ASEAN–NZ Cooperation; and (vii) ASEAN Circle and Promotional Fares providing inexpensive travel within ASEAN.

3.4.7 Obstacles to tourism cooperation

Despite the significant progress in ASEAN cooperation in the field of tourism, there is still great scope for improvement, such as addressing the following problems: (a) Lack of a unified tourism promotion plan and cooperation in developing the ASEAN region as a common destination, rather than as different tourist sites. Although ASEAN cooperation has been strong in this area, additional refinements are required to make the region a more attractive and appealing destination. (b) Lack of cooperation in planning and research. This is probably the most difficult, but most important task because it requires ASEAN cooperation in identifying the region's strengths and weaknesses, and in formulating short-term and long-term plans to take advantage of anticipated tourism opportunities. (c) Travel barriers. The governments of Indonesia, the Philippines and Thailand have imposed travel taxes on departing nationals. (d) Inadequate private sector involvement. The ASEAN NTOs can provide the institutional framework for cooperation, but it is only the private sector which can implement the plans. More frequent and intensive consultations among the representatives of the national airlines and shipping and rail services should take place to provide an integrated logistical support package for tourists in the region.

3.4.7 Conclusion

ASEAN cooperation has been partly responsible for the rapid growth and development of their financial services and tourism subsectors. In the case of financial services, ASEAN cooperation has played a significant role by fostering greater mobility of financial resources, by harmonizing the rules and regulations governing the banking and financial practises in ASEAN and by promoting an exchange of information between their private sectors and government counterparts. With respect to tourism, they have been successful in undertaking cooperative efforts in the area of marketing and promotion. Unlike the financial services and tourism, the growth and development of the transport subsector could not have been partly attributable to ASEAN cooperation due to many factors including the presence of strong national interests.

Suggestions for further reading

For a good historical background of ASEAN cooperation in trade, Meyanathan and Haron (1987), Ooi (1987), Tan (1987) and Rieger (1985) are recommended. Chng (1991) and Chee Peng Lim (1987) are recommended for a comparative study of the industrialization experience of the ASEAN countries.

For a good coverage of ASEAN agricultural development, see Chiew (1987), Cabanilla (1988), pp. 55–68, and Wong (1979), Chapter 4. For a good background reading and evaluation of ASEAN cooperation in transport, see Naidu (1988), pp. 191–204 and Navaratnam (1987), pp. 357–69. On ASEAN cooperation in financial services, read Schulze (1988), pp. 157–88 and on ASEAN cooperation in tourism, read Wong (1987), 372–93 and Puntasen (1988), pp. 205–27.

Notes

1. Commodities sold under these contracts enjoy preferential duties and priority supply in times of worldwide shortage. In 1977 an emergency sharing scheme for petroleum was drawn up. Singapore, Malaysia and Indonesia were given priority over non-ASEAN countries for Thailand's exports of rice in times of shortage.
2. The establishment of preferential trading arrangements represents the first stage in the process of achieving a complete economic integration of ASEAN economies.
3. Until 1992 Malaysia was Singapore's third largest trading partner. In 1994 it overtook the US as Singapore's top trading partner (*The Straits Times*, 16 August, 1996, p. 46).
4. The increasing importance of intra-industry trade is due to the globalization strategies of the multinational companies (MNCs) which undertake the various stages of production across its affiliates in different countries to achieve greater functional specialization and exploit the benefits of comparative advantage.
5. A major objective of the diversification drive is to maximize the role of the private sector in propelling the economy in terms of output turnover and employment creation. For details, see Hashim (1996), pp. 123–4.
6. The virtual guarantee of monopoly power under this exclusivity as well as its small domestic market were the reasons for Singapore's decision not to participate in the AIC scheme on automotive parts.
7. The ASEAN–CCI Secretariat is meant to help foster greater communication and linkages between the policy-making bodies and the private sector, and thus make the private sector closely involved from the early stages of ASEAN economic policy formulation. This has been operational since July, 1996. Further, consultations between high-level private sector representatives and ASEAN Economic Ministers are held every year.
8. However, during the Philippine economic crisis of the 1980s, agriculture posted positive growth rates while all the other sectors experienced negative growth (Esmara, 1988, p. 56).

9. Vietnam is probably the most agricultural economy in ASEAN, but due to its special case, is not included in the analysis.
10. In the 1960s rice productivity in Japan was twice that in Malaysia, three times that in Indonesia and Thailand, and four times that in the Philippines.
11. Thailand was slowest to adopt the modern HYVs since it did not run out of arable lands until the 1970s, reinforced by a buoyant export market and world food crisis. In addition, it has been reported that Thailand is well known for its fragrant Thai rice which is preferred to the miracle rice (of HYVs).
12. Indonesia achieved self-sufficiency in rice in 1985. A heavily managed and generously funded programme of subsidies and extension services overcame bureaucratic inertia, droughts and pests. The Philippines had been a net importer of rice until 1994.
13. This was partly discussed in Chapter 2. For a more detailed discussion of benefits and other issues on new rice technology adoption, Feder et al. (1988) is again recommended.
14. The Sukarno era and the early years of the Suharto regime were politically unstable while the Marcos regime in the 1970s and early 1980s was marred by political and social crisis.
15. This issue will be discussed in more detail later in another chapter.
16. A comparative study on ASEAN ports' efficiency by Tongzon and Ganesalingam (1994) has revealed that except for Singapore and to a certain extent Malaysia, all other ASEAN ports' efficiency are below international standards.
17. There are also costs in terms of the loss of exchange rate flexibility and loss of domestic monetary autonomy.
18. Schulze (1988) classifies obstacles to financial integration in terms of 'ability and willingness barriers'. 'Ability barriers' include capital and foreign exchange controls, government regulations of banks and other financial institutions, government expenditure and official reserves policy. 'Willingness barriers' include fiscal policy, unstable exchange rates, higher cost of acquiring information and greater risks resulting from poor information.
19. ASEAN's collaborative efforts in this field can be grouped into the areas of shipping and ports, land transportation, civil aviation and related services. The ASEAN cooperation in this sector has been enhanced by the recent launching of the Plan of Action in Transport and Communications (1994–1996) to develop multi-modal transport and trade facilitation and to harmonize road transport laws and regulations. This will promote trade, investment and industrial linkages, thus further integrating the ASEAN economies (ASEAN Secretariat, 1995).
20. The recent deregulation of the transport sector in ASEAN are individual members' unilateral actions, rather than joint and cooperative efforts.

4 Sub-regional economic cooperation

Perhaps another significant development in the area of ASEAN economic cooperation is the emergence of economic growth triangles (GTs). This development is part of the overall emergence of several subregional economic cooperation zones in Asia since the 1980s (see Figure 4.1 for other sub-regional development zones in Asia). Min and Myo (1993) define growth triangles as transnational economic zones spread over large but defined, geographically proximate areas covering three or more countries where differences in factor endowments are exploited to promote external trade and investment.[1] Since growth triangles are increasingly becoming an important form of ASEAN economic cooperation, this chapter will examine the rationale for their emergence, their costs and potential benefits, lessons for successful and sustainable growth triangles and how they can facilitate the achievement of a regionwide economic cooperation under ASEAN.

To date, in Southeast Asia SIJORI (consisting of Singapore, Johore of Malaysia, Indonesia's Riau Province of Batam and Bintan, covering 20 000 sq km) is the oldest, having been operational since 1989. It has successfully integrated Singapore's technology and infrastructure with cheap land and labour offered by Johore and the Riau islands, giving rise to proposals for growth areas in other parts of the region (see Figure 4.2).

Three more GTs are in the making: (i) Northern Triangle or IMTGT (comprising North Sumatra of Indonesia, Northern Peninsular Malaysia, and Southern Thailand, covering 180 000 sq km of land) has passed the feasibility study stage and the recent intergovernmental and joint business council meetings on this GT have led to agreements on a range of issues and identified a menu of possible projects and initiatives. Some projects are already in operation. (ii) East ASEAN Growth Area (EAGA) (comprising Mindanao of the Philippines, Kalimantan and Sulawesi of Indonesia, Sarawak, Sabah and Labuan of Malaysia and Brunei, covering an area of 695 000 sq km) aims to take advantage of Brunei's capital, Indonesia and Malaysia's rich natural resources and Mindanao's agricultural output and manpower. (iii) Greater Mekong Economic Sub-region (comprising Cambodia, Laos, Myanmar, Thailand, Vietnam and Yunnan, China) is now on its second phase. The Asian Development Bank (ADB) has played a central role here as facilitator through a regional technical assistance programme (RETA).

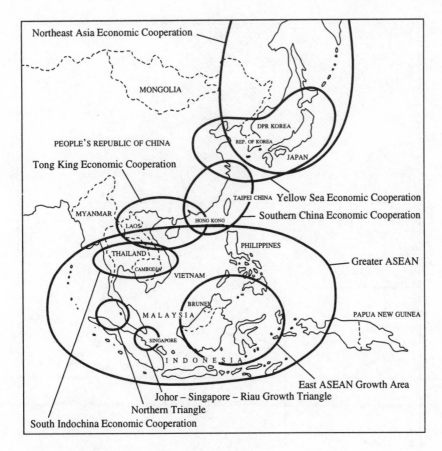

Northeast Asia Economic Cooperation

MONGOLIA

PEOPLE'S REPUBLIC OF CHINA

Tong King Economic Cooperation

DPR KOREA

REP. OF KOREA

JAPAN

MYANMAR

LAOS

HONG KONG

TAIPEI CHINA Yellow Sea Economic Cooperation

— Southern China Economic Cooperation

THAILAND

CAMBODIA

VIETNAM

PHILIPPINES

— Greater ASEAN

BRUNEI

MALAYSIA

SINGAPORE

PAPUA NEW GUINEA

I N D O N E S I A

East ASEAN Growth Area

Johor – Singapore – Riau Growth Triangle

Northern Triangle

South Indochina Economic Cooperation

Source: Based on Perry and Grundy-Warr (1996).

Figure 4.1   Sub-regional development zones in Asia

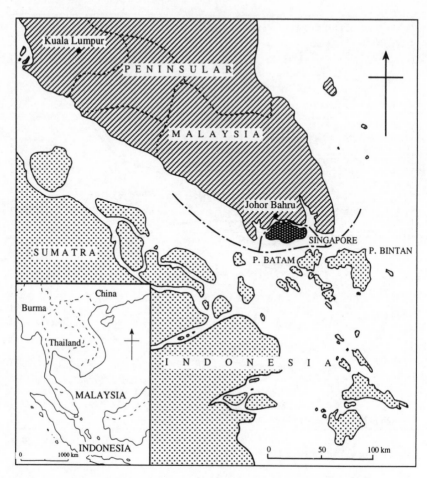

Source: Ghaffar (1996), p. 8.

Figure 4.2   The Indonesia–Malaysia–Singapore growth triangle

The sectors covered for sub-regional cooperation comprise infra-structure, energy, trade, industry, investment, tourism, human resource development, environment and telecommunications.

The success of the SIJORI growth triangle has provided some lessons for the newly emerging growth triangles in the Southeast Asian region. The SIJORI experience has shown the key factors for a successful and sustainable growth triangle and the problems and costs likely to be encountered.

4.1 The emergence of growth triangles

Political and economic factors have explained the emergence of these sub-regional economic zones. The end of the Cold War has left a super-power vacuum in the region. To prevent any nation from filling this superpower vacuum, regional states want to strengthen relationships with each other. Growth triangles are thus seen as apolitical power balancing mechanisms which can build up trust and mutual under-standing among the Asian states.

There is an increasing awareness that bilateral and sub-regional coop-eration is an imperative to cope with increasing international competitive pressure. This will allow them to exploit the complement-arity of factor endowments and proximity for their mutual benefit. The best example is the establishment of SIJORI. Singapore's economy has expanded rapidly, resulting in higher labour and land costs and thus in the erosion of its international competitiveness in many labour-intensive and land-intensive activities. The establishment of the SIJORI has allowed multinational and local industries to redistribute their labour-intensive operations to the lower-cost Batam. The geographical prox-imity of Singapore to Johore and Riau islands also help minimize travel and transport costs, making production and distribution more efficient and competitive. Batam is linked to Singapore by a 30–40 minute ferry ride and Johore to Singapore by a short causeway. On the other hand, for Johore and Riau, Singapore's investments have provided employ-ment opportunities and other spill-over effects into other industries. Apart from its capital and managerial resources, Singapore has provided Batam and Johore with a modern and efficient transportation and tele-communication network and financial infrastructure to support their business operations.

Growth triangles are also seen as a protection against protectionist trends without committing prematurely to the all-or-nothing venture of setting up formal trading blocs of their own. The formation of the North American Free Trade Area (NAFTA) and consolidation of the European Common Market into Economic Union (EU) and the slow progress made in the multilateral trade liberalization have made GTs an alternative of promoting cooperation in the region that are more flexible, less bureaucratic (more activity and project-specific) and more cost-effective than the larger and formal trade blocs of their own.

4.2   Potential benefits

Recent developments in growth theory have emphasized the fact that economic growth is highly concentrated in its location. Under conditions of openness and liberal government policies rapid growth in recent decades has occurred in clusters. Once economic growth in a certain area or region starts to take hold, it quickly spreads to neighbouring locations and transforms the whole region. This is true both within and across national boundaries. The most notable example of the former is the industrial belt of the United States with a concentration in a small part of the northeast and eastern part of the Midwest. An example of the latter is the manufacturing triangle of continental Europe, containing the Ruhr, northern France and Belgium. A similar concentration exists in many other industrialized and newly industrialized Asian countries. In Japan growth is concentrated around Tokyo and Osaka, in Thailand around Bangkok, and in the Philippines around Manila. One major benefit, therefore, from the economic growth triangles is that it allows the policymakers to focus their developmental efforts in economically depressed and peripheral areas of the country.

Since growth triangles are activity specific and project driven, compared with more formal and larger regional arrangements, they incur lesser political and economic complexities and related risks, but yield tangible benefits more quickly and with less uncertainty which can be subsequently applied to the rest of the economy. Flexible, low-cost, fast-track, uncomplicated and well-focussed, they can be started quickly with little fuss. They require no changes in national concepts of sovereignty, administration or national preferences. They do not engage national prestige completely because they require no elaborate political commitments to neighbouring states. They offer the benefits of regional integration without great loss of economic sovereignty. They expand access to key factor inputs and to new markets beyond national boundaries. Each participating state benefits from static gains (increased production and consumption) and dynamic gains (transformation of the economy).

Growth triangles provide a way of addressing their national priorities and concerns in the context of intense global competition. For the capital-rich partners they are a way of sustaining the competitiveness of their exports despite rising wages and increasing shortages of land

and labour. For capital-poor but labour-surplus countries they are a means of speeding up economic development, creating jobs and importing technology. They are an easily organized way of protecting themselves against adverse global economic environment (trade blocs in developed countries), without committing prematurely to the all-or-nothing venture of setting up formal trade blocs of their own.

4.3 Costs and potential problems

Although there are certainly potential economic benefits to be derived from establishing a GT, there are also costs and potential problems which constitute challenges to GTs. There are *direct costs* involved in the provision of infrastructure and energy; *indirect costs* in the form of subsidies, concessions, exemptions from tariff and customs duties and other incentives to attract investors; and *political costs*. Governments involved in GTs could be perceived by their constituents as favouring one portion of their country involved in the GT. These could bring about questions about the concentration of government resources to the 'favoured' GT province, the widening of the income inequality gap and other political issues.[2] There are also *negative externalities* such as environmental degradation, social and ethnic problems, illegal immigration and labour exploitation.

Other costs include *policy adjustment and harmonization costs*. With economic linkage-globalization, states need to adjust domestic policies and programmes to cope with the demanding dynamism of sub-regional cooperation as well as to maximize benefits derived therefrom. From the perspective of the more developed country in the GT, the key issue is 'hollowing out' of industrial capacity. The building of complementarity among the economies of GTs can only be achieved through the enhanced mobility of labour. However, this may conflict with one's national priority and policy. For example, with respect to the mobility of labour, there is a concern that with the availability of cheap labour from other member countries, industries in the labour-shortage country may be encouraged to postpone the decision to restructure into high skill and high technology ones. This concern is reinforced by considerations of the social cost of importing labour. This policy may have to be altered somewhat if greater integration within a GT is considered to be a desirable option.

In the long run, relocation of labour-intensive segments of the industries to the labour-surplus economies may be an optimal solution, but such relocation is not always possible and is limited only to certain industries such as electronics and automobile parts. In addition, many multinationals prefer to relocate not only certain parts or segments of their industries, but also encourage the suppliers of other ancillary equipment to move with them to an adjoining location. Therefore, an attempt to relocate labour-intensive industries could in some degree run the risk of 'hollowing out' the more developed member of the GT.

For the lesser developed members, the question is one of creating employment opportunities for its growing labour force and acquiring and improving the technological base. In the case of the Philippines, the millions of dollars overseas contract workers (OCWs) have brought into the formal and informal sectors of the Philippine economy have not only alleviated its unemployment problem, but have also been a major source of capital for its development process.[3] If not for the steady outflow of millions of Filipinos to the overseas labour market the unemployment situation would have been worse. Between 1975 and 1994 the percentage increases in OCW deployment averaged 18.9 percent or 364 254 employed individuals annually, while unemployment growth averaged 9.1 percent. Apart from the unemployment alleviation, OCW remittances have also been a major source of capital. While FDI as a proportion of the country's GNP declined to below 1 percent for the 1978–87 period before finally recovering in 1988, growing slightly more than one percent between 1989 and 1992, OCW remittances as a proportion of GNP has consistently increased, averaging 4 percent of GNP between 1989–92. It is, therefore, necessary for the members to develop a policy of more systematic and liberal movement of labour within their GT.

There is an old issue of the distribution of gains. Uneven distribution of benefits among member states in a GT could arouse suspicion of exploitative relationships. The SIJORI provides such an example. Some segments of the Indonesian and Malaysian public are of the view that Singapore gains most from the SIJORI partnership. In its early years of implementation, there was some fear in Malaysia that the growth triangle could turn Johore into a 'backyard' of Singapore and Batam (*The Straits Times*, 20 October 1990, p. 23). Jakarta was reportedly sensitive to the fact that Singapore, which occupies only 3 percent of the land area within SIJORI, accounts for about 50 percent of its population and 90 percent of its income (*Time*, 17 January 1994, p. 27). There is, therefore, a need to ensure that benefits derived from GTs are spread to all member states and that regional income inequality is not heightened.

This problem is likely to get worse as competition between Johore and Singapore is growing due largely to growing industrialization in Johore. Johore's recent expression of the possibility of stemming the outflow of labour to Singapore and turning down Singapore's request for more water indicate this growing competition. The upgrading and expansion of port facilities in Johore may also help divert Malaysia's shipping and container traffic from Singapore.

4.4 Growth triangles and ASEAN

President Suharto of Indonesia and Singaporean Prime Minister Goh Chok Tong have recently achieved another milestone in Singapore–Indonesia economic relations by embarking on a new marine and industrial complex in Karimun island, after successful joint ventures in Batam and Bintan (*The Straits Times*, 18 March 1997, p. 20). Both leaders have agreed to increase their level of economic cooperation without involving other ASEAN countries. Do growth triangles conflict or dilute ASEAN solidarity?

GTs can actually facilitate and complement the regionwide ASEAN cooperation in the following ways:

4.4.1 Building blocks

Growth triangles can be perceived as building blocks for economic cooperation in the region. They are complementary, rather than alternatives for the regionwide economic cooperation. The objective remains strengthening the region for foreign investment and opportunities which could reinforce and expand ASEAN cooperation. Member countries could gain confidence and trust in each other, with economic growth as the common goal and binding force. They would then strengthen internal ties among ASEAN states and eventually lead to greater regional economic and political cooperation.

4.4.2 Testing ground

Growth triangles can serve the role of 'reality tests' for selected dimensions or assumptions of AFTA. They can be instrumental in moving them from national comparative advantage to regional competitive advantage. Since GTs are activity-specific, they encourage specific linkages of complementary activities across borders and help promote intra-ASEAN integration and may sharpen and even accelerate certain elements of AFTA's implementation.

4.4.3 National integration and linkage with the rest of Southeast Asia

Growth triangles could also be a means by which the region's economic dynamism could be spread to the lagging parts of the region. Involving economically lagging parts or countries in GTs could spur their domestic growth which will ultimately contribute to the economic robustness of the region as a whole.

Sub-regional cooperation can provide a pragmatic and effective mechanism for linking the ASEAN countries to the rest of Southeast Asia as in the case of the Greater Mekong Sub-region. This is especially significant to ASEAN as an institution, in that the participating countries of this particular sub-region include economies in transition not only domestically but also in their relationship with the region, as future members of ASEAN (Abonyi, 1994).

4.4.4   Economization of politics

The economization of politics is the key to ASEAN success. Regional cooperation was achieved by playing down political and security issues. As long as they are not seen as rival entities but are committed to liberal principles, GTs can provide a venue through which the member states can focus on similarities such as mutual economic gains. In GTs the strong presence of private sector involvement will help hasten the speed of trade liberalization in the region.

4.5   Key factors for successful and sustainable GTs

What lessons, if any, can one derive from the success of the SIJORI for other future growth triangles? As discussed in the preceding section, the main economic aim of SIJORI is to combine the comparative advantages of Singapore, Johore and Riau to attract investment in the manufacturing and services sectors and develop an integrated tourist sector. Has SIJORI achieved this objective?

If we go by the statistics for Johore, it was reported recently that investments in Johore associated with the GT have already reached M\$15 billion since the inception of SIJORI (*The Straits Times*, 4 August 1995). For the first six months of 1995 M\$1.7 billion in investment capital had been poured into Johore. To facilitate continued capital flows, Johore has embarked upon massive infrastructure projects including a second land link to Singapore, a new port, enhanced water and gas supplies to Singapore and expansion of industrial and recreational developments which will increase its integration with Singapore. All these, together with the establishment of a science park in Johore and immigration 'smart cards' for investors, will make Johore the second largest industrial centre in Malaysia after the Klang Valley.

The SIJORI has also kickstarted development in Riau with industrial estates, mega resorts, agribusiness and heavy industrial projects, and has established Riau as a new centre of FDI in Indonesia after Jakarta and West Java. Singapore's involvement is exemplified in Batam Industrial Park (BIP), a joint venture between Singapore GLCs (primarily

Singapore Technologies Industrial Corporation and Jurong Environmental Engineering) and Indonesia's conglomerates.

Can the SIJORI's success be replicated in other emerging growth triangles in the region? It should be pointed out that the circumstances surrounding SIJORI differ from other GTs in the region. First, SIJORI has only three components or legs. The IMTGT has a larger number of states, made up of territories without a clear lead player, although Penang has been recognized for its central location and its more advanced economic and communication status. As they are supposedly equal players, there appear problems of coordination and in identifying major areas of cooperation. Although that may eventually contribute to the developmental goals of the region, it may also become unmanageable, leading to mini growth zones within the larger IMT growth triangle. EAGA is not merely a triangle but a polygon. The entire sub-region constitutes a vast geographical spread covering vast land and sea areas, comprising several diverse entities. Currently, the centre of the polygon's activities seems to be concentrating on the economically vibrant and externally linked areas around Labuan, Brunei, Northern Sarawak, Sabah and Southern Mindanao. The mere physical distance would make communication links a burden. Second, political instability in certain localities in EAGA may raise doubts among prospective investors.

Whether or not the success of SIJORI can be replicated in other emerging GTs would depend on whether or not they are able to meet the following requirements:

4.5.1 Geographical proximity
This is one of the most compelling factors for capital, labour, trade and investment flows among the member states. Similar language and cultural background which can prevail in geographically proximate areas are conducive to close business relationships in GTs. But geographical distance can be overcome by establishing adequate communication links or by capitalizing on certain links between two members. IMTGT and EAGA seem to fulfil this requirement.[4]

4.5.2 Economic complementarity and infrastructure
This is not only a justification but also an important factor for a successful GT. Different stages of economic development and factor endowments can provide an impetus for sub-regional cooperation to achieve an international competitive edge. With cooperation, productive factors such as capital and labour will be more mobile so as to produce goods to be exported outside the sub-region. Infrastructure is a

prerequisite for transforming geographical proximity into economic complementarity. Legal and physical infrastructure can facilitate the flows of resources between member states.

There is some economic complementarity among the member states of IMTGT and EAGA with the active involvement of Penang as a source of industrial know-how and capital for the former, and of Brunei as a source of capital for the latter, but infrastructure in Penang may still be inadequate and Brunei does not have well-developed industrial, communication and financial services sectors.

4.5.3 *Political commitment and private sector participation*
Strong political commitment at the highest level and the will to adjust national policies to effectively participate in the GTs is another key factor. Government policies must encourage the necessary participation of the private sector since the role of the private sector is crucial in determining whether economic linkages actually take place. The government must assure investors of the reduced political risks involved in the sub-regional cooperation.

GTs, to be successful, must be market-driven with the role of the private sector being crucial. There are problems when the private sector is not yet fully developed. Lack of managerial capabilities and less developed financial sector can also constrain the potential benefits of greater complementarities and markets offered by GTs.

Although both IMTGT and EAGA have enjoyed political support at the national level, they seem to be weak in relation to other requirements to attract the private sector such as adequate infrastructure, accessible markets, support services, and a stable social and political climate.

4.5.4 *Presence of a catalyst*
The state must take the lead in proposing and establishing the GT, or a third party like a multilateral institution must act as a catalyst to facilitate the consultative process in forming the GT. But the entrepreneurial function of identifying market opportunities is best left to the private sector. To achieve quick results requires a lead player that sets the agenda for the triangle. In the case of IMTGT and EAGA there is no clear lead player, although Penang and Brunei have been recognized for their central location and relatively advanced economic and communication status.

4.6 Conclusion

Growth triangles are a key indicator of the economic dynamism and growing economic cooperation in the region. They have both positive and negative implications on the domestic, intra- and inter-regional scenes in the economic and political arena. Generally, the GTs are confidence-building and security-enhancing mechanisms. They are instrumental in promoting harmonious relations in the region and in addressing both regional and domestic concerns. Nonetheless, there are challenges to be addressed such as economic and political costs involved in setting up and sustaining the GT, policy adjustment and harmonization, negative externalities, distribution of benefits among member countries and the apprehension that involvement in GTs might diffuse ASEAN. These challenges can be addressed by concerted efforts of participating governments, third party institutions and the private sector.

The SIJORI experience has provided some valuable lessons for other emerging GTs in the region. The different circumstances facing the emerging GTs will make their tasks more difficult to achieve. Their success in forging a sustainable sub-regional cooperation would depend to a large extent on their ability to surmount the constraints facing them and on how they can fulfil such requirements as economic complementarity, adequate infrastructure, political commitment and strong private sector participation, and the presence of a lead player which can set the agenda for the sub-regional consultative and planning process.

Suggestions for further reading

For conceptual issues and operation problems of growth triangles, read Min and Myo (1993); for a wide-ranging collection of papers on growth triangles, Lee (ed.) (1991), Toh Mun Heng and Linda Low (eds) (1993) and Myo and Min (eds) (1996) are recommended.

Notes

1. Growth triangles (GTs) are distinguished from regional groupings in that they are government initiated but business propelled and are based on sub-regional cooperation.
2. A major source of concern for the Malaysian authorities with respect to SIJORI is the accentuation of regional inequalities both within Johore as well as between Johore and other states. The concentration of industrial activities in Johore in the context of SIJORI is seen to have contributed to the polarization of economic growth in Malaysia. The heavy concentration of industrial estates in Johore Bahru is also seen to have aggravated income inequality within Johore.
3. Based on the statistics available from the Philippine Department of Labour and Employment, the Philippine unemployment rate has moved up to 10.4 percent (for the first half of 1995) from 9.9 percent in 1994.
4. Distances are further eased with the recent establishment of six direct shipping routes between the island of Mindanao and neighbouring Southeast Asian cities in the

fledgling East ASEAN Growth Area (EAGA). The six routes are: Zamboanga–Labuan island in Malaysia serviced by 18 vessels; Zamboanga–Sandakan in East Malaysia serviced by one vessel; General Santos City–Bitung port in Manado of Indonesia serviced by two ships; Davao–Bitung serviced by one ship; Zamboanga–Bitung serviced by one ship; and Cotabato–Labuan serviced by one ship. However, poor port infrastructure and facilities remain a road block to increasing trade (*The Business Times Shipping Times*, 6 January 1997, p. 1).

5 The role of government in ASEAN

As discussed in the preceding chapters, the adoption of appropriate economic policies has been a major factor responsible for the significant inflow of foreign direct investment (FDI) and high savings rates experienced by most of the ASEAN countries. In particular, their respective governments have played a critical role by formulating and implementing policies that help them achieve macroeconomic and political stability, a liberal export-oriented economic regime and competitive rates of return for investment. Thus, it can be argued that the differences in development performance among the ASEAN countries could be largely explained by their differences in the nature and quality of government intervention.

Their respective governments have intervened not only on a macro level but also on a micro level.[1] On the microeconomic level, ASEAN governments have intervened by direct and indirect ownership of certain industries, by providing different types of assistance to the private sector and by implementing policies aimed at reducing poverty and income inequality. But the extent and form of microeconomic intervention have varied among the ASEAN countries. This chapter examines the extent and nature of microeconomic intervention in ASEAN and how this type of government intervention has affected their economic development.

5.1 Extent and nature of government intervention

There is a general consensus that one of the major factors behind the economic performance of the newly industrializing countries and the ASEAN group of countries has been the role played by their respective governments particularly in the maintenance of law and order, and in the formulation and implementation of policies to achieve macroeconomic stability (World Bank, 1993b). The role of government and good governance in creating and maintaining political stability, required for effective and efficient implementation of appropriate and usually harsh policies, is quite indisputable.[2]

However, there is still some controversy over whether or not state enterprises (SOEs) have played a positive role in the economic development of the ASEAN countries. Another controversy is whether or not strategic trade policy or industry intervention has played a critical role in ASEAN economic success (Pomfret, 1994).

World Bank (1993b, p. 293) produced a hierarchy of microeconomic interventionism in eight high-performing Asian economies. Singapore among the ASEAN5 was ranked the most interventionist, followed by Indonesia and Malaysia. Thailand and the Philippines were not listed, presumably because they were the least interventionist. With its extensive ownership in diversified industries, ranging from housing, transport and shipbuilding to tourism and lotteries to country club operations, the Singapore government has been acknowledged as the most important entrepreneur in the Singapore economy (Lim Chong Ya, 1991, p. 207).

5.1.1   State enterprises (SOEs)

Although virtually all ASEAN countries have already embarked on privatization, state or public enterprises still remain a significant economic force in their economies. This is one of the most extensively analysed and debated forms of government intervention in the region (Hill, 1994). Their rationale, organization, performance and contribution to economy vary significantly across ASEAN countries (Ng and Wagner, 1991; Ng and Toh, 1992; Mohamed, 1994; Pangestu, 1996). Singapore stands out from the rest of the ASEAN countries in terms of performance and economic contribution. Apart from Singapore, state enterprises in other ASEAN countries have generally performed poorly based on economic criteria for a number of reasons: lack of clear objectives and delineation of functions between state enterprises, some degree of ambiguity on criteria for selecting programmes and projects, inefficient management, lack of transparency and accountability, high gearing ratios, high input costs, inadequate technology and political patronage. In some cases, poor commercial performances have contributed negatively to national fiscal positions (like the Philippine case in the 1970s and Malaysia in the early 1980s). Thus, since the 1980s there has been an increasing trend towards privatization of state enterprises in the ASEAN countries to improve their fiscal position and to improve national efficiency and international competitiveness.

Singapore   The Singapore government has been seen to take a paternalistic role, nurturing and guiding the nation towards the desired goal of economic development. Direct and indirect ownership through state enterprises is, therefore, viewed as the principal means of directing the allocation of its scarce resources. Specifically, the Singapore government's intervention through state enterprises is based on the standard market failure arguments such as the provision of public goods, reduction of income inequality, poverty alleviation and management of externalities and natural monopolies or oligopolies. In addition, even in areas where there is no market failure, the government intervenes to promote basic industries, build public infrastructure, correct entrepreneurial inadequacies and to invest in areas where the private sector is unwilling to bear the risks (Lim Chong Ya, 1991, p. 206).

There are generally two types of state enterprises in Singapore: the government-linked companies (GLCs) and statutory boards. The former operate along business lines like other private sector companies, but they are either directly or indirectly owned or controlled by the government holding companies (namely Temasek, Sheng-Li and the Ministry of National Development). GLCs are operated like private enterprises and are not given privileges or concealed subsidies. GLCs that are well-known in Singapore for their outstanding successes include the Singapore International Airlines (SIA) and the Development Bank of Singapore (DBS).

The statutory boards are autonomous organizations set up by the government for specific functions, such as for public housing, laid down by legislation. They are separate entities from the civil service system, but are placed under the jurisdiction of the relevant ministries. Examples of statutory boards are the Housing Development Board, Port of Singapore Authority, Jurong Town Council and Sembawang. These state enterprises are not intended to replace the private sector, except in special cases. These special cases occur when the private sector has clearly failed to provide proper services. But the state enterprises are not given special privileges or subsidies, and must be competitive with the private sector (Goh Keng Swee, 1977). The government's emphasis has been on performance rather than on ownership *per se*. The state enterprises are required to achieve commercial performance consistent with acceptable financial norms, unless there is an explicit social objective. Clear and unambiguous objectives are assigned to them with commercial autonomy.

The Singaporean experience represents a unique example of how state-owned enterprises (SOEs) can become an effective tool for promoting economic development. They have not imposed any financial burden on the budget but have in fact contributed to the overall budget surpluses.[3] Alten (1995) pointed out that in 1986 the ten top earning statutory boards made profits more than twice as much as the combined earnings of the ten most profitable companies listed on the Singapore stock exchange. Carling (1995) has also noted that in the last three fiscal years statutory boards' contributions to the budget averaged 2.8 percent of total budget revenue while subsidies from the budget to statutory boards averaged only 1 percent of total budget revenue. Likewise, Singapore's GLCs have performed well with higher average sales and average profits per company than foreign MNCs or the local private sector (*The Sunday Times*, 23 August 1992). The state enterprises have created forward and backward linkages since the initial period of Singapore's economic take-off by transmitting growth to other sectors of the economy. Other contributions include capital formation, employment, value-added and technological development.

However, there has been increasing concern among the private local entrepreneurs over the growing involvement of state enterprises in areas viewed as the private sector's domain such as commercial banking and housing. They argued that the state enterprises are not only competing with the private sector with unfair advantages, but are also 'crowding out' the private sector so that they have inhibited the development of local private entrepreneurship. Because of this pressure, and to improve the stake of Singaporeans in the economy, the Singapore government in 1987 formed the Public Sector Divestment Committee to look into ways of divesting and/or privatizing state enterprises. The basic objective was to allow the private sector to play a larger role in the economy. The divestment programme started with the public floating of the Singapore Telecom shares, and more will be carried out in the future.

Despite the privatization drive, the SOEs in Singapore continue to be an important instrument of government microeconomic intervention. They are taking the lead in the new regionalization strategy by developing industrial estates or parks in the region such as Indonesia, China, Vietnam and India, and thus, contributing to the development of an external wing for the economy. On the domestic front, they have also been involved in the continuous restructuring of the economy by venturing into technology-based manufacturing like wafer fabrication and aerospace industries.

Indonesia   Although Indonesia has embarked on a privatization drive since the mid-1980s after the slump in oil prices with an increasing recognition of the importance of the private sector, the absolute size of the state enterprise sector has changed little, if at all (Habir, 1990).

The strong presence of the state in the Indonesian economy is based on such market failure arguments as the provision of public goods, reduction of income inequality and poverty alleviation (Pangestu, 1996). In addition, there is the political argument based on the perceived need to counteract the private sector dominated by Chinese Indonesian business groups and foreign investors.[4] A large state enterprise sector is seen as a desirable counterweight to the non-pribumi dominance of the economy. Thus, ownership issues in the state enterprise sector in

Indonesia have historically been related to the question of 'who controls what' (Habir, 1990). Another argument is to give priority to certain strategic industries aimed at transforming Indonesia into an advanced industrial country. The strategic industries identified are the ten state enterprises which were to be supervised by the Strategic Industry Board (BPIS, Badan Pengelola Industri Strategis).[5] Most of all, there is Article 33 of the Indonesian Constitution which is usually interpreted to mean that economic activities concerned with the daily life of the people should be controlled by the government through state enterprises.[6]

Based on the above arguments, it is not surprising to see that the utilities sector is 100 percent government owned. The Indonesian government also owns 50 percent of shares in the oil and gas sector as well as in the transport and communications sector. The role of state-owned enterprises is also dominant in the financial sector in which 65 percent of the shares is government owned (Hill, 1992). It is also somewhat prevalent in the manufacturing sector accounting for around 24 percent. The role of the state in the agricultural sector, however, has not been through direct ownership, except for the plantation sector comprising a combination of nationalized plantations and those set up under subsidized credit programmes. Government intervention has been in the form of subsidizing inputs and programmes to increase food production. The commitment to achieving rice self-sufficiency after the 1971 drought led to massive investments in supporting infrastructure and services, subsidies for fertilizers and strong central direction for farmers to plant rice. As pointed out previously, this type of government intervention together with the adoption of the high yielding varieties of rice under the Green Revolution has made Indonesia self-sufficient in rice by 1985. The overall state ownership in the economy is slightly under one third (Pangestu, 1996).

SOEs in Indonesia are divided into three broad categories: (a) Perjan which are enterprises responsible for the provision of public services, attached to the ministerial department and financed out of government budget; (b) Perum which comprises of enterprises concerned with profits as well as public services and expected to generate sufficient income; and (c) Persero which are limited liability companies whose shares are owned wholly or partly by the Ministry of Finance on behalf of the government and expected to operate as profit-oriented ventures. Theoretically, government intervention would have differed across categories, but no difference in government control has been observed as many Persero continued to receive government subsidies and have been regulated to support government policies.

An absence of commercial autonomy, unclear economic objectives and political patronage have characterized the Indonesian experience with state enterprises (Hill, 1994).[7] Consequently, only a small portion of these state entities have recorded an acceptable rate of return on investments while most incurred losses with 37 percent and 30 percent recorded in 1985 and 1986, respectively. The SOEs in Indonesia have been the target of economic reforms during the post oil-boom period, but there is little evidence that the presence of the state has diminished.

Malaysia   Microeconomic intervention in the form of SOEs in Malaysia has manifested itself in three main forms: the establishment of new companies with the government as the sole owner; the setting up of joint-venture companies with private entrepreneurs as part owners; and the buying of a proportion of the publicly-traded shares of existing companies (Mohamed, 1994, p. 240).

These SOEs are considered to have a more explicit political objective. From 1970 to 1990 the economic priority was to reduce poverty and ethnic income inequalities in Malaysia. This economic thrust was reinforced by the political pressure to promote *Bumiputra* (indigenous Malay) interests and thus reduce the economic dominance of the nonindigenous people (mainly the Chinese) in Malaysia (Jomo, 1994). In the 1970s and early 1980s the Malaysian government was probably the most active promoter of the interest of the poor in ASEAN through various policy options. From 1956 to 1990 the share of social services had got the highest priority in Malaysia's plans, with the exception of the Second and Fifth Malaysia Plans (Huq, 1994, p. 152).[8]

The introduction of New Economic Policy (NEP) after the racial riots of 1969 marked a shift in the Malaysian government's role from a passive facilitator to a pro-active structuralist one. This shift occurred out of the realization that any effort to alter income distribution must undertake structural changes in terms of redistribution of productive assets. This realization was vindicated by Snodgrass (1980) who found that the former *laissez faire* approach pursued by the Malaysian government in the 1960s could neither accelerate growth from the macroeconomic perspective nor improve the economic well-being of the mainly rural populace from the microeconomic standpoint. Thus, since then, the policy makers of the time have pursued a growth strategy that also takes care of the redistribution of corporate assets along with other expenditure benefits in favour of the underprivileged.

Consequently, the size of its state enterprise sector grew substantially especially in the 1970s and early 1980s as the state took on a pro-active role by participating directly in commercial and industrial activities and acting as a trustee through the various trust agencies to help increase the *Bumiputra*'s share of corporate equity. This assertive role of the state saw the ratio of public sector expenditure rise from 29.2 percent in 1970 to a peak of 58.4 percent in 1981 (Ariff, 1994b, p. 177). Compared to other ASEAN member countries, central government expenditure per capita in Malaysia in 1980 was nearly ten times that of Indonesia, five times that of the Philippines and three times that of Thailand (Chee and Navaratnam, 1992, p. 369).

However, the economic performance of its state enterprise sector was largely disappointing, as reflected in their low rates of return recorded by all sectors with the exception of the extractive industry. Shaikh (1992) noted that the combined rate of return for all SOEs, excluding the extractive industry, was negative in 1986. Chee and Navaratnam (1992) estimated the external debt for 525 government companies at M$14.9 billion and the total accumulated losses for non-financial SOEs at over M$2.3 billion in 1987. But, despite their inefficiencies, they were often shielded from being liquidated or closed down because of their social structuring function. It should be pointed out that the SOEs have played an important role in the social restructuring process. Through SOEs, poverty incidence was reduced significantly to about 17 percent in 1987, and the *Bumiputra*'s share in corporate assets increased from 1.5 percent in 1969 to 19.4 percent in 1988 (Jomo, 1991). It can be argued that by reducing income inequality and poverty incidence in Malaysia, the SOEs have eased the social tensions that could have led to political and social instability and thus have indirectly contributed to Malaysia's economic development.

Its state enterprise sector started to diminish in importance in the 1990s as Malaysia continued to embark on a privatization programme. This policy reversal is aimed at relieving the financial and administrative burden of the government in maintaining its investments in infrastructure and a network of services, promoting competition, efficiency and productivity of the services, stimulating private entrepreneurship and investment. This helped reduce the size of the public sector and contributed towards meeting the objectives of the NEP, especially as *Bumiputra* entrepreneurship and presence has improved and is, therefore, capable of taking a share of the privatized services (Jomo, 1994, p. 271). Various arguments against privatization in Malaysia have also been advanced, but one thing is unequivocally clear, that is, in many instances, especially in public utilities, the government has maintained effective control despite changes in ownership.

Brunei The involvement of the Brunein government in oil and gas exploration and the dominance of oil and gas production and

Table 5.1   Government expenditure as a proportion of GDP (%)

ASEAN	Average 1971–80	1981	1982	1983	1984	1985	1986	1987	1988
Indonesia	20.9	25.8	24.1	24.8	22.3	24.1	22.8	23.5	22.5
Malaysia	30.2	46.6	44.5	39.9	35.0	34.6	38.0	30.1	29.8
Philippines	12.4	15.4	14.8	13.2	11.6	12.8	14.9	17.4	16.7
Singapore	25.9	33.0	30.8	33.1	34.4	45.7	43.3	45.5	34.7
Thailand	16.4	17.6	19.1	18.4	18.7	19.7	18.7	17.2	15.4

Source: Asian Development Bank, *Asian Development Outlook* (1989).

employment in the Brunein economy, as mentioned in Chapter 2, indicate the significant role played by the Brunei government in its economic development. As we saw in Chapter 2, Brunei is a special case with its over-reliance on these two sectors.

Thailand   Table 5.1 shows government expenditures in the ASEAN states as a proportion of their respective GDPs in the 1970s and most of the 1980s. Thailand, compared to the other ASEAN economies, has been relatively non-interventionist, as indicated by its low level of government expenditure as a proportion of GDP relative to the other ASEAN members. Its low levels of government intervention coupled with high levels of growth rates suggest that quality, rather than quantity, of government intervention matters.

Although the size of the government in Thailand has been small and has not assumed a leading role in steering the course of its economic development, its involvement in the economy is quite encompassing. By the end of 1987, these enterprises, which are engaged in almost all sectors of the Thai economy, employed a total of about 257,556 employees which was about half the total number employed in the civil service (Ingavata, 1989).

The state enterprises in Thailand have performed relatively well compared to Malaysia, Indonesia and the Philippines, based on financial profitability criteria. However, despite their profitability, they have relied heavily on foreign borrowing due to insufficient internally generated funds. By 1985 the total outstanding foreign debt of all state enterprises was about US$5 billion – about half of Thailand's public sector foreign debt (Ingavata, 1989). This factor largely accounted for the privatization drive initiated by the then Prime Minister of Thailand Prem Tinsulanond in 1986.

Philippines The Philippines had a small state enterprise sector inherited from the American colonial regime. Such enterprises proliferated during the Marcos era as several 'crony' corporations had become more than extensions of the state apparatus. SOEs increased from 44 in 1966 to 246 in 1985 (Godinez, 1989, p. 261). Since the Aquino administration several of these have been removed from the state sector.

5.1.2 Strategic trade policy (industry intervention) vs neutral trade policy

Among the successful ASEAN economies, Singapore, Indonesia and Malaysia are probably the most interventionist in terms of strategic industry intervention by providing fiscal incentives and subsidies to certain industries.[9] The Singapore government has consistently intervened by providing investment incentives to those favoured industries. Those strategic industries, identified as crucial for Indonesia's economic transformation into an industrialized economy, are granted the exclusive right of operation, preferential access to funds and immunity against bankruptcy (Pangestu, 1996). Indonesia and Malaysia's agricultural sectors, as referred to in the preceding section, have also been accorded a 'strategic' status. Malaysia's policy of developing its automobile, iron and steel, petrochemicals and cement industries under its Heavy Industrialization programme is another example of a strategic trade policy intervention.

That this type of intervention (based on strategic trade policy) has played a critical role in NIEs economic success was first proposed by Johnson (1982). Later, more economists restated this view by saying that a key feature of Japan's development strategy was the targeting of industries on the basis of their perceived potential for economic growth and technological change. Amsden (1989) has argued that similar policies were crucial to South Korea's rapid growth beginning in the 1960s. Wade (1990) has documented the role of interventionist policies in Taiwan's rapid development. Beason and Weinstein (1993) tested the hypothesis that Japanese industrial policy tools (that is, cheap credit, net transfers, tariff protection and tax relief) favoured high growth or increasing returns to scale sectors or enhanced productivity growth. They found that these were directed disproportionally in favour of two sectors, textiles and mining, which had poor growth records, and that there is no evidence that they had any impact on productivity. This hypothesis is difficult to test because the industrial policy in successful economies appears successful if judged by aggregate growth performance; there is no doubt that Japan and South Korea adopted an intervention-based strategic trade policy and no doubt these countries have been economically successful (Pomfret, 1994, p. 5).

The counterargument to the interventionist view is that the NIEs have intervened to neutralize distortions and that the key to their economic success is their policies which match their import barriers with export subsidies and thus create neutral regimes which do not discriminate between industries (Balassa, 1991). In cases where policy makers picked the winners, they were only replicating what market mechanisms would have achieved anyway. According to this view, the role of their respective governments was to provide a stable macro-economic environment conducive to international competition free from distortionary policies, rather than to promote specific industries. Thus, their governments have allowed their economies to do what comes naturally (Riedel, 1988). The recent study by the World Bank (1993b) was in support of this view. It argued that microeconomic inter-ventionism could not explain the economic success of the NIEs. Pomfret (1994) investigated further this issue by correlating the World Bank-based hierarchy of microeconomic interventionism in eight high-per-forming Asian economies (Japan, South Korea, Singapore, Taiwan, Hong Kong, Indonesia, Malaysia and Thailand) with the order of long-term growth performance of these countries, and found that while all these countries enjoyed rapid growth those whose governments tried to direct resources to strategic activities may have performed less well than they would had their policymakers sat on their hands (Pomfret, 1994, p. 9).[10]

There are other theoretical and empirical studies which support the view that neutral policies, rather than microeconomic interventionist policies, were responsible for the success of the ASEAN4 economies (that is, Indonesia, Malaysia, Singapore and Thailand). Theoretically, Romer (1994) pointed to the crucial importance of making the fixed cost of introducing new goods or activities as low as possible, and Riedel (1988) characterized economic success based on doing what comes naturally. According to these models, those governments that succeeded in removing the obstacles that inflate the costs of doing business and in enabling firms to specialize according to their comparative advantage, have successful economies.

Empirical studies (for example, Edwards, 1992) on determinants of growth are inconclusive, but among the consistently significant variables in econometric studies are measures of openness. Although these results are often cited in support of the case for export-led growth, they also support the case for the trade–growth relationship (Levine and Renelt, 1992). Literature surveys have criticized the empirical and conceptual shortcomings of many of these studies and the conditional nature of the trade–growth relationship (Edwards, 1993, p. 1389; Levine and Renelt, 1992). Nevertheless, the presumption remains from the recurring positive correlation between openness measures and growth and from the earlier generation of cross-country trade and development case studies that openness is conducive to growth (Pomfret, 1994, p. 14).

The Malaysian, Indonesian and Singaporean experiences with strategic trade intervention provide further empirical evidence on how strategic industry intervention can affect economic development. The protectionist measures adopted by the Malaysian government under its Heavy Industrialization programme to shield the selected heavy industries from international competition have led to higher production costs and consumer prices. For example, in the cement industry a surcharge of over 50 percent was imposed on imported cement to protect the domestic market.

The poor performance of the steel and cement industry coincided with the generally weak Malaysian economy in the early 1980s. Malaysia's automobile industry protection produced mixed results. In the first decade of its existence, the economic burden of the national car project, Proton, was estimated at M$1.6 billion (Jomo and Edwards, 1993, p. 32). Further, the problem of deepening technological dependence was evident due to Mitsubishi's reluctance to transfer its technology to Proton. However, with continuous protection from the state, Proton's market share steadily increased and has made some inroads into the international markets, particularly in the UK. It is, however, doubtful if Proton can compete with the more established foreign brands once government protection is removed.

Malaysia's strategic industry intervention manifested itself again in its Industrial Master Plans (IMP) which guide the country's industrialization efforts from 1985. The first IMP for the period 1985–95 has identified 12 priority subsectors comprising of seven resource-based industries and five non-resource-based industries for industrial expansion. Malaysia's International Trade and Industry Report (1994) has observed that the state's industry targeting under the IMP has been relatively successful in contributing to Malaysia's economic development based on the following economic indicators: Malaysia's actual growth rate in 1985–92 was 6.7 percent, higher than the targeted growth rate of 6.4 percent; the annual average growth rate of manufacturing value-added was 12.6 percent exceeding the IMP target of 8.8 percent for the entire period; the export performance of all subsectors, with the exception of the palm oil, and iron and steel industries, exceeded the IMP targets; and manufactured exports as a percentage of total exports grew from 43.5 percent in 1986 to 69.0 percent in 1992.

The government of Indonesia has identified the following upstream industries for microeconomic intervention: iron and steel, synthetic fibres, cement, chemicals, fertilizers, motor vehicles' engines, aircraft, telecommunications, electronics and shipbuilding sectors. These sectors are considered to have high growth potential and are important for a diversified and sustainable industrial development. Indonesia's industrial intervention is different from Malaysia's in that its industry targeting is more directed towards its domestic market and employment creation, with little attention given to export promotion. This microeconomic intervention is, therefore, a deviation from Indonesia's overall economic orientation of export promotion and trade liberalization. This inward orientation has been fostered by adopting significant protective measures in the form of tariffs and quantitative restrictions.

Perhaps the most controversial sectors of industry intervention in terms of contribution to Indonesia's economic development are the state-run industries of iron and steel, motor vehicle and aeronautic engineering. The iron and steel industry has been the most controversial because its high capital intensity and limited employment generating capacity render it inconsistent with its factor intensity. Thus, during the developmental stage the government policy had resulted in providing it with a high level of protection. But it is now considered as a success story of Indonesia's industry intervention. The Krakatau Steel company established in 1971 is a good case in point. This company was given virtual monopoly from 1980 to 1990 with full protection. The tariff protection was gradually lowered as the company was developed to a world-class standard. Now it can compete against the best steel producers in the world, and the tariff rate on imported steel products is now only at 5 percent (*The Sunday Times*, 31 March 1996, p. 4).

In contrast, the motor vehicle and components industry has remained inefficient and heavily dependent on government assistance and protection. The recent decision to impose a 20 percent surcharge on imports of propylene (used in the manufacture of plastics) and the granting of tax incentives and tariff exemptions for a private firm and its South Korean counterpart involved in the development of a national car project are recent examples. In addition, it is highly fragmented with five main producers of motor cycles producing approximately 25 separate models and some 40 assemblers of passenger cars and commercial vehicles producing approximately 50 makes and 140 models, all in relatively small numbers. This implies that most producers are prevented from achieving a minimum efficient scale of production.

Similarly, Indonesia has also produced its first domestically designed and built commercial airplane which had its maiden flight in 1995.

However, in spite of this achievement, this venture is likely to be inefficient. The Indonesian government has justified this investment on the grounds of technology acquisition and development, and a range of non-economic considerations such as national prestige (Hill, 1992, p. 217).

As pointed out previously, Singapore was ranked by the World Bank as the most interventionist among the ASEAN5 countries. The state has continually led the private sector to achieve the country's economic development by promoting industries with high growth potential and which are crucial to maintaining its international competitiveness. In the mid-1970s due to tight labour conditions, the state intervened by promoting higher value-added industries such as computers, electronic components, precision engineering and pharmaceuticals, and by offering them investment incentives. After the 1985 recession the Singapore government under its Strategic Economic Plan (1989) identified fourteen industries for industrial clustering – commodity trading, shipping, precision engineering, electronics, information technology, petroleum and petrochemicals, construction, heavy engineering, finance, insurance, general supporting industries, tourism, international hub and domestic industries (Alten, 1995, pp. 128–9).

Since 1992 the Singapore government has been actively promoting and facilitating the 'go-regional' drive to maintain Singapore's international competitiveness and thus sustain its economic development. Through regionalization Singapore would be able to tap the growth potential in the other parts of the region where it can relocate its labour-intensive operations.

Singapore's continued economic dynamism is highly attributable to the government's foresight and effective leadership in providing the guiding framework which has prepared the private sector for coping with the changing challenges of global competition.

5.3 Conclusion

The preceding discussion has shown that the nature, extent and effects on economic development of microeconomic intervention have varied significantly among the ASEAN countries. It has also demonstrated that the quality, rather than the extent of microeconomic intervention in terms of state-owned enterprises, has played the most critical role in ASEAN economic development experiences. ASEAN government intervention by way of direct and indirect ownership of certain enterprises has generally resulted in economic efficiency loss and lower growth, except for the case of Singapore. Consequently, the recent attempts at deregulation and privatization of state enterprises in

Indonesia, Malaysia, the Philippines and Thailand are designed mainly to improve their overall productivity and efficiency. The privatization drive by Singapore is mainly the government's deliberate policy of allowing the private sector to be more directly involved in economic development and to increase the stakes of Singaporeans in their economy. It was announced by the Singapore government that the recent public floatation of Singapore Telecom shares was intended to allow more Singaporeans to own shares and thus distribute the fruits of economic growth more widely.

With respect to the link between strategic industry intervention and economic development, the evidence is also varied. Industrial intervention has proven quite successful in Singapore, but to a lesser extent in Malaysia and a very limited extent in Indonesia. The main factor explaining these differences is the general orientation of the government intervention. There seems to be a pattern that an export-oriented government intervention encourages firms to be efficient as they know they have to compete in the international market in the long run. A domestic market-oriented intervention encourages rent-seeking activities and inefficiency as the firms are shielded from foreign competition in the short term and longer term. Further, there is no conclusive evidence from the experiences of the ASEAN countries that strategic industry intervention has been a significant factor behind their strong economic performance.

Suggestions for further reading
Ng and Wagner (1991) have a fairly comprehensive account of the rationale, organization, performance and economic contribution of ASEAN state enterprises, while Pomfret (1994) has surveyed the different viewpoints on the role of strategic industry intervention in the development of the highly successful East Asian economies.

Notes
1. Government intervention on a micro level can take many forms. In this chapter it may be in the form of direct allocation of resources (via state enterprises) or in the form of indirect allocation of resources to certain industries through targeted and subsidized credit to selected industries, low deposit rates and ceilings on borrowing rates, protection from import competition, subsidies to declining industries, establishment and financial support of government banks, development of export-marketing institutions and cooperative venture between the private and public sector.
2. Good governance is built on three interrelated principles: democratic accountability, long-term orientation and social justice.
3. Statutory boards are required to transfer 20 percent of their annual operating surplus to the government; this transfer is broadly equivalent in its impact to the imposition of a corporate income tax.
4. It is reported that, although ethnic Chinese Indonesians represent only 3 percent of

the nearly 200 million population in Indonesia, they control about 70 percent of the Indonesian economy (*Asiaweek*, 24 January 1997, p. 23). The economic dominance of ethnic Chinese businessmen in ASEAN economies will be discussed again in Chapter 13.

5. The ten are PT IPTN (aircraft manufacturing), PT PAL Indonesia (shipbuilding), PT PINDAD (ammunition), Perum Dahana (explosives), PT Krakatau Steel, PT Barata Indonesia (machine working), PT Boma Bisma Indra (machine working), PT INKA (rail industry), PT Inti (telecommunications) and Unit Produksi Lembaga Elektronika Nasional Lembaga Ilmu Pengetauhan (electronics). For a more detailed discussion, see Habir (1990).

6. This philosophy reflects the influence of socialist traditions in Western Europe before World War II on the founding fathers of Indonesia (Pangestu, 1996).

7. Despite the financial crisis in the state oil company Pertamina in 1975–76, large investments were directed to oil refining, fertilizer, cement, aircraft and other sectors until the oil price slump forced a cancellation of these projects.

8. Social services include expenditure on health, education and other social welfare expenditures including transfers.

9. Intervention here refers to microeconomic policies aimed at directing resources to the production of specific goods or services.

10. Thailand is cited as a good example. Thailand recorded the highest per capita income growth rate between 1987 and 1992. Government has been an important factor, especially in the creation of macroeconomic stability in the 1980s and investment in primary education, but the government has not been interventionist at the micro-economic level. Policies to influence the sectoral and spatial distribution of activities pursued during the 1970s were abandoned later.

PART TWO

ASEAN EXTERNAL ECONOMIC RELATIONS

6 ASEAN economic relations: the US, Japan, the EU, China and Vietnam

The export-oriented industrialization policy of the ASEAN countries has made their economic relations with developed and developing countries an important part of their overall economic development. This chapter will evaluate the ASEAN external economic relations particularly with the US, Japan and the European Union (EU), their major trading and investment partners, and two important newly emerging market economies in Asia.

6.1 Developed countries

Although the ASEAN countries have expanded trading and investment links among themselves and with other Asian countries, as a group their trade and investments are still concentrated with developed countries. ASEAN economic relations with developed countries (the US, Japan and the EU) have essentially revolved around three major issues: (a) trade and market access; (b) foreign investments and technology; (c) foreign aid.

In the past the dominant issues were aid and development assistance in the era of 'non-reciprocity' in multilateral relations. Over time as the ASEAN countries continued to grow, the issues of trade, market access and investments based on reciprocity have increasingly been gaining prominence in ASEAN–developed countries' economic relations. The ASEAN countries continue to demand access to the markets of the industrialized countries for their manufactures in the context of rising nontariff barriers while the developed economies continually demand market access for their financial and other services, and for effective protection of intellectual property rights. The continued dynamism in the Asian region and the persistent recession in Western Europe have made ASEAN an important market for the developed countries. On the other hand, there is a growing misconception that strong economic growth in developing countries has occurred at the expense of the developed countries' prosperity, based on the belief that the inflow of goods from the developing countries has resulted in more job losses for their domestic industries. This has allegedly fuelled protectionist pressures in the developed countries by linking trade with labour standards and human rights.

Table 6.1   ASEAN major trading partners (% of total)

Country	Exports		Imports	
	1980	1995	1980	1995
US	16.9	19.2	15.4	14.1
Japan	26.8	14.3	21.8	23.1
European Union	13.4	14.4	12.7	15.7
NEA NICs	5.3	12.7	3.4	12.5
ASEAN	16.7	22.4	13.3	17.3
Australia	2.2	1.8	3.1	2.4
Others	18.7	15.2	30.3	14.9
Total	100.0	100.0	100.0	100.0

Source: IMF, *Direction of Trade Statistics Yearbook* (various issues).

6.1.1   United States

The United States is still ASEAN's largest export market and source of foreign investment. Between 1980 and 1995 ASEAN exports to the US as a proportion of total ASEAN exports increased from 16.9 to 19.2 percent while the share of exports to Japan declined from 26.8 to 14.3 percent so that in 1995 the US had replaced Japan as ASEAN's largest export market, as Table 6.1 shows. It is also an important source of imports for the ASEAN countries, accounting for about 14.1 percent of ASEAN imports in 1995.

The importance of the US as an export market varies between ASEAN countries. Table 6.2 shows that the Philippines has the highest proportion of exports to and imports from the US due to historical reasons while Brunei has the lowest proportion of exports to and imports from the US. The other ASEAN countries have proportions of their exports to the US in the range of 15.9 and 20.7 percent. On the import side, the US is not as prominent, although the share of the US in the individual ASEAN countries' imports is considerable ranging from 5.9 to 18.4 percent. Over the same period 1980–95, the ASEAN countries have increased their trade surpluses with the US significantly, starting with US$1549.0 million surplus in 1980 and increasing to US$14118.0 million in 1995.

The significant US–ASEAN bilateral trade is largely due to a substantial inter-industry trade owing to strong economic complementarities. ASEAN countries are major exporters of such goods as petroleum, rubber, sugar, tin, textiles, garments and other labour-intensive products, and these items are imported by the US. Indonesia and

Table 6.2   Share of the US in ASEAN total trade, 1995 (%)

ASEAN countries	Share in ASEAN exports	Share in ASEAN imports
Brunei	1.7	5.9
Indonesia	15.9	9.1
Malaysia	20.7	12.7
Philippines	35.3	18.4
Singapore	18.2	15.0
Thailand	17.8	15.6

Source: IMF, *Direction of Trade Statistics Yearbook* (1996).

Thailand have the highest proportion of exports to the US in the form of labour-intensive manufactures such as textiles, clothing and footwear. The US in turn exports capital-intensive, technically-intensive goods such as chemicals, electrical and nonelectrical goods, and these goods are in turn heavily imported by the ASEAN countries.

The US is also becoming an important destination of high value-added manufactured products from ASEAN. Except for Brunei, the largest share of ASEAN exports to the US is made up of manufactured goods. Over the years, there has been a shift in ASEAN from exporting primary and labour-intensive manufactured goods to capital-intensive and higher value-added manufactured goods to the US. At least more than half of ASEAN total exports in the category of machinery and miscellaneous manufactures go to the US market. Singapore and Malaysia have the highest proportion of exports to the US made up of electronic components such as memory chips, transistors and integrated circuits, followed by Thailand.[1] A significant portion of ASEAN–US bilateral trade is intra-industry due to the global strategy adopted by the US MNCs aimed at locating the various stages of production in different countries to exploit the differences in comparative advantage.

The US is the most significant source of FDI in the ASEAN region. The US direct investment in the ASEAN region has also doubled over the same period. This topic will be discussed in more detail in Chapter 9. Although the US is a very important trading partner to ASEAN, it is not as dependent on the ASEAN countries as the ASEAN countries are on the US. Even so, the US is seeking to expand its exports to the ASEAN region as it is a fast growing market, and this would also help the US to overcome its trade deficit in the region.

One of the areas where the US wants to expand is in the exports of services to the ASEAN markets. In ASEAN several barriers to trade in the service sector currently exist, including leasing restrictions, motion picture limitations, limited foreign ownership of banking, advertising restrictions and preferential treatment of domestic transportation. The US, too, is not without its share of barriers in this sector, especially at the state level. The conflict between the US and ASEAN has generally been over the US legislative measures in areas such as patents, copyrights and intellectual property rights. The US has been pressuring developing countries including ASEAN to step up intellectual property rights protection efforts, and threatening retaliatory measures against those that fail to do so (for example the latest US/China dispute on piracy). The ASEAN countries have stepped up efforts, but the US has not been satisfied.

6.1.2   Japan

The declining importance of Japan as a market for ASEAN exports since 1980 was noted in Table 6.1, indicating a significant drop in the Japanese share of ASEAN total exports from a high 26.8 percent in 1980 to 14.3 percent in 1995. In 1980 Japan was ASEAN's biggest export market. In contrast, Japan remains the largest source of ASEAN imports, accounting for 23.1 percent in 1995.

Table 6.3 shows that Japan is a very important export market for Brunei and Indonesia, accounting for 57.3 and 28.4 percent, respectively, of total ASEAN exports in 1995. This is because these countries are relatively endowed with mineral resources which Japan needs. Japan is also important for Thailand and Philippine exports primarily because of Thailand's exports of crude materials and oils and fats, and of the Philippines' exports of crude materials and mineral fuels.

ASEAN imports from Japan are dominated by capital-intensive manufactures such as machinery. Japan is also a significant source of imports of capital-intensive manufactures for all ASEAN countries, as well as imports of chemicals and miscellaneous manufactures in all ASEAN countries, except Brunei. Thus, there is a symbiotic trade relationship between ASEAN and Japan. Japan relies on ASEAN for its supply of strategic raw materials and as a market for its industrial exports. ASEAN, on the other hand, relies on Japan for its capital and technology.

The ASEAN countries as a group have had a balance of trade deficit with Japan. In 1995 this deficit amounted to US$31,134 million. On an individual country basis, only Indonesia and Brunei have enjoyed a positive trade balance with Japan due to the nature of their exports. The other four ASEAN countries have had negative trade balances

Table 6.3   Share of Japan in ASEAN total trade, 1995 (%)

ASEAN Countries	Share in ASEAN exports	Share in ASEAN imports
Brunei	57.3	4.1
Indonesia	28.4	26.8
Malaysia	12.7	20.5
Philippines	15.8	22.4
Singapore	7.8	21.1
Thailand	16.7	30.2

Source: IMF, *Direction of Trade Statistics Yearbook* (1996).

because they import a great deal of manufactured products particularly in the form of machinery and manufactured goods from Japan, but Japan does not import as much in return.

It is likely that as intra-ASEAN trade continues to grow, there will be an increase in ASEAN–Japan bilateral trade. Growing economic interdependence among Pacific basin countries is also likely to improve Japan–ASEAN trade relations. Further, Japan should continue to shift its exports to ASEAN due to ASEAN's growing industrialization and trade restrictions in the US and the EU.

Japan has always been an important source of foreign investment for ASEAN countries. By 1990 a third of total foreign direct investment in ASEAN was accounted for by Japanese foreign direct investment. Indonesia is the second largest recipient of Japanese foreign direct investment after the US, particularly in oil. Japanese investments in the Philippines are mainly in copper, and in other ASEAN countries they are mainly in manufacturing, particularly in textiles, iron and non-ferrous metals, chemicals, transport equipment and electrical machinery. Japanese investments are generally directed to obtain or produce components at low cost. There is also a strong link between parent companies and their overseas affiliates. The average size of investments is small, and usually takes the form of joint ventures with strong Japanese control. They are largely import substituting investments and are located close to consuming centres.

ASEAN has traditionally been a priority region for Japanese economic assistance. About a third of total Japanese official assistance goes to ASEAN. Indonesia and the Philippines are the main recipients in the form of technical assistance.

*Table 6.4   Share of the European Union in ASEAN total trade, 1995
            (%)*

ASEAN Countries	Share in ASEAN exports	Share in ASEAN imports
Brunei	9.1	22.0
Indonesia	16.2	20.4
Malaysia	14.2	15.2
Philippines	17.1	10.9
Singapore	13.4	13.3
Thailand	15.0	20.6

Source: IMF, *Direction of Trade Statistics Yearbook* (1996).

6.1.3   European Union (EU)

The European Union (formerly known as European Economic Community) has been traditionally not as important a market for ASEAN exports as the US or Japan. Its share of total ASEAN exports was 13.4 percent in 1980, which only slightly increased to 14.4 percent in 1995. Considering that there are a number of countries comprising the EU, this share is indeed quite small compared to the US and Japanese shares. The EU shares in individual ASEAN countries' exports do not vary significantly, with Brunei having the lowest proportion of exports going to the EU.

The trade relationship between ASEAN and the EU is characterized by dependence rather than interdependence. The share of ASEAN in the EU total exports has been roughly less than 1 percent, quite marginal compared to the EU share in total ASEAN exports. For the ASEAN countries, except for Brunei, the EU is an important market particularly for their manufactured exports. Unlike the US and Japan, the ASEAN countries export to the EU a substantial amount of primary products as well as manufactures. ASEAN's major export items to the EU include timber, rubber and tin (mostly from Malaysia), tapioca and cassava (mostly from Thailand), palm oil (mostly from Malaysia), machinery (mostly from Singapore), basic manufactures and miscellaneous manufactures. ASEAN imports from the EU are predominantly manufactures and chemicals. Almost half are machinery and transport equipment.

The EU is ASEAN's third largest source of foreign direct investment (FDI). But its share has been declining due to increasing Japanese and US shares. From 1982 to 1992 only 1 percent of the EU's cumulative

FDI went to East Asia, compared with 18 percent to the US (*The Straits Times*, 23 September, 1995).

The declining share is due to the lack of encouragement from the national governments to invest in Asia and the absence of significant business links between business communities in the EU and in ASEAN, for example, the lack of a real European counterpart to the grouping of Chambers of Commerce of ASEAN as a whole. And ASEAN did not rate high in Europe's range of interests.

The ASEAN countries have always considered the EU an important market for their exports in the context of their export-oriented and market diversification policies. This importance was demonstrated by the establishment of a Commission of the European Community for South and Southeast Asia in Bangkok in 1979, and the signing of the ASEAN–EC Cooperation Agreement at the Second ASEAN–EC Ministerial Meeting in Kuala Lumpur in 1980 to assess and monitor ASEAN–EU cooperation. The most recent ASEAN initiatives have been the establishment of regular ASEAN–EU dialogues and Asia–Europe ministerial meetings which began in Singapore in 1996.

The EU policies, on the other hand, towards developing countries are designed to stimulate trade and investment. Since 1972 the EU has adopted the Generalized System of Preferences to assist developing countries in gaining access to the EU market. The ASEAN countries have been recipients of EU financial and technical assistance to promote industrial development and cooperation in the ASEAN region. However, the introduction of the Multifibre Arrangement has been a major concern for the ASEAN countries as it imposes trade restrictions on their textile exports where they have a comparative advantage.

The future of ASEAN–EU economic relations depends to a large extent on ASEAN's continued surge in growth, greater integration in ASEAN, success of the implementation of the agreements under the Uruguay Round and future economic conditions in Europe.

6.2 Newly emerging market economies of China and Vietnam
Although the newly emerging Asian economies are not ASEAN countries' major trading and investment partners, they are fast expanding markets for ASEAN exports and for some capital-rich ASEAN countries a growing destination for their capital and managerial expertise. This is particularly true with respect to the newly emerging market economies of China and Vietnam.

6.2.1 China

Before normalization, bilateral trade with China was largely indirect, except for Singapore. Bilateral trade remains small but has been increasing since normalization. In absolute levels, total two-way trade with China rose from US$3.9 billion in 1985 to US$18.7 billion in 1995, faster than the growth of China's global trade.

From the ASEAN perspective, China remains a small trading partner, and China's share in ASEAN's total direct trade slightly decreased from 3.1 percent in 1985 to 2.9 percent in 1995. ASEAN is more dependent on China as a source of imports than as a market for exports. However, a new trend seems to be emerging since the latter half of the 1980s as the import share declined from 5.1 percent in 1985 to 3.1 percent in 1995 and the export share rose from 1.3 percent in 1985 to 2.7 percent in 1995. The export shares could be higher if the indirect trade via Hong Kong is fully considered.

Among the ASEAN countries, Singapore is China's largest trading partner. In fact, Singapore accounted for 36.5 percent of the ASEAN–China trade in 1995. From China's perspective, the share of ASEAN in China's trade increased from 5.6 percent in 1985 to 7.0 percent in 1995.

Promotion of foreign investment has been one important element of China's industrialization programme. A number of incentives have been offered to foreign investors: in Special Economic Zones (SEZs) there is preferential taxation treatment, eased restrictions on entry of foreign personnel, and better access to foreign exchange and working capital; in coastal cities there are infrastructural facilities and preferential treatment. Among ASEAN Singapore has the largest number of investment projects in China, which are diverse and technologically sophisticated. While China offers great opportunities to ASEAN for its huge market potentials and for ASEAN's export diversification policy, China is also a source of competition in third country markets.

6.2.2 Vietnam

From the ASEAN perspective, ASEAN–Vietnam bilateral trade is very low by international standards. ASEAN's total exports to Vietnam as a percentage of its total exports is very insignificant with less than 1 percent, although it went up from 0.002 percent in 1985 to 0.89 percent in 1995. Similarly, the ratio of imports from Vietnam was also less than 1 percent, but slightly increased from 0.001 percent in 1985 to 0.20 percent in 1995. However, trade volume is fast increasing. For the same period, bilateral trade between ASEAN6 and Vietnam grew by 148.9 percent per annum on average. But, from the Vietnamese perspective, ASEAN is one of its major trading partners. Vietnamese exports to

ASEAN as a proportion of its total exports was 11.6 percent while its imports from ASEAN as a proportion of its total imports was 26.1 percent in 1995.[2] Major exports of Vietnam to ASEAN are natural rubber, vegetables and fruits, coal, chromium, and footwear. Its major imports are machinery and equipment, petroleum, fertilizers, corn, maize, sugar, wool and cotton fabrics.

Foreign direct investment between ASEAN and Vietnam has also grown in recent years. FDI from ASEAN countries accounted for 15.5 percent of Vietnam's total cumulative investments at the end of 1993 compared to a mere 7 percent in 1991. Over the 1995–1997 period the ASEAN share of total FDI commitments and legal capital has grown significantly. Construction and related real estate have been the main focus of ASEAN investments followed by agricultural processing and textiles.

Singapore is Vietnam's top ASEAN investor particularly in the areas of tourism and infrastructure. Singapore has worked with Vietnam to promote tourism, build an industrial estate and develop its port and shipbuilding industry. To date, the number of licensed projects held by Singapore investors is 120, and the capital pumped in is about US$2 billion (*The Straits Times,* 5 October 1996).

To promote foreign investments, Vietnam has been building its legal framework starting with the promulgation of the new law on foreign investment in 1987. Subsequent amendments in 1990 and 1992 allowed joint ventures between domestic private and foreign firms, the establishment of Export Processing Zones (EPZs), and 100 percent foreign-owned investments with no fixed minimum or maximum amount of FDI stipulated. They also contained various fiscal incentives such as a two-year tax moratorium for joint ventures, tax exemption for certain exports and imports and guarantees against capital expropriation and nationalization (*Vietnam Jewel of Asia,* 1993).

A number of problems, however, have hindered the inflow of FDI such as underdeveloped infrastructure, bureaucratic delays, massive and widespread corruption, and unclear ownership guidelines.[3] Despite these difficulties, foreign investments in Vietnam have been growing. In 1992 Vietnam attracted a total invested capital of US$6.320 billion in 724 projects in the form of joint ventures. Investments are largely from the non-ASEAN countries. Singapore is the largest ASEAN trading and investment partner, accounting for 3.6 percent of total foreign investment in Vietnam in 1992.

The prospect for ASEAN–Vietnam economic relations is bright due to Vietnam's policy of giving priority to developing cooperative relations with neighbouring Asian countries, its political stability, improvement in its bureaucratic machinery and infrastructure, its policy of export market diversification for ASEAN and lately because of its recent membership in ASEAN in July, 1995.[4]

Suggestions for further reading
For a good general background on ASEAN economic relations with their major trading and investment partners such as the US, Japan and the EU, read Sandhu et al. (eds) (1992), pp. 321–8, 329–34, 335–9. Harris and Bridges (1983) is also worth reading with respect to ASEAN–EU economic relations. For ASEAN–China and ASEAN–Indo-China economic relations, Sandhu et al. (eds) (1992), pp. 340–51 is recommended.

Notes
1. Singapore is the world's largest producer of hard disk drives and the third largest producer of headphone stereos. Thailand is the world's second largest producer of hard disk drives while Malaysia is the world's third largest producer of radio cassette players. This observation is based on Table 16 of United Nations Economic and Social Commission for Asia and the Pacific (1994).
2. With the fall of the CMEA, Vietnam's trade orientation has shifted from the former Soviet Union and East European bloc to Asia. In 1992 Singapore emerged as Vietnam's top trading partner. The other top four trading partners were Japan, Hong Kong, France and Taiwan.
3. Vietnam is now considering amending and simplifying its tax and foreign investment laws and procedures to make it easier and more attractive for foreign investors. See *The Straits Times*, 5 October 1996.
4. The economic implications of Vietnam's entry into ASEAN and AFTA will be discussed in detail in Chapter 11.

7 ASEAN and other regional trading arrangements

Another source of serious concern for ASEAN countries in their dealings with developed countries is the likely negative impact of regionalism in these economies. This chapter will examine two major regional economic initiatives recently formed by Western developed countries and their likely impact on ASEAN economies: the deepening and enlargement of European integration and the establishment of the North American Free Trade Area (NAFTA).

The late 1980s witnessed a growing interest in regionalism as an alternative to multilateralism. During this period important steps were taken to establish and deepen existing levels of economic integration. The European Community (EC) led the way by first aiming for a Single European Market (SEM), then forming the European Union (EU) and later a European Economic Area (EEA) that includes four members of the European Free Trade Area (EFTA). In 1992 the North American countries, the US, Canada and Mexico, signed a free trade agreement (NAFTA). These developments seem to indicate the emergence of two trading blocs and have caused the fear that the EU and NAFTA could turn into inward-looking blocs, thereby posing a threat to the openness of the world multilateral trading system.

Theoretically, an economic grouping becomes a bloc only when the members adopt a common economic policy in their dealings with non-members and use it to divert trade and investment from the latter. Thus, while an economic union such as the EU can be considered a bloc, a free trade area cannot be because it does not have a common external policy. That is why the US has always insisted that NAFTA would not become a protectionist bloc. In practice, however, the fact that the EU and NAFTA do not benefit non-members means that trade and investment diversion could take place.

The first impact comes in the form of *trade diversion*, the extent of which depends on the degree to which commodity exports to an integrating country, say the US, overlap that of a partner country, say Mexico (elasticity of substitution) and on the degree of discrimination against outsiders in the matched commodities (margin of trade preference).

The second impact is in the form of *investment diversion*, as domestic and foreign investment shift away from non-members to member countries within an FTA or a customs union zone. The effect would be particularly pronounced in industries sustaining acute trade diversion.

However, the picture is not all gloomy for non-members if we take into account the dynamic and long-run effect of economic integration. The growth of income in the integrating area will accelerate due to expanded market size, leading to an increase in demand for foreign imports. The size of this increase depends on the income elasticity of import demand. Along with other sources, ASEAN exports to the integrating area will also expand, but this effect may be offset wholly or partly by the dynamic counterpart of trade diversion, which implies shrinkage of the nonmember economies as their exports contract.

7.1 ASEAN and European integration

European integration is a process that commenced more than 30 years ago. In the late 1950s, the original six members started the formation of a customs union and Common Agricultural Policy (CAP), a process which was completed ten years later. During the 1960s and 1970s the EC set up a web of preferential arrangements with various countries such as Greece and Turkey, EFTA countries in Europe and Associated states in Africa and the Caribbean (ACF). The EC was enlarged in the 1970s from six to nine members with the accession of the United Kingdom, Ireland and Denmark. In the 1980s it was further enlarged to twelve members with the accession of Greece (1981) and then Spain and Portugal (1986). On December 3, 1992 the Common Market came into being. The EC is now embarking on the task of establishing a common currency.

7.1.1 Trade diversion

The European integration poses a protectionist challenge to ASEAN in the form of a trade-diverting common external trade policy where efficient low-cost ASEAN producers may be discriminated against. Since it is impossible to estimate the trade diversion effect without the knowledge of the relevant elasticities, qualitative observations are made here. Trade diversion will come from the following measures adopted by the EC:

- the abolition of all intracommunity nontariff barriers (NTBs), including the technical barriers to trade, which result from differential product standards between member states. Products where such technical barriers are important are: electrical engineering products, mechanical engineering equipment, medical equipment, pharmaceutical products, motor vehicles, foodstuffs, metal articles, mineral products and rubber products. The abolition of intra-EC NTBs will enhance discrimination against the ASEAN countries.

- the conversion of national quotas on sensitive products into EC-wide quotas. Whether or not this conversion is trade-diverting or trade-creating depends on whether the EC-wide quotas will be more restrictive than the ones now in existence.[1] The uncertainty it creates could be trade-diverting.
- the elimination of national preferences on government contracts and the opening of government procurement bids only to the Community members will discriminate against ASEAN bidders for public contracts.[2]
- the increasing use of anti-dumping measures by the EC as a vehicle for protection.

ASEAN exporters of manufactures are expected to be most hurt as the EU imports a large amount of manufactures from ASEAN. EU imports of ASEAN manufactures have increased from 48 percent in 1980 to 64 percent in 1988, as a proportion of total EU imports from ASEAN.

The European integration also poses a competitive challenge in the third markets. Competition among EU firms will intensify due to the extension of trade preferences among themselves, which could lead to more efficiency. Industries that will face strong EU competition are cars, electronic goods, textiles and clothing.

7.1.2 Investment diversion

Apart from trade diversion, there may be investment diversion. Foreign direct investment has been one of the factors responsible for the economic dynamism of ASEAN by providing an important source of capital, technology and management skills and by stimulating exports. The creation of a large EU market means that more firms will establish their operations in Europe to benefit from this enlarged market. Third country investment could also flow in to avoid protectionist barriers maintained by the EU. Investment diversion in ASEAN could occur in machinery and transport equipment, food, chemicals, textiles, metals and electronics.

Substantial trade and investment diversion may slow down ASEAN growth. The effects of trade and foreign investment have generally been favourable for ASEAN in terms of technology transfer and employment creation. If such diversions are great, sustaining the present growth momentum might be a problem.

7.2   ASEAN and North American integration

On December 17, 1992, the US, Canada and Mexico signed a trade accord to eliminate trade barriers and form a continental-wide single market. Coming into force on January 1, 1994, it has established a free trade area of 370 million people producing and consuming goods and services valued at US$6.8 trillion a year. An agreement of such a size will certainly have widespread implications for member and non-member countries.

The objectives of NAFTA are (a) to eliminate trade barriers, (b) to promote conditions of fair competition, (c) to increase investment opportunities, (d) to provide adequate protection of intellectual property rights, (e) to establish effective procedures for the implementation and application of the Agreement and for the resolution of disputes, and finally (f) to improve further trilateral regional and multilateral cooperation.

When NAFTA came into force, tariffs on approximately 50 percent of the 9000 traded items covered by the treaty were eliminated with immediate effect. Within the next five years, 15 percent more of the items are to have zero tariffs with the remainder following in the next ten years. In addition, remaining licensing requirements and quotas were also eliminated with immediate effect.

To qualify for the preferential access, a commodity must be wholly produced within that particular member country or if imported materials are used, they must be subject to 'substantial transformation' within the country. At least 35 percent of the value of the commodity exported has to be accounted for by the beneficiary country in question. This is known as the 'rules of origin'.

NAFTA investors also receive more favourable treatment in setting up operations or acquiring firms. Existing requirements, including specified export levels, minimum domestic content, preferences for domestic sourcing, trade balancing and technology transfer, are being phased out over periods of up to ten years.

Following the US and Canada, Mexico is committed to the removal of various restrictions on service transactions. Mexico will eliminate its restrictions on banks and insurance companies by January 2000, and on brokerage firms within ten years so that wholly-owned subsidiaries that may be established will be subjected to non-discriminatory treatment.

US trucking firms, which were barred from carrying cargo into Mexico, are now permitted to carry international cargo into the Mexican states and to the rest of Mexico by the year 2000. Full reciprocal access for trucking firms will be permitted by around 2000. The US and Mexico will allow charter and tour bus operations in the cross-border market with full access in all three countries. US railroads are now able to serve Mexico generally. US investments are permitted in landside port services. The majority of Mexico's tariff and non-tariff barriers on tele-communication equipment are now eliminated. And NAFTA allows the three countries to follow their own environmental, health and safety standards.

The same theoretical framework used in the case of the European integration can be used here. The economic implications of NAFTA for the ASEAN countries can be assessed in terms of trade and diversion effects. Also, if the dynamic perspective is adopted, it is possible that the growth-enhancing effects of NAFTA may be significant enough to reduce the negative short-run implications of trade and investment diversion.

The US is the largest market for ASEAN and competition from Mexico in the US market has caused greatest concern among the ASEAN countries, as the Mexican economy resembles the ASEAN economies most, and as the Canadian and Mexican markets are relatively insignificant to ASEAN. Direct competition from Mexico is likely to occur in food, petroleum and petroleum products, organic and inorganic compounds, machinery, telecom equipment, electronics and in miscellaneous manufactures such as clothing and footwear. For these items Mexico has demonstrated some productive capacity and thus, its export elasticities in these products are relatively high.[3] Diversion of investments to Mexico, particularly in labour-intensive products, is also likely due to lower labour costs and its proximity to the US market.

There are, however, a number of forces which can mitigate the trade and investment diversion effects of the European and North American integration on ASEAN. First, due to the successful completion of the Uruguay Round of Trade Negotiations under GATT, the barriers that North America and Europe have against foreign countries will be reduced substantially over the next ten years (2003, roughly at the same time as NAFTA and AFTA). The Uruguay Round aims to cut tariffs by 37 percent on average on industrial and farm goods as well as liberalizing trade in agriculture and services. It also intends to replace non-tariffs such as quotas with tariffs. Athough it does not have the scope and depth of NAFTA, a successful implementation of the new GATT treaty can mitigate the trade and investment diversion effects of NAFTA from ASEAN.

The ASEAN countries also have a competitive edge over Mexico in terms of infrastructure and management (*The Straits Times*, 27 August 1992). Based on The World Competitiveness Report (1992, 1994),

Mexico was behind Singapore, Malaysia and Thailand in terms of overall world competitiveness. Based on The World Competitiveness Report (1995), Mexico was ranked behind all the ASEAN5 countries, that is, Singapore, Malaysia, Thailand, Indonesia and the Philippines.

Continued dynamism in the Asian region, fuelled by greater regional trade liberalization and the enlargement of markets with the opening up of China, India and Indo-China, will make ASEAN an attractive region for investments. That is why the US and Canada have increased their trade with ASEAN even after the US–Canada free trade agreement was implemented in 1989.

7.3   Counter strategy for ASEAN

7.3.1   AFTA and linkages with NAFTA and the EU
The response of the ASEAN countries to the growing regionalism in Europe and North America has been one of retaliation and reconciliation. First, the 1992 decision by the ASEAN countries to establish an ASEAN free trade area by the year 2008 and the recent decision to speed up the process by moving the implementation date to 2003 reflected the ASEAN effort to maintain, if not improve, the attractiveness of the ASEAN region for trade and investment. At the same time, there has been an attempt to forge linkages with NAFTA and EU countries. Such linkages are taking shape already. An initial link between NAFTA and AFTA countries was forged in November, 1991 when a trade and investment framework agreement was signed between the US and Singapore. For example, a Mexican manufacturer of sheet glass has a technology-sharing agreement with US firms in glass-making machines and moulds. This firm hopes to manufacture glass products in Thailand and then use Singapore as a purchasing, distribution and financing centre. Similar arrangements are being sought for textiles and garments manufacturing between Mexican and Indonesian parties.

Dialogues between ASEAN and the EU to discuss the prospects for cooperation on trade with each other have started under the Asia–Europe Meeting (ASEM). An Investment Promotion Action plan under the Asia–Europe Cooperation framework has been proposed to strengthen the multilateral trading system.

7.3.2   Formation of Asia–Pacific Economic Community (APEC)
Since APEC was formed in 1989, it has become the primary regional vehicle for promoting trade and investment cooperation in the Asia–Pacific region.[4] ASEAN has joined APEC initially on the understanding that the grouping is informal, with no legal binding power. But, since

1993 the development of APEC into a more formal grouping is taking shape.[5] This trend is a response to the rising regionalism in Europe and to the possibility of the world splitting into blocs. This grouping can, therefore, be viewed as a cooperative venture between East Asia and North America to promote an open global trading system.

Apart from the vision statement and general framework for trade liberalization in the Asia–Pacific region, the APEC leaders have also expanded the trade and investment facilitation programme to include the endorsement of non-binding investment principles to facilitate investments in the region, improve customs procedures,[6] establish common standards and lower administrative barriers to market access and establish a dispute settlement mechanism to supplement that of the World Trade Organization. They have also agreed to expand regional cooperation in education and training, science and technology, small and medium enterprises, sustainable development and infrastructure (including energy, transportation, telecommunications and tourism).

Given APEC's commitment to the principle of open regionalism, APEC can complement ASEAN's long-term interest in establishing a freer multilateral trading environment. ASEAN have much to gain from APEC not only because the Asia–Pacific region is economically important for them, but also because of the political leverage from being part of APEC. Since APEC will offer to extend its liberalization to non-members who are willing to reciprocate, barriers are likely to fall inside and outside the region.

In the Osaka Summit meeting in November 1995, the action agenda for trade liberalization to ensure compatibility of balance of interests among member countries was approved, but the scope of coverage remained unresolved. APEC members were divided on whether or not certain sectors would have to be exempted from trade liberalization. Japan, South Korea and China wanted to shelter their farmers from free trade while the US and Australia, APEC's biggest food exporters, insisted on no exceptions.

In the last APEC Summit Meeting in Subic Bay, the Philippines in November 1996 the APEC leaders took another step by endorsing a detailed action plan (Manila Action Plan for the Asia–Pacific Economic Cooperation) for achieving the goal of free trade and investment within the region by the year 2020. Each individual member's action plan details plans to reduce tariffs, commencing in January 1997, gradually to zero (by 2010 for developed countries and 2020 for developing countries), and to speed up the movement of goods and people throughout the region by harmonizing customs and immigration procedures. On the unfinished issue of coverage, the APEC members have reaffirmed their commitment to a voluntary non-binding structure, instead of the formal and legal structure of other trading arrangements such as the EU and NAFTA. Unlike previous summits, they have also expressed their commitment to improve their less-developed members' ability to compete and benefit from a larger market by fostering a programme of economic and technical cooperation. Further, they have expressed support for a leading role for the private sector in boosting trade and investment in the region and in providing a 'reality check' for political leaders and officials. They have also demonstrated their concern for small and medium-scale enterprises by agreeing to provide training resources and information on potential new markets.

Suggestions for further reading

For an industry by industry assessment of the effect of the North American Free Trade Area (NAFTA) and the Economic Community post-1992 on the Association of Southeast Asian Nations, see Kreinin and Plummer (1992). For a general assessment of the relationship between the ASEAN Free Trade Area (AFTA) and NAFTA, read Pupphavesa and Geeve (1994), Chapter 8.

Notes

1. EC-wide quotas are in a way trade liberalizing compared to the existing ones. Under the current system, if the import quota of EC country A has not been filled, while in country B the quota is binding, it is not possible to use the slack in A to increase imports into B.
2. Products where public procurement accounts for a large share of the market and where discrimination against imports is important are: defence equipment, aircraft and space equipment, electric power-generating machinery, medical equipment, railway equipment, ships, telephone exchanges, computers and metal constructions (Kreinin and Plummer, 1992, p. 1362).
3. A large proportion of ASEAN exports to the US are likely to be affected as the US is the largest export market for the Philippines, Singapore and Thailand and the second largest for Indonesia and Malaysia (*The Straits Times*, 1 October 1992).
4. The APEC concept was initiated in January 1989 by the then Australian Prime Minister Bob Hawke. At his invitation trade and foreign ministers met in Canberra and created APEC. The founding members include Australia, Canada, Japan, South Korea, New Zealand, the US and all members of ASEAN. Memberships were subsequently extended to China, Hong Kong, Taiwan, Mexico, Papua New Guinea and Chile, bringing the total membership to 18 nations. This grouping is committed to regional economic cooperation and open regionalism.
5. At the pathbreaking 1993 Summit meeting in Seattle, the APEC leaders issued a vision statement and endorsed the Report of the Eminent Persons Group. At the second Summit meeting in 1994 in Bogor, Indonesia, they produced commitments including the setting of 2020 as the dateline for a free and open trade in the Asia–Pacific, 2010 for the industrialized economies.
6. APEC Subcommittee on Customs procedure has just reached an accord to adopt common customs checks by 2000. The accord contains nine technical steps needed to

ensure that goods pass through the same customs clearance procedures including common rules for valuing goods to assess import tariffs, wider enforcement of copyrights, adoption of a single APEC customs declaration form, and the computerization of clearance procedures in line with UN rules.

8 Regionalism, multilateralism and the World Trade Organization

It is implied from the preceding chapters that the ASEAN countries in negotiating with countries outside the region for freer trade and more secure market access have reinforced their bargaining position by negotiating as a group and taking a common position, rather than individually. They have also pursued a regional approach to trade liberalization. But it is quite clear from their policy announcements that they prefer a freer global trade to a freer regional trade and that the multilateral approach is the best tool for achieving a freer global trade. This chapter will explore the factors behind the worldwide revival of interest in regionalism, analyse the major achievements of the last round of multilateral trade negotiations and its implications for the ASEAN countries and the role and challenges facing the World Trade Organization (WTO). The last section considers the advantages and disadvantages of regionalism *vis-à-vis* multilateralism.

8.1 Reasons for the revival of regionalism

Created in Geneva on 30 October 1947 by 23 founding nations, the General Agreement on Tariffs and Trade (GATT), now known as the World Trade Organization (WTO), membership increased to over 100 countries. As believers in an open market and fair competition secured through multilateral rules and discipline, the GATT members had, over seven rounds of negotiations, slashed average tariffs on manufactured goods from more than 40 percent in the 1940s to less than 5 percent today. The rounds were: the Geneva Round in 1947, the Annecy Round in 1949, the Torquay Round in 1950–51, the Geneva Round in 1955–56, the Dillion Round in 1961–62, the Kennedy Round in 1964–67, and the Tokyo Round in 1974–79.

Despite the substantial tariff reduction on manufactured goods, there has been a growing dissatisfaction over the multilateral approach to trade liberalization under the auspices of GATT for a number of reasons. New forms of trade restrictions such as the Voluntary Export Restraints (VERs), Orderly Marketing Arrangements (OMAs), technical standards, customs procedures and others have emerged as disguised forms of protectionism. The large membership of GATT has made negotiations more complicated and difficult to resolve, let alone monitor compliances. The Western countries, particularly Western Europe and the US are increasingly disillusioned with GATT and there is a growing perception that multilateralism has failed to provide a level playing field. The Special and Differential treatment (S & D) accorded to developing countries in the form of the Generalized System of Preferences has been cited as an example.

There is a perception that the European market is becoming more inward-looking with the establishment of the European Union (EU) and the extension of integration to the European Free Trade Area (EFTA) and Eastern European countries. The decline in US economic dominance and increased competition from Europe and Japan has reduced US commitment to multilateralism and pushed it to form a countervailing bloc. The US–Canada Free Trade Area (FTA) was later followed by the North America Free Trade Area (NAFTA). The enterprise for the Americas' initiative envisages more FTAs with South American countries.

The delayed conclusion of the Uruguay Round has made countries pessimistic of the effectiveness of multilateralism and has driven a number of countries to form regional groupings as an insurance policy.[1] Finally, faltering support of the US and Western Europe for the multilateral system has created a sense elsewhere that regionalism is the order of the day. Smaller countries are seeking regional trading arrangements with their large neighbours. Ex-President of Mexico Salinas pushed Mexico into NAFTA because of concern that European investments would be diverted to Eastern Europe and that domestic reforms in Mexico might be derailed under political pressure. On the other hand, there was the US concern with cross-border problems should the Mexican economy collapse. Due to the above sources of dissatisfaction over the GATT-sponsored multilateral approach there has been a proliferation of regional trading pacts. According to the WTO report (1995), 109 regional trading arrangements were notified to GATT between 1947 and 1994. There were 33 registered pacts between 1990 and 1994.

8.2 Achievements of the Uruguay Round and ASEAN
During these seven rounds the ASEAN countries did not benefit as much as the developed industrialized countries because they chose to remain on the sidelines. The recent successful conclusion of the Uruguay Round (1986–93), where the ASEAN countries had been more active participants in the negotiation process, has achieved the following agreements beneficial to the ASEAN countries:

(a) Tariff reduction on industrial and farm goods by an average of 37 percent and the replacement of non-tariffs with tariffs. The tariff equivalents are to be reduced by a simple average of 24 percent over a ten-year period for the developing countries and by a simple average of 36 percent over a six-year period for the developed countries subject to a minimum of 15 percent (ESCAP, 1995, p. 90);

(b) The tariffication of non-tariff barriers and reduction of farm subsidies. All border non-tariff measures applied on imports of agricultural products are converted into tariff equivalents and subjected to the same tariff reductions and datelines as in the imports of industrial products. Subsidization of domestic producers of agricultural products is reduced equal to a 20 percent reduction of the aggregate measure of support with the exception of subsidies with a minimal impact on trade (the 'Green Box'), cases where domestic support constitutes less than 10 percent of the total value of production for developing countries or 5 percent for developed countries on a general or product-specific basis and direct payments under production-limiting programmes. The developing countries are provided with exemptions with respect to investment subsidies, agricultural input subsidies, or those applied to encourage diversification out of illicit narcotic crops;

(c) Liberalization of the trade in services. The General Agreement on Trade and Services (GATS) extends basic MFN obligations to services, thus bringing this sector for the first time into the auspices of GATT. Agreements include elimination of limits on the number of service providers, total value of service transactions, kind of legal entity or joint ventures and foreign capital related to maximum foreign participation;

(d) Protection of trade-related intellectual property rights (TRIPs). The TRIPs Agreement establishes disciplines for copyright, trade marks, geographical indications, industrial designs, patents, layout designs of integrated circuits and protection of undisclosed information;

(e) Strengthening of the rules for settling international trade disputes and clarification of the anti-dumping rules. The Agreement provides more detailed rules in defining dumping, and procedures and methods for initiating investigations. These rules are aimed to make domestic legislations more transparent, greater scrutiny of information contained in the complaint, positive action to ascertain industry support for the complaint and reviews of anti-dumping measures within five-year intervals;

(f)   Transformation of GATT into a permanent watchdog, called the World Trade Organization (WTO), with status equal to the International Monetary Fund and the World Bank.

The success of the long-drawn-out Uruguay Round has certainly been a boost to the multilateral process as an approach to global trade liberalization. The pessimism that prevailed during Uruguay talks about the inability of the process to strike general agreements on rules governing international trade has been to a large extent translated into new hopes and reinvigorated the world trading environment. Apart from the psychological boost, there are also benefits derived for the ASEAN countries. On the first agreement, a freer trade in agriculture and manufactures will benefit particularly Malaysia and Thailand. Malaysia's exports of palm oil have been facing quotas in the European market with its common agricultural policy. Thailand's exports of rice have faced significant tariffs and global quotas in Japan and the European Community (EC); its cassava exports are subject to the EC's voluntary export restraints (VERs).

The Philippines and Indonesia will also benefit from the agreed phasing out of import quotas under the Multifibre Arrangement (MFA), particularly for their exports of textiles, clothing and footwear. The reduction of farm subsidies should also benefit particularly Malaysia's export of palm oil in the EC since soya bean oil (its competing substitute) in the EC is heavily subsidized.

The basic obligations incorporated in the Services Agreement and the commitments undertaken by the countries lay the groundwork for progressive liberalization of international trade in services through successive rounds of negotiations. The impact of this on ASEAN is likely to be varied as their services sectors vary in terms of efficiency and development. Singapore, having the most developed financial sector, is likely to benefit from the liberalization of trade in professional and technical services such as banking and finance, transport, tourism, engineering consultancies, medical services and computer software. But Indonesia, Malaysia and the Philippines may experience substantial deficits in services account resulting from the liberalization of trade in services.

The protection of intellectual property rights would seem to inconvenience the ASEAN countries at first reading. But in the long term this agreement would lower the risk of investment for foreign businesses, making the ASEAN region more attractive to foreign direct investment (FDI). Further, an effective enforcement against any breach

of copyright will encourage greater indigenous innovation and technological progress.

The agreement on the rules on anti-dumping should also benefit the
ASEAN countries as problems relating to the application and administration of anti-dumping systems and the increased recourse to anti-
dumping actions have become more pronounced.

8.3   The role and challenges of the WTO

The main task of the trading community now is to implement the
results of the Uruguay Round in order to bring about a world trade
liberalization. This enormous task can better be managed within an
institutional framework – the WTO – encompassing the GATT and
having the status of an Inter-Governmental Organization like the World
Bank. Also, a more credible system for managing disputes has been
established within the WTO, which is crucial to the successful enforcement of the commitments under the Uruguay Round.

To be able to effectively implement the Uruguay agreements and
become the motor of world trade liberalization, the WTO needs to
resolve the following issues:

- The WTO must be able to maintain a motivated Secretariat so
  that it can be adequately equipped with resources to deal with
  its enormous work. Although the key posts in the WTO Secretariat are filled, the team in the Secretariat has been
  overstretched and has been demanding improved pay and work
  conditions.[2]
- There are over 200 notification requirements arising from the
  Marrakesh decisions and member countries are behind schedule
  in meeting many of them.[3]
- The Uruguay Round has agreed on a set of principles to govern
  services trade, but only a few barriers have been reduced. There
  is still the remaining task of resolving negotiations in the area
  of agricultural trade, financial services, telecommunications and
  maritime transport.[4]
- There are a few dynamic countries such as China, Russia and
  Taiwan that are still outside the WTO. Global free trade cannot
  be achieved if such countries remain outside the organization.
  Yet some of the non-members seem unable or unwilling to align
  their rules with WTO norms. The challenge is how to accelerate their entry without any sacrifice of principles. If the
  accession negotiations get stuck, how long will the WTO survive
  as a motor of trade liberalization? Some new formula may be

needed to enable them to engage in the coming initiatives even if they have not yet become full members.

- There are a number of current members of the WTO, mainly developing countries, whose governments and economies are not effectively plugged either to the world economy or the Geneva decision-making process due mainly to low income and high indebtedness. These countries may not see any benefits from an open trading system and from the additional efforts launched in WTO.

- There is a challenge to secure for the WTO and the open trading system the support of the voters whose opinions drive policy in an increasingly democratic world. Despite the unprecedented support for freer trade around the world, considerable protectionist pressures remain. The WTO is seen in some quarters as contributing to the violation of human rights and labour exploitation. The WTO needs to spearhead a global educational campaign on the benefits of free trade, apart from individual countries' campaigns on the merits of the strategy.

- There is the unsettled issue of whether or not the principle of fairness, human rights, child labour and the right to collective bargaining must be linked to trade. The US has proposed that WTO members proclaim the desirability of five core labour standards, and set up a committee to examine the links between trade and the observance of these standards. This question is related to defining the meaning of 'free trade'. Countries are divided on this. Norway has made similar proposals and some EU countries, notably France, are sympathetic. The ASEAN countries have already made their position clear. In contrast to the countries of North America and Western Europe, they prefer to take up this issue under the auspices of the International Labour Organization (ILO), rather than under the WTO. This issue could delay the progress for establishing a freer world trade unless properly managed.

- Finally, the need for the WTO to set the course for the global trading system and for the world economy for the next millenium.

8.4 Multilateralism vs regionalism

Given that there are a number of challenges facing the WTO, it is not an irrelevant question to ask whether or not regionalism is better than the multilateral approach towards worldwide trade liberalization. The case for free trade was advocated by Adam Smith and David Ricardo and later was rigorously proved in a number of theoretical studies (for example Samuelson, 1939 and Kemp, 1962). Viner's analysis of trade creation and trade diversion has also shown that preferential trading arrangements are not necessarily welfare-enhancing, either from the members' viewpoint or from the world's. Preferential trading arrangements are second best solutions, as shown by Meade (1955, 1956), Johnson (1958) and others.

The key issues in the multilateralism versus regionalism debate are: Will regionalism in the form of free trade arrangements (FTAs) and customs union (CUs) bring quicker results in trade liberalization? Will regionalism increase or reduce world welfare? Will regionalism ultimately support and reinforce the multilateral free trade system and therefore should it be welcomed, or will it undermine the system and deserve condemnation? Should regionalism be accepted as a second best solution to the breakdown of the GATT-based multilateral system, given that the first best solution is unattainable?

Critics of the GATT-based multilateral approach to free trade who are frustrated with the slow progress made under GATT in trade liberalization have translated the GATT acronym as a general agreement to talk and talk. They have argued that regional trading arrangements among like-minded nations produce faster agreements on trade liberalization. On the other hand, supporters of the GATT approach have pointed to the slow implementation of an FTA or CU. For example, the European Community (EC) started in 1957 and the integration process has been slow. It took ASEAN ten years after its formation to draw its agenda for economic cooperation, and 25 years to agree to establish an FTA. The ASEAN FTA immediately faced hitches in implementation and the time frame for implementation was reduced from 15 to ten years largely because the implementation of the Uruguay Round agreements would be completed within a ten-year time frame.

A regional trading arrangement is designed to promote trade among its members at the expense of non-members. It, therefore, produces a trade-creating effect (generating trade with one more efficient member at the expense of another less efficient member) and a trade-diverting effect (taking trade away from efficient outside suppliers and giving it to inefficient member countries). Which effect would be dominant depends on the proportion of trade between members and non-members, on the expenditure share between imports and domestic production and on the elasticity of substitution between goods. It is not certain that the trade diversion effect is minimized if the regional trade arrangement is confined to proximate countries.[5]

It is suggested that certain disciplines must be observed to minimize the incidence of trade diversion; for example, that the common external tariff in a CU is not higher or more restrictive than the pre-CU level, that duties and regulations in an FTA are not higher than the pre-FTA level, and that greater discipline is exercised with regard to antidumping and VER actions.

Will regionalism support or undermine multilateralism? One view is that regionalism can serve as a building block for multilateralism.[6] The threat of regionalism could produce multilateral trade agreements that otherwise would have been held up. It was reported that one of the forces that prompted the eventual successful conclusion of the Uruguay Round in 1993 was the decision of the EU to form a Single Common Market in 1992. Thus, there could be a positive interaction between the regional and global approach to trade liberalization.

In a political economy sense, negotiations and agreements where few parties are involved are easier to achieve than in situations where a number of parties are involved. There are over a hundred countries currently involved in the process of multilateral trade negotiations which makes the achievement of agreements and resolutions under the Most Favoured Nation (MFN) principle much more complex and diffi-cult than if negotiations are conducted with few parties under regional reciprocity. The free rider problem has constrained groups of countries to extend preferential arrangements under the MFN principle.

Further, public support for a regional trading arrangement tends to be more focussed and mobilized than support for multilateralism. The politics of preferential trade arrangements implies that it is easier for businessmen to secure trade diversionary deals in a Free Trade Area or Customs Union than in the non-discriminatory world of the General Agreement on Tariffs and Trade.

On the other hand, regionalism could also undermine multilateralism. The unwillingness of the EC to start the multilateral trade negotiations in 1982 and its foot-dragging in the Uruguay Round reflect to some extent the availability of regionalism as an option. Under this scenario the world will be divided into three or two trading blocs.

To date, regional trading arrangements have been positive forces in driving global liberalization with initiatives to establish free trade between regional groupings.[7] This goal of global free trade is quite feasible. As Table 8.1 shows, over 60 percent of world trade now occurs within regional groupings that have already achieved free trade such as the EU and Australia–New Zealand, or have signed an agreement that will achieve it such as NAFTA and AFTA, or have made a political commitment to do so by a certain date such as APEC, the Free Trade of the Americas and EUROMED. On the other hand, the prolifer-ation of regional arrangements could also make it difficult to maintain

Table 8.1   Regional free trade arrangements (share of world trade, 1994)[a]

European Union	22.8%
EUROMED	2.3%
NAFTA	7.9%
Mercosur	0.3%
Free Trade Area of the Americas	2.6%[b]
ASEAN Free Trade Area	1.3%
Australia–New Zealand	0.1%
APEC	23.7[b]
Total	61.0

Notes:
[a] Trade among the members of each regional group.
[b] Excluding trade among the members of their own sub-regional groups.

Source: Bergsten (1996).

consistency with the global system. For example, the next potential regional arrangement, a Transatlantic Free Trade Area (TAFTA) between North America and Europe, could have a negative impact on the global trading system by encompassing new discrimination against the poor by the rich and thus reversing the progress towards North–South trade cooperation.

Whether regionalism will lead to a fragmented world economy or to non-discriminatory free trade through building blocs depends on the willingness of member governments, the behaviour of interest groups and the reactions of governments and interest groups in non-member countries.

Suggestions for further reading
Martin and Winters (eds) (1995) provides an assessment of the recently-concluded Uruguay Round of Trade Negotiations and its implications for the developing countries covering a wide range of issues. Bergsten (1996) and Brittan (1996) provide an introduction into the challenges and opportunities the World Trade Organization (WTO) is facing. On multilateralism versus regionalism, Schultz (1996) is recommended.

Notes
1.   Commencing in 1986, it was finally concluded in December, 1993.
2.   Taken from the speech of Sir Leon Brittan, Vice President of the Commission of the European Communities, 24 April 1996.

3.   Ibid.
4.   In 1999 a new round of negotiations on freeing agricultural trade, which began during the Uruguay Round, is due to start; in 1997 more talks on services trade are scheduled to begin.
5.   For a more detailed discussion of this issue, see Bhagwati (1996).
6.   The phrase 'building or stumbling blocks' is owed to Bhagwati (1991, p. 77) who refers to the expansion of membership as a test of preferential trading arrangements (PTA) serving as building blocs for global freeing of trade. He also pointed out that if going down the PTA path itself can trigger multilateral negotiations and their successful conclusion, that too can be a way in which PTAs may serve as building blocs.
7.   For example, Mercosur is a free trade agreement between the South American Market and the European Union; Free Trade Area of the Americas is between NAFTA and South America.

9 Role of foreign direct investment (FDI) in ASEAN

We have seen previously that foreign direct investment (FDI) in the form of MNCs has played a significant role in ASEAN economic development by providing the required capital, technology and access to the external markets through their international marketing networks. This chapter will discuss in more detail the benefits and costs associated with FDI, and the policies adopted by the ASEAN countries to maximize the benefits of FDI and counteract its potential negative consequences.

9.1 Foreign direct investment

Foreign direct investment is differentiated from other forms of investment by the former's ability to have a direct control over the invested capital. Usually in the form of multinational corporations (MNCs), foreign investors are driven to invest overseas due to their possession of superior technology or some type of comparative advantage, to maintain international competitiveness in the midst of rising production costs at home, or/and to counter certain moves of their rivals.

9.1.1 Forms of foreign direct investment

The activities of MNCs may take the form of *horizontal integration* in which case large corporations open new subsidiaries worldwide, or one or several existing firms competing in the host country may be bought up by a large international corporation, and competition is reduced and market divided in oligopolistic fashion. Horizontal integration may be domestic market-oriented or export-oriented investments. For example, Toyota setting up an assembly plant in ASEAN is a domestic market-oriented investment whereas Sumitomo's chemical complex in Singapore is an export-oriented one. They may also take the form of *vertical integration* by keeping control of the various stages of a production process. For example, Unilever in the Philippines sets up a coconut oil production plant for soap production in its American factories.

9.1.2 FDI trends in ASEAN

Since the late 1970s the ASEAN region has been one of the most attractive investment locations in the developing world. Its share in the total stock of FDI in developing countries increased from 9 percent in

1980 to 24 percent in 1992 (UNCTAD, 1994). Its share in global FDI flows increased from less than 1 percent to 9 percent over the same period (Athukorala and Menon, 1996, p. 77). The growth of FDI into ASEAN was rapid particularly in the 1987–91 period (see Table 9.1). The importance of FDI varies, however, among individual ASEAN countries. FDI in aggregate plays a more important role in Singapore and Malaysia than in the other three remaining ASEAN economies, as Table 2.5 and Table 9.1 reveal.

Developed countries have been the largest source of FDI, accounting for the vast majority of outflows in all years, but the share of developing economies has grown rapidly due to the significant increase in outflows from the NIEs (see Table 9.1). Japan and the US remain the major sources of FDI.

Foreign firms are directly involved in the host country trade to a large extent complementing the outward-looking strategies of ASEAN, particularly important in resource extraction, manufacturing and services. The manufacturing sector has been the prime mover of industrial expansion, evident in the rapid rise of MNCs in the ASEAN growth economies.

FDI flows have accounted for a significant portion of total foreign capital flows in ASEAN, but have been small as a source of ASEAN total investment, as Table 9.2 shows, with the exception of Singapore. This means that capital movements associated with FDI are generally of limited consequences for most of the ASEAN countries. A downturn in FDI flows generally has little implication for their aggregate investment flows.

Although extra-regional investments are still dominant, there is a rising share of Northeast Asian investments (that is, Japan, Hong Kong, Taiwan, South Korea and China) due to relocation of manufacturing industries and appreciation of currency. The share of NIEs' investment in ASEAN overtook that of Japan in 1990 which emphasizes the NIEs growing importance within ASEAN as a source of FDI.[1] Intra-ASEAN investment is also growing with Singapore as the leading supplier of foreign capital to the rest of the ASEAN region.[2]

It is likely that inward investment in the area of labour-intensive manufactures will fall as they are facing increasing competition from the lower wage-cost emerging economies of China and Vietnam. It is, however, uncertain whether or not the aggregate level of inward investment will fall. It largely depends on how the ASEAN countries can maintain their attractiveness to foreign investors. There are other parameters foreign investors consider important in choosing their

Table 9.1 Outward and inward FDI flows ($USmillion)

	Average (1976–80)	Average (1981–85)	1986	1987	1988	1989	1990	1976–90	1991
Outward flows									
World	42 030	44 178	92 963	138 196	170 725	212 463	230 305	1 275 693	–
DCs	41 265	43 080	91 058	135 617	164 614	202 666	221 861	1 237 541	–
Europe	19 477	25 467	50 692	73 135	100 984	119 269	136 774	705 570	–
Japan	2 255	5 094	14 480	19 520	34 210	44 130	48 024	197 108	30 726
USA	16 881	7 706	18 690	28 980	17 871	30 167	34 111	252 757	28 197
Others	2 652	4 813	7 196	13 982	11 549	9 100	2 952	82 106	–
Inward flows									
World	32 474	53 115	70 874	126 199	150 750	190 740	187 988	1 154 494	–
ASEAN	1 524	3 012	2 847	4 303	6 983	8 902	11 580	57 291	–
Indonesia	253	237	258	385	576	682	964	5 312	1 482
Malaysia	559	1 083	489	423	719	1 668	2 902	14 412	–
Philippines	69	63	127	307	936	563	530	3 120	–
Singapore	545	1 349	1 710	2 836	3 647	4 212	4 808	26 684	–
Thailand	98	280	263	352	1 105	1 777	2 376	7 763	2 015

Note: –: not available.

Source: Ramstetter (1993), Table 1.

Table 9.2 Ratios of inward flows of FDI to foreign capital flows and fixed capital formation (%)

	1976–80	1981–85	1986	1987	1988	1989	1990	1986–90	1991	1992	1993	1994
Ratios to foreign capital flows												
Indonesia	out	7.4	6.6	18.4	41.2	61.6	40.7	–	–	–	–	–
Malaysia	out	45.8	400.8	out	out	953.1	235.7	–	–	–	–	–
Philippines	5.4	3.4	out	69.1	240.0	38.7	19.7	–	–	–	–	–
Singapore	75.4	179.3	out	out	out	out	out	–	–	–	–	–
Thailand	7.1	13.9	out	21.4	71.2	73.6	57.5	–	–	–	–	–
Ratios to fixed capital formation												
Indonesia	2.4	1.2	1.3	2.0	2.6	2.6	–	2.1	3.6	3.9	3.8	3.6
Malaysia	12.3	10.9	6.7	5.8	8.6	14.9	20.7	11.7	24.0	26.0	23.7	16.1
Philippines	1.1	0.8	3.2	6.2	15.6	7.3	6.2	6.7	6.0	2.1	7.9	9.6
Singapore	17.7	17.8	26.0	39.4	42.3	39.7	36.6	35.0	32.7	13.3	24.6	23.5
Thailand	1.6	3.1	2.9	3.1	6.9	8.4	8.6	6.5	4.9	4.8	3.5	1.1

Notes:
–: not available.
out = net capital outflow; total capital inflows = the negative of the current account balance.

Sources: Ramstetter (1993), Table 3; UNCTAD, *World Investment Report* (1995), Annex Table 5; *World Investment Report* (1996), Annex Table 5.

investment locations including political stability, proximity to markets and productive resources, infrastructure and administrative efficiency.

9.2   Benefits and costs

During their initial stages of economic development the ASEAN countries, like other developing countries, were constrained by the shortage of capital. Low output, high unemployment and poverty were largely attributable to low productivity and poor productive capacity. The inflow of foreign direct investment has provided not only more employment opportunities, much required capital and technology to boost its productivity and output, but has also reinforced its export competitiveness through the outward-oriented foreign investments and the foreign firms' international networks and management knowhow.

Although the growth in employment has been slower than the growth of FDI flows, FDI has provided employment opportunities directly and indirectly resulting from the growth of local ancillary industries via the linkage effect. The direct and indirect employment effects of FDI work through the multiplier effect on income emanating from the increase in investment which raises demand and leads to the subsequent expansion of production in other industries, resulting in the expansion of local employment. The possible offsets to such positive effects include the high import intensity of foreign firms and the possible crowding out of indigenous firms due to the large market power of foreign firms. Besides, if the capital intensity of foreign firms is higher than that of local firms, there will be employment displacing effects with the inflow of FDI. For the ASEAN countries, FDI has resulted in the generation of employment opportunities due to the substantial linkage effect, less significant crowding out and direct employment effects.

The greater export-orientation of foreign firms, as evidenced by their shares in export sales as compared to domestic firms in ASEAN (see Table 9.3), appears to exert a demonstration effect for the local firms. This, coupled with the increasing competitiveness brought about by the diffusion of new technologies as well as management skills of the foreign enterprise, has served to stimulate the host country's exports. Singapore is a striking example among the ASEAN countries that has effectively used FDI to spearhead an export-led growth. The Singapore government has been instrumental in making FDI more export oriented which subsequently leads to a large FDI contribution to the export sector. In this respect, the government policy of minimal restrictive trade policy has been crucial.

But, there are also costs associated with the inflow of FDI. A signifi-

Table 9.3 Foreign firm shares of employment, total sales and exports in non-petroleum manufacturing industries

Countries	1977			1986			1989		
	Employment	Sales	Exports	Employment	Sales	Exports	Employment	Sales	Exports
Indonesia	10.6	21.0	–	8.9	17.2	–	–	16.7	–
Malaysia	33.6	43.9	–	30.3	36.7	–	36.2	40.7	–
Singapore	53.8	72.8	84.7	54.2	63.4	74.9	59.6	76.4	86.1
Thailand	7.6	9.2	11.3	5.7	6.1	15.9	–	–	27.3

Note: –: not available.

Source: Ramstetter (1993), Table 10.

149

cant inflow of capital is usually accompanied by a deterioration of the current account, as a rise in domestic demand induces an increase in imports or as the currency appreciates accompanied by a substantial repatriation of profits. It could also lead to inflationary tendencies. The type and size of macroeconomic impacts depend on the size of the foreign capital relative to the resource utilization level prior to the capital inflow and on the exchange rate regime adopted. Under a fixed exchange rate regime, the impact is via the income channel. The deterioration in the current account is due to a higher level of domestic demand and a rise in international reserves. The extent of current account deterioration depends on the import intensity of domestic demand and the resulting decline in the price of tradables relative to nontradable goods. A higher monetary growth could lead to lower interest rates or to a higher inflation. Under a flexible exchange rate regime, the deterioration in the current account is due to a currency appreciation. A currency appreciation, *ceteris paribus*, means a lowering of the price of importables and an increase in imports with detrimental effects on export competitiveness.

Having a current account deficit is not necessarily bad. It makes sense for growing economies like ASEAN to import the necessary capital to increase their productive capacities. This investment-driven deficit is sustainable. It is only when the deficit is driven by consumer spending and when the current account deficit leads to unsustainable foreign debt that a current account deficit becomes a real cause for concern. Second, it is also dangerous if it could lead to a money supply-caused asset price bubble that then bursts leaving banks with huge bad loans. Third, it is also a cause for concern if the current account deficit is a reflection of a budget deficit. Based on past experiences, the track record of the private sector in its ability to settle its debt is satisfactory partly due to the fact that the private sector is usually profit-oriented and thus will try to ensure they have made calculated risks.

Further, domestic savings might weaken. Reduction in domestic savings may occur when the availability of foreign capital can deter efforts of domestic financial institutions to mobilize domestic savings, and when it allows the government to increase its expenditure in less or unproductive areas and not to increase taxes which could lead to lower public sector savings.

There is the danger of losing some political autonomy as the economy becomes too dependent on foreign firms and foreign technology. There is also the danger of it becoming a 'dumping ground' of outdated, environmentally harmful and energy inefficient technology.

9.3 Managing foreign capital

During the 1960s the ASEAN countries, except Singapore, had looked at MNCs with distrust because of the possible adverse effects of FDI including those that were presented in the preceding section.[3] Japanese MNCs received the strongest distrust due to the rapid expansion of Japanese investment and the fear of Japanese domination in the region (Pussarangsri and Chamnivickorn, 1995). During this period they had adopted restrictive regulations in an attempt to control FDI and thus avoid its possible harmful effects.

Since the late 1970s there has been a change in attitude towards FDI for several reasons including the debt crisis and the benefits of FDI in the NIEs. Although the ASEAN debt crisis was not as severe as that in Latin American countries, it raised some concern to ASEAN policy-makers, in particular in Indonesia, Malaysia and the Philippines. FDI was accepted as a means to alleviate their debt crises.

9.3.1 Maximization of benefits of FDI

In an attempt to attract FDI into their respective economies, the ASEAN countries have some form of guarantee against nationaliz-ation.[4] They have relaxed their restrictive rules and regulations on FDI and changed their policy orientation to create an environment con-ducive for investment. The change in policy has been moderate in Thailand and Singapore, but has been drastic in Malaysia, Indonesia and the Philippines.

Singapore's attitude towards foreign investment has always been favourable. Its rules and regulations governing the operation of a foreign juristic person have always been quite lenient. Thailand's case is also unique. No significant change in its Alien Business Law has occurred since its enactment in 1957, although the interpretations of the Law are becoming more favourable with more exemptions granted to foreign investors (Pussarangsri and Chamnivickorn, 1995, p. 17). In Indonesia since its trade liberalization in 1986, restrictions and barriers applied to foreign investors have been modified or removed. In the Philippines the rules and regulations for foreign investors have been relaxed with the enactment of the Foreign Investment Act of 1991. In Malaysia many new incentives have been introduced since 1986 with a reduced role of government intervention.

The following are some of the areas where rules and regulations for foreign investment have been relaxed.

Foreign ownership of business Total foreign ownership of business is allowed in most industries. In many cases exemptions are granted to foreign investors in activities that are closed to foreign investment. In areas where national security and use of domestic natural resources are at stake joint ventures are preferred. However, there is still some variation in terms of restrictiveness within the ASEAN countries. Singapore has the most liberal policies on foreign ownership of business with no specific rules and regulations for foreign investors except in banking and brokerage. There are now no restrictions on foreign participation even in telecommunications and public utilities. Malaysia's policy on foreign ownership is also quite liberal. Practically all businesses are open to foreign investors, except in the news media industry. The proportion of foreign ownership allowed is tied to the performance of firms and not to the type of business activities. A 100 percent foreign ownership is allowed when a firm exports at least 80 percent of its production, and 51 percent foreign ownership is allowed if a firm uses high technology in production. The Philippines and Thailand have moderately liberal policies. Based on the Foreign Investment Act of 1991 the Philippines has a negative list of business activities restraining foreign investment. The business activities in the negative list are classified according to the level of restrictions applied to foreign investors. The industries in the most restrictive group are completely closed to foreign investors. The second and third most restrictive groups refer to industries where up to 25 percent and 30 percent of foreign ownership is allowed, respectively. In the least restrictive group foreign investors can own up to 40 percent of the business equity. The rules are rigid with very few exemptions. Similar to the Philippines, Thailand has classified business activities into three types according to the level of restrictions. Under the Treaty of Amity and Economic Relations between the US and Thailand, US companies are not subject to restrictions imposed by their Alien Business Law, except in some specific areas. Indonesia has the most stringent policy towards FDI. Apart from the negative list of industries where foreign investors are restricted, joint ventures are preferred with the majority of shares to be held by the Indonesian partners for at least 15 years, with a few conditions for possible exemptions.

Land ownership   Although the Philippines, Thailand and Indonesia prohibit foreign juristic persons from owning land, they allow foreign firms long-term leasing agreements. In Thailand promoted firms are, however, allowed to own land and foreign juristic persons to own land in industrial estates. Malaysia and Singapore are most liberal with no restrictions on land ownership by foreign investors. Only approval from the Foreign Investment Committee is needed in Malaysia.

Foreign exchange control   As discussed in Chapter 2, foreign exchange control in ASEAN countries is virtually minimal. International transfers are permitted with a few restrictions. For example, profit remitted out of Thailand is subject to 20 percent tax, except for those promoted firms. In the Philippines a specific amount of capital is allowed to be transferred abroad each year, and any additional amount to be transferred requires approval from the Central Bank of the Philippines.

9.3.2 Minimization of costs

Given that there are potential costs associated with FDI inflows, the ASEAN governments have adopted appropriate policies to neutralize or minimize the disadvantages of FDI. Generally, they have relied on three sets of policy measures. The first type, some of which was discussed previously, are the rules and regulations governing FDIs such as equity ownership, restricted sectors, foreign exchange control and performance requirements such as local content, export-production ratio and manpower training. The second set of policies refers to the system of promotion measures and incentives such as income tax reductions or exemptions, import duty exemptions, investment and depreciation allowances. These incentives are tied to certain criteria consistent with their development objectives. The third set refers to policies affecting intra-industrial linkages through subcontracting arrangements.

Deterioration of the current account and inflation   As can be gleaned from Table 2.6, all the ASEAN countries, except Thailand, have experienced a significant improvement in their current account balance during the 1987–96 period when there was also a massive inflow of FDI into their respective economies. Singapore, being the most FDI-dependent ASEAN country, has the most spectacular achievement in counteracting the negative consequence of FDI in terms of current account deterioration. Apart from Singapore's surplus in the services account, it has been successful in attracting export-oriented FDI with its generous scheme of fiscal incentives, superior legal and physical infrastructure, political and social stability, harmonious industrial relations and liberal trade policies.[5] The export orientation of these foreign firms has contributed greatly to the surge in exports and reinvestments by MNCs and thus more than compensated for the repatriation of profits by MNCs. The negative impact of the appreciation of the Singapore dollar has also been neutralized by the government policy of encouraging firms to produce high value-added products and improve productivity using various incentives. The government's emphasis on education and training has also facilitated the technology transfer.

The other ASEAN countries, which were traditionally less open, have reduced import leakages by imposing a local content rule in the production of exportables. The Philippines among the ASEAN countries has relied on this most heavily. Malaysia is the first ASEAN country to adopt positive measures to induce higher local content in the automobile industry. Credits in the form of points are given to producers whose production exceeds the required local content level.

With the exception of Singapore, whose tariffs are already very low, they have encouraged exports by also eliminating or reducing import tariffs on capital goods and raw materials used by export-oriented firms. Virtually all ASEAN countries, except Singapore, grant import duty exemptions to imports of raw materials and machineries used for producing goods for export based on the concept of export-processing zones.

There are other incentives such as tax holidays, investment allowances and accelerated depreciation allowances and the recent initiatives by Indonesia to allow foreign-owned firms to provide services to export-oriented firms (*The Straits Times*, 5 March 1996).[6] Previously this privilege was only given to joint-venture firms. Further, private firms are now allowed to operate bonded zones.

Prudent fiscal policy has also contributed to a healthy current account balance.[7] Under the twin deficit phenomenon there is a link between trade balance and budget balance. Most ASEAN countries have not experienced budget deficits and thus their healthy budgetary positions have contributed to their favourable trade balance positions.

Although Thailand's current deficit as a proportion of its GDP did not improve for the 1987–96 period (as Table 2.6 shows), it succeeded in arresting the upward pressure on inflation resulting from the surge of foreign capital particularly during the period 1987–92.[8] Thailand, with its fixed exchange rate regime, was able to contain the inflationary pressures by implementing effective liquidity control measures. Its monetary policy was aimed at neutralizing the monetary impact of the capital inflows while other policies were aimed at encountering the tendency for the inflows in the overall balance of payments. To reduce domestic liquidity, mopping up operations were conducted through the issuance of the Bank of Thailand's own securities while the Bank of Thailand exercised moral suasion asking commercial banks to limit their lending to speculative activities. The monetary restraint was supported by a fiscal policy that emphasized a sizeable fiscal surplus. Central government's budgetary surplus averaging about 3 percent of GDP was maintained from 1987–92. This policy stance helped boost national savings and made room for higher investment and export.

Weak domestic savings The negative impact of FDI on domestic savings has been neutralized by requiring their residents to save part of their earnings in a provident fund which has become a major source of investment funds. This is particularly true for Singapore and Malaysia through their compulsory savings schemes. In addition, low inflation and an efficient banking system achieved through the process of deregulation have contributed to more confidence in the financial system, and thus to greater savings.

Loss of political autonomy This is minimized by diversifying the source of FDI and allowing market forces to determine the final composition. In the 1960s petroleum refining, metals and food and beverages were the main sources of growth in Singapore. By the 1980s skill-intensive industries such as industrial electronics, computers, industrial machinery and high value-added petroleum products had taken over.

The local firms have also prospered despite the dominance of the foreign firms. This has been due to the assistance from the ASEAN governments and the initiative from local entrepreneurs. For instance, the ASEAN governments have tried to forge a better relationship between foreign firms and local suppliers of parts and components.

Lack of technology transfer To ensure a real transfer of technology from the foreign investors to the local firms, the ASEAN countries have adopted various measures to promote subcontracting arrangements. Malaysia has the most comprehensive scheme which includes tax incentives and specific institutional arrangements such as the umbrella strategy, vendor development scheme, local content requirement and cluster creation. Under the umbrella strategy one large enterprise, called the umbrella company, provides assistance to small local companies in production and marketing. The umbrella company gets rewards in return, say awarding of government contracts without contest bidding. Under the vendor development scheme MNCs assist local counterparts in the production of parts and components for them. INTEL and PROTON car producers are participants in this vendor development scheme. Under cluster creation small local enterprises are relocated to the same area to become a cluster of vendors of the same industries. Information about buyers (large enterprises) and sellers (small local subcontractors) is conducted by the Subcontract Exchange scheme.

Singapore has introduced a subcontracting scheme similar to Malaysia. However, unlike Malaysia Singapore does not have a local content requirement. The specific institutional arrangement consists of the Local Industry Upgrading programme managed by MNC engineers on a rotational basis in which MNCs are encouraged to provide technical and other types of assistance to small local enterprises. In return the MNC engineers receive compensation from Singapore's Economic Development Board (EDB). Indonesia's subcontract arrangement is called the Foster Father Plan where large enterprises provide financial assistance to and market the products of small enterprises.

The Philippines and Thailand have not promoted interfirm technology transfer as vigorously as Malaysia, Singapore and Indonesia. The Philippines has simply relied on the local content requirement. In addition, Thailand has an information provision and exchange programme operated by Thailand's Board of Investment Unit for Industrial Linkages.

9.4 Conclusion

In conclusion, the impact of FDI on the ASEAN has been more positive than negative. Effective implementation of appropriate policies played an essential role in ensuring that the FDI flow complemented their national development strategy (such as encouraging the export orientation of FDI which is in line with the export-led growth strategy), assimilating the appropriate technology to local economy and minimizing the negative impacts of FDI. Singapore is a good example illustrating the appropriate use of government policies to ensure the effective use of FDI, which resulted in the overall positive impact of FDI on Singapore.

Greater cooperation in the area of investment will go a long way in increasing the bargaining power of the ASEAN countries and their attractiveness as an investment location in the context of a tighter global capital market. It is heartening to note that the ASEAN countries at their 28th ASEAN Economic Ministers (AEM) Meeting in Jakarta in September 1996 agreed to establish an ASEAN Investment Area (AIA) with the objective to increase substantially the flow of investment into ASEAN from member and non-member sources. They suggested such measures as allowing ASEAN companies to be listed on other ASEAN stock exchanges, establishing an enhanced ASEAN agreement on investment promotion and protection and joint promotion of ASEAN as an investment location. Apart from this, they have also agreed to set in motion another investment liberalization scheme – the ASEAN Industrial Cooperation Scheme – by November 1 1996, as mentioned previously.

Suggestions for further reading

For a general review of the literature on FDI, see Hill (1990) and Pussarangsri and Chamnivickorn (1995). Studies published over the last few years on ASEAN include Ramstetter (1993) and Chia Siow Yue (1993). In addition, there are country studies: on Singapore, see Lim and Associates (1988), Chapter 9; on Indonesia, see Hill (1988) and Thee (1991); on Thailand, see Tambunlertchai (1993).

Notes

1. Taken from APEC Report: Vision for the Economies of the Asia Pacific Region in the Year 2000 and Tasks Ahead, Report to the Ad Hoc Group of Economic Trends and Issues, APEC, September 1993.

2. Singapore emerged as Malaysia's top foreign investor for the first time in 1996, with total approved investments in the manufacturing sector rising sharply to M$4.8 billion (S$2.7 billion) from a mere M$1 billion in 1995 (*The Straits Times*, 24 January 1997, p. 80).

3. Other possible negative consequences of great concern to ASEAN are excessive repatriation of profits, increase in market concentration and worsening income inequality (Naya and Imada, 1990).

4. Malaysia has the strongest guarantee by constitution. Indonesia and the Philippines are less liberal but also have a guarantee by law. Nationalization is flexible in these countries, but there is a provision of compensation. Thailand and Singapore do not have a guarantee by law but have signed bilateral treaties with their major foreign investors for protection. FDI in ASEAN countries is also under the protection of the Multilateral Investment Guarantee Agency which assures against non-commercial risks (Pussarangsri and Chamnivickorn, 1995, pp. 20–21).

5. Singapore has provided a relatively more elaborate incentive scheme such as tax holidays, investment allowances, accelerated depreciation allowances and reinvestment incentives.

6. Indonesia is the only ASEAN country that has not offered income tax privileges for foreign investors. However, Indonesia is reportedly considering offering tax holidays to selected companies in strategic industries to lure them away from competing countries (*The Straits Times*, 7 January 1997, p. 38).

7. This point is supported by the twin deficit argument which establishes the link between budget deficit and trade deficit. For more detailed arguments, see Feldstein (1986), Hooper and Mann (1989).

8. The rate of inflation decelerated from 6 percent in 1990 to 5.7 percent in 1991. For a detailed explanation, see Nijathaworn (1993), pp. 18–19.

PART THREE

FUTURE ASEAN ECONOMIC COOPERATION AND CHALLENGES

10 ASEAN economic cooperation under AFTA

If one has to assess the performance of ASEAN as a political and economic grouping since its formation in 1967, two remarkable political achievements can be noted: first, ASEAN has promoted peace and stability in the region; second, it has strengthened ASEAN's bargaining position and influence in international negotiations. But ASEAN's efforts at trade liberalization, as indicated by the level of intra-ASEAN trade and industrial cooperation, have met only with limited success due to a number of factors, as explained in previous chapters. The 1992 agreement at the Fourth ASEAN Summit in Singapore to form a free trade area among the ASEAN countries by the year 2008 (the target date was later moved forward to the year 2003) represents a milestone as well as the greatest challenge in the entire history of ASEAN economic cooperation.

This chapter discusses the prospect for greater ASEAN economic cooperation and the challenges facing the ASEAN countries in the process of achieving this vision. Specifically, it tries to examine the economic benefits and challenges the AFTA agreement presents for these economies.

10.1 Rationale of AFTA

The 1992 ASEAN Free Trade Agreement (AFTA) is a watershed, as it represents a significant change in the economic policy orientation of the ASEAN countries, with the exception of Singapore who had long cherished the idea of regional free trade. A number of internal and external developments have made free trade politically acceptable. First, the ASEAN economies have become more diversified in production structure and more complementary to each other, raising potential for greater regional trade. Growing intra-industry trade resulting from the activities of MNCs and increasing levels of industrialization achieved by most ASEAN members have strengthened this complementarity. Second, since the 1980s ASEAN economies have been undertaking unilateral policy reforms to liberalize trade and deregulate foreign investments, resulting in a more outward-oriented industrial sector. Third, perceived protectionism in their major Western trading partners in the form of emerging regional arrangements (such as NAFTA, the

EU) and emergence of non-tariff barriers (such as VERs and anti-dumping duties) pointed to the need to reinforce intra-ASEAN cooperation as a safety net and as a counterstrategy to maintain their bargaining position *vis-à-vis* these emerging trading blocs in market share and in attracting investments. Fourth, the newly emerging market economies of China, Indo-China and Eastern Europe have posed a new threat and challenge for investment attraction as these countries have huge domestic markets and/or highly competitive cost structures. Last, but not least, the private sector, realizing the potential benefits of greater regional integration and frustrated with the slow progress in trade liberalization, have intensified their pressure on their respective governments to achieve greater ASEAN integration.

10.2   Objectives of AFTA

The main objective of AFTA is to increase the international competitiveness of ASEAN industries and the ASEAN region as an investment location. Specifically, the objectives are to increase intra-ASEAN trade by abolishing intra-regional trade barriers while allowing member countries to keep their respective trade policies towards the rest of the world, to attract local and foreign investors to invest in the region and to make their manufacturing sector more efficient and internationally competitive within a liberalizing global market. An integrated regional market is expected to produce economic benefits from greater consumer surplus, exploitation of economies of scale, competition-induced efficiency, industrial rationalization, inter-industry linkages and intra-industry trade.

To realize these benefits, the ASEAN Free Trade Agreement (AFTA) seeks to reduce tariffs on all commodities traded within the member countries to between 0 and 5 percent *ad valorem* and remove all other trade restrictions by the year 2003 under the Common Effective Preferential Tariff (CEPT) – the main instrument of AFTA. The agreement also lays down the rules for fair competition and identified a number of measures to enhance economic cooperation such as harmonization of standards, macroeconomic consultations and improved reciprocal recognition of product testing and certification, coordination of foreign investment policies, joint investment promotion strategies and cooperation in transport systems. Further, it contains measures of contingent protection and allows the reintroduction of trade barriers in case of balance of payments difficulties.

10.3   Elements of the CEPT scheme

Under the CEPT scheme the ASEAN countries have agreed to include unprocessed agricultural products. And to ensure that the benefits of the scheme are restricted within the member countries a minimum of 40 percent of the value must originate within AFTA, if the products are not wholly produced within AFTA countries.

The tariff reduction schedules are classified into two tracks. The list of products subjected to accelerated tariff reductions are in the fast track. Those products in the fast track with tariffs at 20 percent or less will have their tariffs reduced to 0–5 percent by 1998, and those whose tariffs are above 20 percent will have their tariffs reduced to 0–5 percent by the year 2000.[1] Other products are in the normal track. Under the normal track tariffs at 20 percent or below will be reduced to 0–5 percent by the year 2000, and tariffs above 20 percent by the year 2003.

There are also exclusions (products that will not be given preferential tariffs, if exported). The first type of exclusions refer to those products in the Temporary Exclusion List (TEL). These products will be gradually transferred, on equal instalments, to the Inclusion List starting in 1996 and finishing in 2000. Motor vehicles and mineral fuels are examples. The second type refers to the goods excluded for national security reasons, protection of public morals, human, animal and plant life and health, and the protection of articles of artistic, historic or archaeological value. Examples of items in this list are armaments, live plants and animals, and alcoholic beverages. The third type refers to those products in the Sensitive List. These products due to their special nature and political importance are accorded special treatment compared with the products in the Inclusion and Temporary Exclusion Lists. This means that the time frame may be longer than 2003 and tariff rates are not required to be reduced to the 0–5 percent range as in the CEPT. A working group under the purview of both the Senior Economic Officials Meeting (SEOM) and the Senior Officials of the ASEAN Ministers on Agriculture and Forestry (SOM AMAF) has been created to work out the features of the special arrangement. This working group has met twice already, once in Jakarta in December 1994 and again in April 1995 in Kuala Lumpur. The outcome of these meetings has been the submission of the three lists from each country as well as initial discussions on the features of the special arrangement.

Most products are covered by the CEPT. As of 1994, 87 percent of all tariff lines were covered by the CEPT and in 2003, it is expected that 99 percent of products will be brought under the CEPT.

10.4   Free trade and opportunities

Existing theories of regional integration which provide a general framework for what economic results to expect from joining a free trade area have already been discussed in Chapter 3. A recent study by Imada, Montes and Naya (1991), using a partial equilibrium framework, shows that AFTA would result in a net welfare gain for the ASEAN members. With free trade the growth of intra-ASEAN imports would increase between 40 percent (for Malaysia) and 70 percent (for Thailand). The only exception is Singapore whose imports will only increase slightly. This increase is partly due to the diversion of imports from non-partner countries, but the trade diverting effects are lower than the trade creating effects.

Total exports of ASEAN would increase between 1.5 percent (for Singapore) and 5 percent (for Thailand). The increase in exports would not be at the expense of exports to the rest of the world. It also shows that there would be shifts in the distribution of industrial activities, but that no country will dominate the region.

Apart from the static gains, there would also be dynamic gains associated with the growth of internal markets, greater intra-ASEAN trade and investment and others which are not captured by the partial equilibrium framework. These dynamic effects have already been discussed in Chapter 3.

10.5   Costs and challenges under AFTA

The foregoing discussion has emphasized the potential economic benefits from the establishment of AFTA based on existing theories of regional integration. However, what is not clearly spelled out are the possible social costs and adjustment problems associated with trade liberalization.

First, the perfect competition assumption of the above model of integration may be violated in the real world (for example, the energy, chemicals and other heavy industry markets are dominated by a few large multinational companies (MNCs)). Thus, the enlargement of markets caused by economic integration is likely to lead to market consolidation by the big MNCs through mergers and acquisitions which already have significant market power based on their capital, technology, marketing and management advantages to keep away potential competitors. Under these market conditions oligopoly or monopoly might be a more appropriate model to use in analysing the effects of economic integration under AFTA.

The loss of national control and regulation over certain industries, resulting from economic integration, may lead to the entrenchment of

MNCs' market power to the possible detriment of consumers and workers' welfare. This happens when their oligopolistic or monopolistic power is being exploited to increase or consolidate their control over resources and profits.[2]

Further, greater competition fostered by the enlargement of markets will further reinforce the trend in MNCs towards restructuring and rationalization to concentrate on their core activities. These industrial changes have already caused a significant decline in employment security and job losses. In particular, these have resulted in the replacement of permanent workers by externally-hired contractors. Consequently, there has been a growing army of casual or part-time workers without enjoying the benefits of job security. Due to the multinationalization of production, occupational and health hazards have increased for workers everywhere. Attempts to impose high health and safety standards in the workplace have been constrained by the use of outside contractors to maintain and run the plant and machinery, and by the desperate need for foreign direct investment in some developing countries (ICEF–MIF Merger Congress, *World Industry Trends*, 1995).

Second, the establishment of an ASEAN FTA will produce equilibrium adjustments involving other variables, apart from the abolition of trade impediments such as tariffs and non-tariff barriers, affecting the entire member country economies. There will be adjustments in production, employment, price, wage structures and exchange rate alignments, as the cost structure and resource allocation in the region changes.

Shifts in production, employment and wage structures will occur based on the principle of comparative advantage. The ASEAN region is heterogeneous in terms of resources, and thus based on the principle of comparative advantage, industries that use relatively large amounts of labour and natural resources are likely to shift their labour-intensive and natural resource-intensive operations to relatively labour and natural resource-rich countries such as the Philippines, Thailand, Indonesia and Vietnam. In fact, this shift is already occurring in the region and the abolition of trade and investment barriers under AFTA will reinforce this trend.[3]

We will, therefore, expect with high probability employment levels and wages for certain industries in some countries in AFTA to decline. But wages in other lower-cost countries in AFTA, where the relocation of production takes place, may not increase (although employment levels are expected to rise in the short run) in the short and longer terms as long as there is an infinite supply of unskilled labour available to take on the labour-intensive operations of the MNCs. This type of wage adjustment will be reflected in greater profits for the MNCs, and may not be reflected in lower consumer prices. Under this scenario there will be repercussions on the price structure of the AFTA area and on real exchange rates of member countries.

Third, there will be obvious fiscal implications. The role of international trade taxes as a major source of government revenue will lose its significance and this will create financial problems for the ruling government. Governments that are unable to restructure their source of fiscal revenue will have to resort to social expenditure-cutting measures to the detriment of the needy and the disadvantaged. The underprovision of public goods will have significant ramifications for the rest of the economy.

Fourth, as trade liberalization proceeds, the growing interdependence among member economies will reduce a member nation's degree of national autonomy in terms of effective policy making. As economies become more interdependent, the need for coordination of policies becomes essential. Economic interdependence in Asia is already occurring due to greater intra-regional trade and investment.

Intra-regional trade is likely to gain further momentum in the coming years due to the following factors: the rapid growth and expanding markets of the region's developing economies, increasing outward orientation in trade policies, increasing intra-regional investment and relocation of production facilities from Japan and the NIEs to other countries in the Asian region.

The last factor is particularly important in the context of the recent decision to eliminate the performance requirements and trade-related investment measures (TRIMs) by the members of the World Trade Organization (WTO). Intra-regional investment within ASEAN and recent booming investment from ASEAN to Vietnam, Laos and Myanmar indicate that ASEAN has begun to build up its own outward investment momentum and may emerge as an important regional capital supplier in the future.

As investment deregulation brought about by trade liberalization under AFTA will further reinforce this growing regional interdependence, the need for policy coordination implies giving up one's national autonomy and independence in policy making. It means an equalization and/or enforcement of a regulatory framework, not only in relation to customs procedures and other non-tariff barriers, but also in relation to labour and environmental standards. Labour standards are particularly important and vary within the ASEAN member countries. In the process of policy coordination national governments may lose control over the activities of the MNCs especially in relation to individual governments' policies on wages and enforcement of national environmental standards. Due to ASEAN's different levels of economic development and differences in priorities, the ASEAN countries tend to adopt different policies with respect to these areas.

Finally, there is the issue of division of costs and gains. An increase in output could occur at the cost of greater inequality across countries as well as within countries. The relocation of resources from high-cost to low-cost countries will not only result in lower wages but will also cause inequality in wages. Competition for foreign investment and for exports to other countries outside AFTA could lead to greater problems associated with the distribution of gains. Unlike the European Union where intra-trade accounts for a substantial portion of each member's total trade, intra-ASEAN trade accounts for only about 20 percent of their total trade. The bulk of their trade is external. Consequently, an ASEAN AFTA is likely to result in substantial trade diversion.

Since there are benefits and costs associated with AFTA, it is uncertain whether the creation of AFTA will be beneficial overall.[4] This brings us to the next point: is economic growth necessarily incompatible with the attainment of social objectives of poverty alleviation and reduced income inequality?

As discussed in Chapter 2, the experiences of most ASEAN countries have shown that the economic objectives of growth and efficiency can be achieved under a liberal regime without necessarily sacrificing the social dimensions of development. This was made possible by their effective implementation of appropriate policies that minimize or neutralize the social costs of trade liberalization. This remarkable economic achievement has been fuelled, among other things, by the massive inflow of foreign direct investments fostered by their liberal policies.

10.6 Factors affecting the implementation of AFTA

Will the ASEAN countries be able to implement their commitments to trade liberalization and thus promote economic growth by increasing intra-ASEAN trade and investment? A successful implementation of AFTA depends very much on how they can resolve the following:

(a) low economic complementarity and trade diversion effects;
(b) macroeconomic imbalances;
(c) high and variable inflation in some member countries;
(d) losses of fiscal revenue;
(e) uncoordinated policies;
(f) divergent views on the degree of market decentralization and government intervention;

(g)   an unbalanced distribution of costs and benefits and acceptance of the overall social benefits; and

(h)   absence of adequate institutions.

10.6.1   Low economic complementarity and trade diversion effects

According to Meade (1955), the trade diversion effects will be smaller if countries are initially competitive but potentially complementary or dissimilar. This means that due to protection, similar goods are produced before the integration. After the integration, the differences in unit costs in the previously protected industries will be large, providing greater opportunity for more efficient producers to expand trade in an enlarged market.

Although most ASEAN economies have achieved a high degree of industrialization with a dramatic increase in the share of manufactured goods in their overall exports and a large increase in intra-industry trade in manufactured goods, the degree of complementarity, particularly in the primary and low value-added sectors, is still generally low due to the similarity of factor endowments. Similarity of factor endowments (as indicated by the fact that ASEAN's extra-regional trade still accounts for the bulk of ASEAN's total trade) will produce significant trade diversions,[5] thereby increasing the need for macroeconomic adjustments. Price and wage flexibility and factor mobility will be necessary. These are attributes that most ASEAN countries do not possess.

10.6.2   Macroeconomic imbalances

The experiences of the Central American Common Market (CACM) and the Latin American Integration Association (LAIA, formerly LAFTA) have shown that macroeconomic imbalances such as external and fiscal disequilibria will not only cause real exchange rate overvaluation but also large real exchange rate variability. In 80 percent of trade liberalization reversals in Latin America, persistent external and fiscal deficits were the cause.

As pointed out in Chapter 9, current account deficits are not necessarily bad. However, at some level a deficit becomes unsustainable. Indonesia, Malaysia, the Philippines and Thailand already have larger foreign debts as a share of GDP than did Mexico in 1994. Thailand and Malaysia are forecast to run external deficits at 8 to 10 percent of GDP if the trend continues.

Indonesia and Vietnam are still running huge fiscal deficits, although there has been an improvement in their budget deficits. All these will make trade liberalization for these ASEAN countries more difficult.

10.6.3 High and variable inflation

High and variable inflation in some member countries reduces the static and dynamic gains of market integration by increasing real exchange rate variability, by hindering the development of capital markets and by increasing the risk of longer-term projects (related to horizontal and vertical integration). In the period 1968–85 ASEAN countries that had relatively high inflation also had more exchange rate variability (Nadal De Simone, 1995).

10.6.4 Losses of fiscal revenue

As pointed out earlier, in the process of trade liberalization, there will be a substantial loss of fiscal revenue for countries who are relying on international trade levies. With the exception of Singapore, whose reliance on these sources is very little, all other ASEAN member governments, especially Indonesia, the Philippines, Thailand and Vietnam, will be losing a significant source of fiscal revenue.[6] Thus, the formation of an AFTA will require a restrictive policy stance in most ASEAN countries, or structural fiscal reforms and the establishment of efficient transfer mechanisms. The required structural reforms may meet with political opposition and thus this may impede the process of fiscal reforms.[7]

10.6.5 Uncoordinated policies

As market integration proceeds resulting in growing economic interdependence within ASEAN, brought about by increased intra-ASEAN trade and investments, uncoordinated policies will increase the variability of real exchange rates and the international spillover effects of domestic policies, and thus reduces the gains from integration. Moreover, the lack of coordinated policies with respect to foreign investment reduces the attractiveness for and the ability of ASEAN to maximize the benefits from foreign investment. However, AFTA does not include measures for effective policy coordination.

10.6.6 Divergent views on the degree of market decentralization and government intervention

If there are large gaps in national lobby groups' preferences and the level of government intervention, constraining national sovereignty in a free trade agreement may become too costly for a government as it will bear the full cost of a failure to satisfy politically important groups. The inclusion of untraded and irrelevant items within the ASEAN PTA and the existence of products in the Sensitive and General Exclusion lists are the manifestations of strong import-competing groups that led governments to refrain from fully liberalizing trade.

10.6.7   Unbalanced distribution of costs and benefits

Unbalanced distribution of costs among the ASEAN countries due to significant disparities in per capita income, investment rates and in unemployment rates will render AFTA unstable. The solution is usually to provide training programmes and safety nets. Fiscal expenditures will rise. It is therefore necessary for the richer member countries to compensate poorer members to settle disputes over an unbalanced distribution of the costs and benefits of AFTA. But AFTA does not have this provision and thus this reduces AFTA's chance of success.

10.6.8   Absence of adequate institutions

Institutions and rules introduce stability and continuity in the process of integration by increasing the probability that future policymakers will consider the effects of their policies on the current decisions of economic agents. The EU provides an example where institutions have played an important role in its evolution from a free trade area to a common market and now on its way towards complete economic integration. The ASEAN countries are now in the process of harmonizing standards, tariff classification, customs valuation and procedures. But in ASEAN there is still a need to establish a mechanism to enforce AFTA decisions and rules, and a clear procedure for monitoring and settling disputes.

10.7   Conclusion

The emergence of new domestic and external developments have made the formation of AFTA politically acceptable. The recent decision to speed up the process by advancing the target date to the year 2003 from 2008 is a clear manifestation of a high level of political commitment and confidence in greater regional integration, despite its accompanying short-term costs and sacrifices.

But whether or not AFTA can in fact increase intra-ASEAN trade and promote regional growth depends on their success or failure in resolving the implementation problems discussed. The ASEAN governments have only seven years to resolve these problems. It is argued that apart from policy coordination, macroeconomic policy discipline is required to reap the benefits of integration. The ASEAN countries have to resolve the following problems: low production and trade complementarity; macroeconomic imbalances; high inflation; the need to reduce reliance on international trade taxes; unbalanced distribution of costs and benefits; and the absence of institutions to enforce decisions and to ensure coordination in policy making.

AFTA is only at an early stage of its development. Many technical issues, therefore, have to be resolved. Given the strong political will to surge forward, these obstacles are not insurmountable. Already a significant unilateral liberalization process in ASEAN has begun, particularly in the previously high tariff economies of Indonesia, the Philippines and Thailand. This has resulted in the harmonization of tariff structures to a considerable degree. Deregulation and privatization have also complemented this trend. On the assumption that these trends continue, it is highly likely that AFTA will achieve its objectives.

Suggestions for further reading
AFTA Reader provides regularly an update of decisions, developments and statistical data on AFTA and progress made in the implementation of AFTA commitments by individual ASEAN countries. For a discussion of the prospects and problems of AFTA, see Naya and Barretto (1994) and Nadal De Simone (1995).

Notes
1. The products in the fast track list are: electronics, copper cathodes, ceramics/glass, leather, gems/jewellery, fertilizers, pharmaceuticals, wooden/rattan furniture, chemicals, cement, pulp/paper, rubber, vegetable oil, plastics and textiles.
2. The 1994 European Energy Charter signed by countries including Japan, Australia and other non-European countries, which seeks to establish a level playing field for multinational companies in the signatory states, does not contain a social dimension protecting workers within the industries affected.
3. This is demonstrated worldwide particularly in the chemicals industry. A number of chemicals companies based in Europe have already shifted their production operations to some low-cost economies of Asia such as India, Vietnam, China and Indonesia. The rise in investments in Asia contrasts with the decline in Europe where capital investment by the chemicals industry declines (ESCAP, 1994, p. 51).
4. It is impossible to quantify the gains and costs of trade liberalization unless we can disentangle the equilibrium adjustment process.
5. The competitive nature of their agricultural sector is demonstrated by Thailand's initial reluctance to include palm oil in the CEPT, fearing that it will face competition from more productive Indonesian and Malaysian palm oil producers, once the market is liberalized.
6. Vietnam and the Philippines are considerably dependent on tariffs as a source of fiscal revenue, accounting for about 23 to 28 percent of their budget (Le, 1995, p. 11).
7. The recent experience of the Philippines, when the introduction of the value-added tax (VAT) was delayed due to the strong opposition from political and civil groups, is one example.

11 ASEAN free trade area and the newly emerging Southeast Asian economies

The most recent admission of Laos and Myanmar to ASEAN has almost fulfilled the ASEAN founding fathers' dream to establish an ASEAN10, a grouping covering all countries in Southeast Asia. It is now just a matter of time before this vision can be realised.

Vietnam became officially the seventh member of the Association of Southeast Asian Nations (ASEAN) on the 28 July 1995. It has also officially declared in principle its intention to join the ASEAN Free Trade Area (AFTA).[1] At about the same time Myanmar, emerging from its self-imposed isolation, ceded to the ASEAN Treaty of Amity and Cooperation and is opening up to join the rest of Southeast Asia in terms of economic orientation and objectives. In 1992 Laos was granted an observer status in ASEAN. At the 30th Annual Ministerial Meeting in Kuala Lumpur in July 1997, Laos together with Myanmar was admitted as a full member of ASEAN. Membership of ASEAN brings with it membership of AFTA. Myanmar and Laos are expected to fully implement their AFTA commitments by the year 2008, two years after Vietnam's target year. Cambodia's admission has been deferred until its current domestic political crisis is resolved.

As ASEAN members, these newly emerging Southeast Asian economies will have to deal with the important question of how they can maximize the benefits of trade liberalization as proposed under AFTA. In the light of this, the objective of this chapter is to consider and to assess to what extent they meet the requirements to enjoy the benefits of AFTA. More specifically, it deals with the following policy questions: What are the potential benefits associated with their becoming AFTA members? Which areas require further economic reforms in order to make these countries ready to become active and benefiting members of AFTA? Due to insufficient data on Cambodia and Laos, this chapter will only deal with the case of Vietnam and Myanmar. The subsequent analysis, however, can also be applied to Cambodia and Laos due to their similar economic structures and characteristics.

The balance of this chapter is organized as follows: Section 1 deals with the potential benefits from the membership of Vietnam and Myanmar, and Section 2 examines how Vietnam and Myanmar have measured up to the preconditions required to benefit from regional integration, followed by recommendations on what should be done to make them ready to reap the economic benefits of economic integration.

11.1 Potential benefits from Vietnam and Myanmar's membership

11.1.1 From the ASEAN6 perspectives

The membership of Vietnam and Myanmar in AFTA can bring additional benefits to other ASEAN countries. In economic terms, Vietnam and Myanmar offer a substantial market and are a good source of cheap labour and natural resources. Thus, with their abundant human and natural resources they can complement the capital-rich and tech-nology-rich members of AFTA (especially Singapore and Malaysia), which are facing severe labour and natural resource constraints. The 'flying geese' model of development will take place under a liberal regional trading environment. In a political sense, the engagement and integration of Vietnam and Myanmar into the region reinforces the foundation for political peace and stability in the region. It must be remembered that Vietnam was once considered a source of threat to the democratic and capitalistic systems of ASEAN, but its recent policy of economic renovation (*doi moi*) under a market-oriented philosophy and its adoption of an export-oriented strategy augur well for the region's future. Any potential conflicts can be resolved diplomatically and peacefully using the instutional machinery of ASEAN, and thus reduces the possibility of a violent confrontation.

The current political instability in Myanmar, caused by the military's alleged refusal to hand over the political leadership to the winning National League for Democracy Party in the 1990 national election, can also be better settled through an open and constructive dialogue with the military junta in Myanmar than through confrontation.

11.1.2 From Vietnam and Myanmar's perspectives

The potential benefits they can derive from joining ASEAN and AFTA are enormous both in political and economic terms. In political terms, Vietnam shares the same security and political interests with the other ASEAN countries. Vietnam considers joining ASEAN as an oppor-tunity to make friends with other countries in the region and thus contribute to the creation of a more friendly and conducive environment for economic development. Vietnam also needs ASEAN to have a more significant and influential voice in the international arena. In addition, its membership is necessary in order to maintain the balance of power in the region. The emergence of China with its potential to become a super military power must be balanced in order to avoid any dominance by one country in the region. The superpower vacuum that has been created in the region with the end of the Cold War must not be filled in. Vietnam's entry into ASEAN is necessary as an important step in its policy of transition from a centrally-planned to a market economy and thus of integration into the world community.

Myanmar's successful entry into ASEAN and AFTA is important to the present military junta in the light of persistent calls for an imposition of economic and political sanctions on Myanmar due to the former's alleged violation of democratic principles and human rights. While the ASEAN countries have repeatedly declared their policy of constructive engagement for Myanmar, its membership can be perceived as a victory for the current leadership and thus, as an indication of a lack of political support for the opposition party.

The potential economic benefits are more contentious and more difficult to identify. As discussed in the previous chapter, there are economic benefits and costs from trade liberalization. The theory of economic integration has also predicted two opposite outcomes, and posited that in the short run trade creation must outweigh trade diversion in order to have a beneficial trade liberalization. The main factors largely influencing this outcome are the degree of complementarity among the member countries, the ability of the member countries to respond to the opportunities offered in a larger and liberal market, and the degree of their trade links with the non-member countries.

On the first two factors, it is fair to say that relative to their other ASEAN neighbours Vietnam and Myanmar enjoy a comparative advantage in the production of mineral products such as oil and gas, primary commodities such as rice, marine products and soybean, and low skill-intensive and labour-intensive manufacturing. These products are facing increasing demand in the fast-growing resource-poor economies in the Asian region.

AFTA will also reinforce further investment flows into these economies from firms seeking a cheaper source of raw materials and labour in areas of economic complementarity such as tourism, infrastructural projects, trade, and banking. Manufacturing opportunities can take the form of agricultural and marine processing, textile production and assembly of electrical and labour-intensive electronic components.

Le (1995) has shown that since Vietnam embarked on economic liberalization, its total volume of exports has grown rapidly, averaging 20 percent annually for the period 1990–95. Trade deficits have also gone down during the same period, from US$1.5 billion in 1987 to US$600 million in 1989. Vietnam then achieved a surplus in 1992.

Although Vietnam's trade balance went to a deficit again in 1993, there is a decreasing pattern.

On the third factor, Vietnam trade links with its old allies has been in decline, but its trade with its ASEAN neighbours has grown in recent years by leaps and bounds, for example from US$163.2 million in 1989 (when the economic transformation started) to US$1,643.8 million in 1992. Singapore is Vietnam's main ASEAN export market and Vietnam's export to Singapore has increased about tenfold for the period 1985–93.

Myanmar, on the other hand, since it ended its self-imposed isolation in 1988, has increased its trade and investment links with its ASEAN neighbours, especially Singapore and Thailand.

There are, however, specific-country costs that deserve some discussion. In addition to the costs associated with AFTA as mentioned in the previous chapter, there are potential short-term adjustment costs specific to Vietnam and Myanmar. Unemployment has already emerged as a serious problem in the process of their transition. In addition to the impact of the recent repatriation of Vietnamese refugees and the restructuring of their state-owned enterprises, there will be those that will be laid off as weaker industries close down in the face of greater competition. It is expected that producers in Vietnam and Myanmar will face strong competition in skill-intensive and capital-intensive industries such as vehicles, electronics, petroleum products, chemicals, machinery and consumer items.

Another potential problem is the increasing pressure that will be exerted on their existing institutions as they have more contact with the relatively liberal regimes of their ASEAN neighbours. The existing institutions and political machinery are currently geared for a centrally-planned economy, although there have been concerted efforts since the 1980s to restructure their institutions in line with their policy of economic transformation (*doi moi*). The liberal concept of private ownership and free market enterprise will put increasing pressures on the present system of ownership and the dominant role of the government in the economy.

11.2 Priority areas requiring further reforms
There are some areas requiring further reforms in Vietnam and Myanmar to make them ready to benefit from a greater regional market and cope with the costs of adjustment. This section will focus on the priority areas requiring further reforms.

Table 11.1   Vietnam's gross output of industry by ownership types (%)

Year	1990	1991	1992	1993	1994	1995
Industry total	100.0	100.0	100.0	100.0	100.0	100.0
State	67.6	68.5	70.5	71.3	72.4	72.4
Non-state of which:	32.4	31.5	29.5	28.7	27.6	27.6
cooperative	9.1	4.8	2.8	2.1	1.1	–
private	1.0	1.5	2.9	4.5	5.1	–
household	22.3	25.2	23.8	22.1	21.4	–

Note: –: not available.

Source: Vietnam's General Statistical Office, *Statistical Yearbook 1993, 1995*.

11.2.1   Development of an internationally competitive private sector

The economic benefits of free trade can only be reaped by the most competitive economy or industry. Under a more competitive environment a country must continually improve its international competitiveness. Further, to have a strong private sector is an important requirement given that the performance of their state sector has so far been poor based on economic criteria. Since private capitalism is new to these economies, the promotion of an environment conducive to the development of the private sector should be given top priority in order to be best prepared for the AFTA challenge and opportunities.

As public enterprises face the problem of restructuring due to inefficiency and lack of financial resources accompanied by cuts to employment, the private sector can also be the answer to the output and unemployment problems.[2] Table 11.1 shows the distribution of industrial output by various ownership types (in percentages) in Vietnam for selected years.

The state sector, consisting of state-owned enterprises (SOEs) and large and medium joint state–private enterprises (JSPEs), accounted for about 70 percent of the gross industry output, whereas the non-state contribution largely attributed to the private household sector accounted for less. However, the percentage change in gross output for the private sector had generally increased while that of the cooperative had declined, which meant that the rate of expansion of the private sector had generally been above that of other sectors, signifying its growth potential.[3] In terms of employment, the private sector accounted for a larger portion of national employment and a dominant portion of the total private employment has been in the agricultural, forestry and construction sectors. Agriculture has accounted for the largest share of total employment in Vietnam. The capital/labour ratio of the private sector is less than that of the state sector, which means that the same amount of capital in the private sector can provide more employment opportunities than the state sector (Ronnas, 1992). This indicates a great capacity for employment generation in the private sector for labour-abundant Vietnam. While the promotion of an internationally competitive private sector should be given priority, the important role of SOEs in Vietnam's economic development, however, should not be ignored. The reformation of SOEs should continue to make them more efficient.

Vietnam has rightly embarked on privatization. Vietnam has prepared some SOEs for privatization with the help of foreign financial institutions. It indicates the present government's intention to stop the draining of public funds, promote competition, increase state revenues and move towards the reintroduction of private ownership. However, the authorities have been slow and cautious. There is a growing concern that it could lead to more job cuts and the worry that the government may lose control of the economy. In this case the government should be selective and adopt an effective regulatory scheme. It should be pointed out that the mere transfer of assets and service functions to the private sector is not a sufficient condition for the establisment of an internationally competitive private sector. It must result in greater competition for privatization to become effective.

Myanmar's private sector is still weak compared to other ASEAN countries. The government must create an environment conducive for the development of an internationally competitive private sector. There is a strong tendency for the government in Myanmar to revert to its old policy of isolationism and protectionism. But the experiences of most successful economies of ASEAN have shown that protectionism is not the answer. To develop an internationally competitive private sector, an introduction of market-oriented policies and incentives, where success is based on merits and hard work is appropriately rewarded, is essential. Further, the development of private entrepreneurship can only occur in a liberal environment and in an atmosphere of open competition.

However, a strong and internationally competitive private sector, although necessary, is not a sufficient condition for realizing the benefits of AFTA. There are other policy-related domestic prerequisites that these countries must meet to derive the potential benefits from a free trade area.

11.2.2 External stability

Sound economic management, as reflected in manageable current account and fiscal deficits, will not only lead to a greater level of investors' confidence, but will also result in economic stability and strong currency. In contrast, huge and persistent external imbalances will result in real exchange rate overvaluation and instability, thereby making trade liberalization more difficult and less sustainable. Countries with severe current account deficits usually have a high real exchange rate variability and overvalued currency, which in turn produces balance of payments crises. Exchange rate misalignments may hamper integration by distorting the functioning of clearing and payments systems.

Although Vietnam has reduced significantly its current account deficit from 17 percent of its GDP over the 1980–86 period to 7.9 percent of its GDP over the 1987–96 period (see Table 2.6), it is still high relative to its ASEAN neighbours. The rapid growth of imports, fuelled by the easy credit policies of the State Bank and by the increase in government expenditure, is the main factor behind this large current account deficit. Wide fluctuations in annual growth of imports and exports have also occurred, indicating external instability. Government expenditure rose at a rapid rate, mostly for recurrent items, resulting in large budgetary deficits. This points to a growing need for resources to finance these deficits, but with a small amount of international reserves, Vietnam is unlikely to benefit from the trade liberalization within the region under AFTA. Since 1993 Vietnam has continuously experienced trade and current account deficits with the trade deficit reaching an alarming 15 percent of GDP in 1996. Having a current account deficit is not bad *per se*, especially when the excessive rise in imports is due to imports of necessary inputs for productive capacity expansion and long-term growth. Although the bulk of Vietnam's imports have been in the form of raw materials and capital goods used for investment and production, the destination of these imports has been for import-substituting industries with the structure of imports determined by trade policy rather than pure market forces.

For Vietnam to be ready for a beneficial free trade, the government must focus its activities more sharply and give a greater role to the private sector. More fiscal incentives for exporters must also be considered to stimulate more exports. Since the link between monetary policy and external deficit is very direct inasmuch as much of the country's money supply consists of foreign currency deposits, a tighter monetary policy may be called for to reduce its external deficit.

Compared to other ASEAN countries, Myanmar's past record in this area indicates that a lot of work is required. Myanmar's huge external debt and poor export performance, aggravated by the wide fluctuations in annual growth of its exports, are the main factors behind its large current account deficit. A low savings rate and a limited inflow of foreign capital due to its present political instability have constrained the process of its economic transition. Without a significant improvement in this area, Myanmar would be unable to benefit from the trade liberalization under AFTA.

11.2.3 Price stability
Vietnam is one of the most successful historically planned economies in reducing inflation. After experiencing a double and triple digit inflation in the 1980s and early 1990s, Vietnam has enjoyed a single digit inflation since 1993. Its inflation rate was estimated at 8.3 percent and 6 percent for 1993 and 1994, respectively, comparable with other ASEAN neighbours. An important task for the government now is to consolidate these gains and to develop the monetary policy instruments that will permit effective control of inflationary forces. This includes developing indicators and instruments, as well as skills in interpreting and utilizing them.

Myanmar's rampant inflation, officially about 20 percent to 30 percent per annum, is not only reducing Myanmar's competitiveness, but is also discouraging short-term and longer-term investments. An important task for the government of Myanmar is now to develop policies effective enough to control this rampant inflation. A low and stable inflation rate is also conducive for long-term and substantial investments. On the other hand, high and variable inflation hinders the development of capital markets. Further, it increases the risk of longer-term projects, and thus reduces the level of long-term investments crucial in developing the infrastructure of a developing economy.

11.2.4 Adequate institutional environment
Their existing economic institutions and political machinery are currently geared for a centrally-planned economy and may constrain their ability to take advantage of the opportunities offered by ASEAN and AFTA. The concept of private ownership and free market enterprise is relatively new as their economies are government-dominated. To face the challenge of greater competition and take advantage of greater economic opportunities, one must have an institutional capacity: an appropriate and adequate legal, political and regulatory framework. If this framework is deficient, investments and other risk-taking activities (such as business ventures and adoption of technological advances) will be reduced. Indicators of institutional environment include quality of

bureaucracy, degree of corruption in government, presence/absence of guarantee against expropriation of private investments and repudiation of contracts by government, and infrastructure quality.

The principal consequence of an inadequate institutional environment is insecure property rights (which can be broadly defined as the rights of a firm or individual to assets, to the revenue streams generated by assets and to any other contractual obligations due to a firm or individual). Inadequate protection of property rights adversely affects the development of an internationally competitive private sector. Competitiveness requires the adoption of new technologies which are usually embodied in highly expensive capital assets. Local and foreign entrepreneurs will be reluctant to invest in these assets in an environment where property rights are uncertain. The greater risks implied by the long-term nature of investments are likely to encourage entrepreneurs to prefer to engage in short-term investments.

It is obvious from the above that the private sector has great potential to become their engine of growth, but there have to be sound policies and a supportive environment before it can effectively play a significant role in their economic transformation. A legal and contractual framework needs to be further developed to facilitate transactions and protect private property. Since Vietnam decided to move away from a centrally-planned model to a market-oriented model of development, it has enacted a number of changes in the law and the legal infrastructure to meet the new demands of the market economy. New laws enacted in specific areas in 1987–90, such as foreign investment, contracts, companies and private enterprises, were followed by the new constitution in 1992 which clarified and protected the right of private ownership. Since then, other specialized laws have been enacted, such as land law, bankruptcy law, and environmental protection in 1993, and a labour code and domestic investment promotion law in 1994. Preparations are continuing to develop the civil code and commercial law.

There are, however, a few implementation issues that need further clarification and further development: the procedure and in the case of foreigners the right to mortgage land use rights; simplification of rules and creation of a level playing field among the economic actors; development and nurturing of the new dispute resolution mechanism; and development of the legal profession. There is a need in particular to encourage the development of the private sector by adopting pro-active policies and market incentives such as, for instance, the granting of more tax relief, assistance in the procurement of capital and making banking credit available to the private sector. There is a need for an adequate infrastructure such as the provision of efficient telecommunications, transport and power supply for the private sector to function efficiently.

Trade liberalization within AFTA would bring about costs in the form of unemployment particularly in weaker industries. This requires labour market regulations to increase labour mobility. The setting up of training programmes and safety nets, for example, may be required.

Although Vietnam has already launched a number of initiatives to ensure protection of property rights, there is still some feeling of insecurity to the extent that political and legal institutions can still make unilateral decisions that reassign rights. What are needed are independent judiciaries and well-defined administrative procedures to make firms and individuals feel secure from violation of their property rights.

One factor that explains the economic success of many newly industrialized countries in Asia is the quality of government intervention particularly in the area of implementing the required policy reforms. Corruption, red tape and inefficiencies in the process of implementation are largely responsible for the failure of many countries to achieve a sustainable growth and development.

11.2.5 Reform of international trade policies

The Vietnamese government has initiated major steps towards full liberalization of its export sector. The granting of the authority to export and import is now solely based on the condition that the enterprise has prospects for receiving an export order. Similarly, export permits and shipment licensing requirements have been lifted for all items, except oil, rice and wood products. Products are no longer subject to export quotas and export taxes have been eliminated or reduced to minimal levels, except on raw materials. The duty exemption system for inputs used to produce for export has been improved in 1994 so that exporting firms need not pay import duties on imported inputs, provided that they are processed for export within three months.

However, there are still a few areas that need further reforms to make the export sector internationally competitive. Apart from providing export incentives, the export-oriented industries must be exposed to greater competition. Although the Vietnamese government has recently announced the reduction of most of its tariffs for imports from other ASEAN nations to below 60 percent as part of its steps towards joining the planned free trade area, the structure of tariffs is still complex and designed to provide greater protection to higher value-added industries. Moreover, even with the planned tariff reductions,

Vietnam's import tariffs will still be generally much higher than other ASEAN countries.

Another issue is the appropriate speed for tariff reduction. In the last Annual ASEAN Ministerial Meeting (July, 1995) in Brunei, Vietnam was allowed extra time to cut its tariffs to between zero and 5 percent for most goods due to the weakness of its economy and its poor tax base. It is therefore advisable that the Vietnamese authorities start to consider alternative sources of revenue to compensate for the revenue loss from tariff reductions.[4]

11.2.6   Consistent policy reform goals

To maintain a conducive environment for international competitiveness, the government must be credible in its policies. Inconsistent policies are not only confusing, but could also have a negative impact. The recent decision by the Officials of the National Assembly and the Vietnamese government to examine a new land law that would allow companies to mortgage land, use it as collateral or transfer it to other parties is a reversal of their current land law which revokes the land use rights of local businessmen and which require them to lease land from the state. The government recently did a U-turn on a ban on converting rice fields for industrial use after foreign investors complained. All these are cases of inconsistent economic policies in Vietnam.

11.3   Conclusion

There are benefits as well as costs associated with being a member of a free trade area. Vietnam, by joining ASEAN and announcing its intention to become an AFTA member, followed by Myanmar's announcement to join ASEAN, indicates their sense of confidence that AFTA membership will bring with it a number of opportunities, outweighing its associated costs, mostly costs of transition. This chapter argues that they must meet certain requirements in order to maximize the benefits from greater regional integration. First, an internationally competitive private sector must be developed to take advantage of the economies of scale and larger market in the face of greater competition. Although some degree of complementarity exists between them and their other ASEAN partners, there is also some degree of substitution and hence a fair degree of competition is expected. Crucial to the development of the private sector is the provision of an adequate and appropriate institutional environment. Vietnam and Myanmar must also consolidate an economic reform process and meet the criteria of macroeconomic stability. Until these criteria are fully satisfied, they are unlikely to maximize the economic benefits from their membership in AFTA.

Suggestions for further reading

For more discussions on the economic opportunities, challenges and implications of Vietnam's entry into ASEAN, see Piei and Khalifah (1996) and Dollar (1996). A succinct analysis of the economic and political implications of Myanmar's admission to ASEAN can be found in *Myan View* (1997, pp. 1–3). Menon (1997) provides a preliminary assessment of the likely economic impact on the Lao economy of joining AFTA.

For a collection of articles covering a wide range of issues on economic management and the transition of historically planned economies of Asia towards a market economy, see Chin and Ng (eds) (1995).

Notes

1. As discussed in the previous chapter, the target date for the implementation of AFTA has been set for the year 2003. However, as an exception, Vietnam was granted an additional grace period of three years, until 2006.
2. The private sector in Vietnam consists of the private capitalist sector, the household and individual sector, but not the collective sector.
3. The collective sector, consisting of agricultural, industrial and commercial cooperatives, was in decline due to reforms favouring the household and individual sectors. The number of state-owned enterprises in Vietnam has declined from 14 000 in 1992 to 6000 in 1994. Only 300 of these are making profits. In contrast, private enterprises increased from 3000 in 1990 to 280 000 in 1994.
4. To reduce its dependence on taxes from international trade, Vietnam's emphasis has been so far to improve its export performance and the efficiency of its tax collection.

12 Economic interdependence in ASEAN

As indicated in Chapters 3 and 6, the 1980s and the first half of the 1990s have witnessed an absolute rise in the level of intra-ASEAN trade, but this rise has not been significant enough to increase the share of intra-ASEAN trade. Extra-ASEAN trade has remained the bulk of ASEAN trade. The same pattern can be observed for intra-ASEAN investment flows to a certain extent.

In this light, this chapter considers a related question of whether or not the ASEAN countries are economically interdependent. Specifically, it tries to explore any interrelationships and commonalities in cycles that might exist among the ASEAN countries, and the extent to which the ASEAN economies are affected by economic developments in their major trading partners. There is a presumption that in the light of growing intra-ASEAN trade and investment, brought about by their outward-looking policies, preferential trading arrangements and unilateral trade and investment deregulations, the ASEAN countries might be expected to share a common cycle,[1] especially in the past decade. If commonality of business cycles is found, suggesting economic interdependence and integration, then there may be a case for policy coordination to the mutual benefit of the ASEAN countries.[2]

Moreover, understanding the nature and characteristics of aggregate economic fluctuations (business cycles) is crucial in providing insights into the workings of an economy.[3]

The rest of the chapter is organized as follows. Section 12.1 addresses the main issue of whether there is a common ASEAN business cycle. Section 12.2 explores the nexus between business and investment cycles in the ASEAN group of countries. Sections 12.3 and 12.4 identify the causes of ASEAN business cycles and gauge the extent to which US and Japanese business and investment cycles contribute to similar cycles in the ASEAN, and section 12.5 presents some policy implications.

12.1 Is there a common ASEAN business cycle?

12.1.1 Generation of business cycles
There are basically two concepts of business cycles. The first one (conventional) identifies cycles as deviations from the economy's growth path (deterministic trend). The other one (nonconventional) views cycles as transitory fluctuations around a stochastic growth trend.

The first one entails fitting a log linear trend to GNP or GDP of the form,

$$\log Y_t = \beta_0 + \beta_1 T + \beta_2 T^2 + \varepsilon_t \qquad (12.1)$$

where Y = real GNP or GDP, T = time, and ε_t is the error term which is assumed to be stationary, implying that all shocks are necessarily temporary or cyclical in nature, and the path of Y_t is completely deterministic in the long run. The residuals from equation (12.1) are identified as cycles and consequently should display significant serial correlation. If β_1, the coefficient of time, is found to be significantly different from zero, the series exhibits a long term trend. In addition, β_1 provides an estimate of the rate of growth of the series. The time squared variable (T^2) is included in the regression to account for any slowdown in the rate of growth of aggregate output. Thus, if β_2 is significantly different from zero, this implies a slowdown in the series.

The nonconventional concept generates business cycles by treating the trend growth rate in real output (Y) to be stochastic, and views cycles as transitory fluctuations around the stochastic trend. This amounts to subjecting the trend growth to shocks, thus allowing shocks to have permanent effects on the economy. A popular test to determine whether the trend growth is stochastic is to determine whether the series has a 'unit root', by applying the Dickey–Fuller (DF) test or its variant the augmented Dickey–Fuller (ADF) test. If the DF test allows us to reject the null hypothesis of no unit root, then the error process is not stationary around the trend, and the appropriate model is a difference stationary model (see Nelson and Plosser, 1982). This can be represented as the first difference of the trend stationary model given by equation (12.1).

One procedure to generate the nonconventional business cycles is that suggested by Beveridge and Nelson (1981), which decomposes a nonstationary time series into permanent and transitory components. The former takes the place of the deterministic trend and is defined as the value the series would have if it were on its long-term path in the current period. If a variable experiences a shock to its permanent component, the effects should persist over time and hence, the permanent component is a random walk. The transitory component is then identified as the cyclical variation representing the forecastable momentum present at each time period, which is expected to dissipate as the series tends to its permanent level.

To generate the permanent and cyclical components of the nonstationary real output series, the stochastic structure of the time series is first identified. Next, an autoregressive model is used to forecast future changes in the real output series beyond the mean rate of drift. The forecasts from this model represent the permanent components, and the difference between the forecast and the actual values of the output series represent the cyclical components.

The business cycles, represented by real output and capital stock fluctuations and generated based on the conventional and nonconventional concepts using the time-domain techniques, are graphically depicted in Figures 12.1 and 12.2, respectively. The residual plots indicate that the observed cycles have low frequency and vary in amplitude. A striking feature in both graphs is the obvious economic contraction suffered by all ASEAN countries in the sample in 1985, although the severity of the contraction varied, from very severe in Thailand and Malaysia to almost imperceptible in Indonesia. This was because of the influence of domestic factors peculiar to each of the ASEAN countries. For example, in the case of the Philippines, the political and economic uncertainty precipitated by the Aquino assassination had adversely affected the level of investments in the Philippines. In the case of Indonesia, its substantial reliance on oil exports in the context of declining oil prices in the 1983–86 period had led to lower export revenues and thus economic slowdown in 1985. Malaysia was also hit by the oil shock of the mid-1980s, although its oil exports accounted for only a smaller share of its total exports. In response to the deteriorating trade balance in the early 1980s partly due to the global recession, Thailand pursued a tighter monetary policy by raising the discount rate and restricting import credit. Consequently, the recession became worse. In the case of Singapore, the rise in labour costs and loss of international competitiveness pushed the economy into a mild recession in 1985.

12.1.2   Commonality of business cycles

The extent of synchronization of business cycles is usually measured in two ways. One approach is to use bivariate techniques such as correlation analysis to study the relationship between business cycles in pairs of countries (for example, Dellas, 1986; Baxter and Stockman, 1989). The other approach is by the use of cross-spectral analysis (for example, Saidi and Huber, 1983; Gerlach, 1988).

Few studies have identified the nature and characteristics of fluctuations in ASEAN aggregate economic activity. The Institute of Developing Economies in Japan (1988) has produced a series of studies on the nature and causes of ASEAN business cycles since 1984. The main objective of these studies was to identify the causes of the business cycles for the five members of ASEAN (that is, Indonesia, Malaysia,

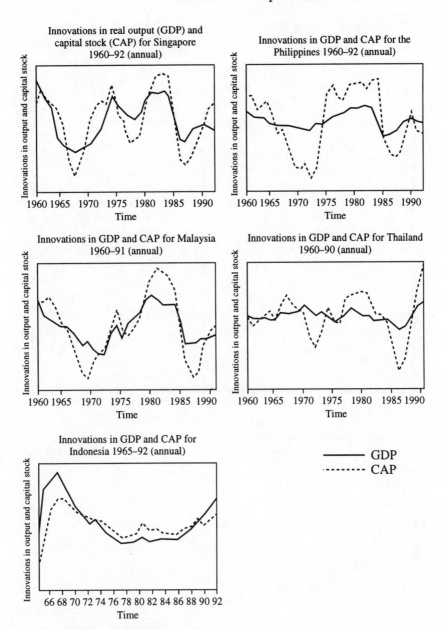

Source: Mookerjee and Tongzon (1997)

Figure 12.1 Business cycles under the conventional method

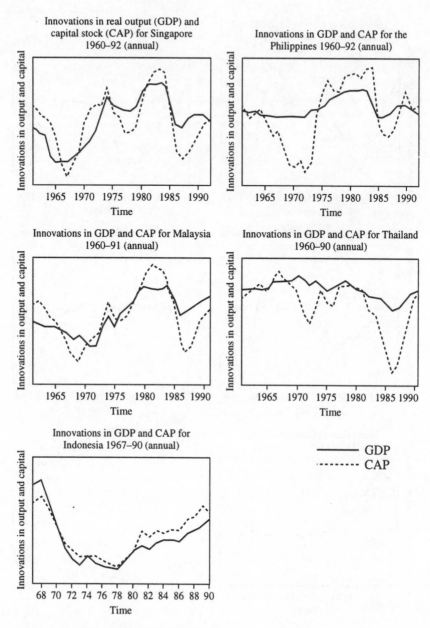

Source: Mookerjee and Tongzon (1997)

Figure 12.2   Business cycles under the nonconventional method

the Philippines, Singapore and Thailand) and develop leading indicators based on annual rates of growth of GDP from 1960 to 1987. However, only two most recent studies by Mookerjee and Tongzon (1997), and Nadal De Simone and Tongzon (1997) investigated the issue of commonality of business cycles among the ASEAN group of countries. Morkerjee and Tongzon (1997) explored, based on annual real GDP series for the period of 1960 to 1992, the issue of commonality using time-domain techniques. Nadal De Simone and Tongzon (1997), using quarterly data for the period of 1975 to 1993, have explored the same issue, with cross-spectral and factor analysis.

Table 12.1(A) presents the results of the investigation made by Mookerjee and Tongzon (1997) on commonality of business (output) cycles for the five ASEAN countries using the conventional and nonconventional concepts. The first part of the table reports the correlation coefficients between countries for the entire sample period (1960–92). The results show that there are two groups of countries that share common business cycles. The first group comprises Singapore, Malaysia and the Philippines. The second group consists of Indonesia and Thailand. Within the first group one can observe statistically significant correlation coefficients ranging from 0.8 to 0.6.[4] This suggests that fluctuations in aggregate output in any one country within this group can significantly explain 36 to 64 percent of the fluctuations in another country.[5] In the second group, the computed correlation coefficient is smaller (0.48), but is nevertheless highly significant. Interestingly, the magnitude of the correlation coefficient is approximately the same under both conventional and nonconventional approaches.[6]

Nadal De Simone and Tongzon (1997) found somewhat similar results, using cross-spectral techniques. Table 12.2 presents the findings where pairwise squared coherences (significant at the 5 and 1 percent level) among the five ASEAN countries are reported. Output fluctuations in Singapore and other ASEAN countries have significant coherences, and the coherences are quite significant especially for Malaysia, the Philippines and Thailand.

What accounts for these findings? One explanation could be that countries in the first group have largely relied on trade to sustain their high economic growth rates, although the contributions of their respective manufacturing sectors to their trade performance vary. Further, in addition to being highly open economies, Malaysia, Singapore and the Philippines have something in common: a great proportion of their exports is destined for the US market. Indonesia and Thailand, on the other hand, have relatively closed economies, and particularly in the case of Indonesia, its export performance is largely tied to its oil

Table 12.1 Correlation coefficients for cyclical components of real output series for five ASEAN countries (full sample)

(A)	Conventional approach					Nonconventional approach				
	S	M	I	T	P	S	M	I	T	P
S	1.00	0.774*	−0.598	−0.221	0.604*	1.00	0.812*	−0.466**	−0.366**	0.796*
M		1.00	−0.562*	−0.200	0.688*		1.00	−0.223	−0.513*	0.792*
I			1.00	0.482*	−0.329			1.00	0.107	−0.401**
T				1.00	0.209				1.00	−0.069
P					1.00					1.00

(B)	Conventional approach					Nonconventional approach				
	S	M	I	T	P	S	M	I	T	P
S	1.00	0.962*	−0.497	−0.007	0.644**	1.00	0.932*	−0.654**	0.505	0.838*
		0.663**	**−0.667***	**−0.397**	**0.670****		**0.647****	**−0.694****	**−0.173**	**0.772***
M			1.00	−0.571**	−0.128	0.558**		1.00	−0.436	0.608*	0.773*
				−0.642*	**−0.220**	**0.940***			**−0.509**	**−0.279**	**0.919***
I				1.00	0.847*	−0.026			1.00	0.054	−0.490
					0.565	**−0.678****				**0.473**	**−0.580****
T					1.00	0.404				1.00	0.739*
						−0.193					**−0.106**
P						1.00					1.00

Notes: S = Singapore, M = Malaysia, I = Indonesia, T = Thailand, P = Philippines. Bold-faced figures are for 1960–79. * significant at 1% level. ** significant at 5% level.

Source: Mookerjee and Tongzon (1997).

190

Table 12.2   Significant coherences[a] of Singapore GDP against selected countries' GDP (1975:1–1993:4)

Periodicity (months)	Indonesia (crossed series)	Malaysia (crossed series)	Philippines (crossed series)	Thailand (crossed series)	Japan (crossed series)	USA (crossed series)
128.0		0.99*		0.99*		
64.0		0.99*		0.99*		0.56
42.7		0.99*		0.99*	0.59	0.58
32.0		0.98*		0.97*		
25.6		0.98*		0.97*		
21.3		0.97*		0.95*		
18.3		0.92*		0.86*		
16.0		0.89*		0.79*		0.58
14.2		0.90*		0.73*		0.58
12.8		0.94*	0.80*	0.72*		0.71*
11.6		0.94*	0.78*	0.69*		0.58
10.7	0.65	0.82*	0.86*		0.56	
9.8	0.86*	0.65	0.84*		0.82*	
9.1	0.91*	0.66*	0.83*	0.57	0.80*	0.59
8.5	0.88*	0.73*	0.73*	0.63	0.71*	0.62
8.0	0.82*	0.73*				0.63
7.5	0.88*	0.66*	0.60		0.56	0.71*
7.1	0.83*	0.64				0.66*
6.7	0.79*	0.65				
6.4	0.71*	0.74*				
6.1		0.75*	0.56			
5.8		0.77*				
5.6		0.73*	0.59			
5.3		0.69*	0.58	0.66*		
5.1		0.62	0.57	0.71*		
4.9		0.57	0.63	0.67*		
4.7	0.56	0.68*	0.73*	0.67*		
4.6	0.59	0.75*	0.75*	0.68*		
4.4	0.59	0.80*	0.74*	0.74*		
4.3		0.85*	0.72*	0.84*		
4.1		0.74*	0.61	0.83*		0.65
4.0		0.62				
3.9		0.88*	0.56	0.70*		0.65
3.8		0.82*	0.72*	0.73*		0.67*
3.7		0.58	0.70*	0.76*		
3.6			0.59	0.78*		
3.5				0.77*		
3.4				0.80*	0.63	
3.3				0.77*		

Table 12.2 cont.

Periodicity (months)	Indonesia (crossed series)	Malaysia (crossed series)	Philippines (crossed series)	Thailand (crossed series)	Japan (crossed series)	USA (crossed series)
3.2				0.75*	0.58	
3.1				0.76*	0.58	
3.0				0.66*		
2.9				0.63		
2.8				0.63		
2.7				0.74*		0.59
2.6				0.77*		0.68*
2.5				0.78*		0.70*
2.4			0.66*		0.71*	0.64
2.3			0.71*	0.60	0.79*	
2.2		0.65	0.69*	0.73*	0.77*	
2.1		0.77*	0.75*	0.80*	0.68*	0.60
2.0		0.71*	0.66*	0.73*		0.71*

Notes: ^a F-statistics are distributed with 2 and 4d degrees of freedom, where d = (m − 1)/2, and m = 9. Only the highest value for the periodicity range is included. Significance is at the 5 percent level. An (*) denotes significance at the 1 percent level.

Source: Taken from Nadal De Simone and Tongzon (1997).

and gas exports which are by nature relatively insensitive to changes in foreign demand. Moreover, there have been very few intra-ASEAN components in Indonesia and Thailand's external trade.[7]

12.2   Role of investment cycles

Investment cycles have been identified as a major source of business cycles in both market-oriented economies and centrally planned economies.[8] In the context of the ASEAN countries, investment cycles are likely to play an important role in business cycles, given the important role of investment in their economic success.[9] To empirically gauge the extent to which investment cycles contribute to business cycles, Mookerjee and Tongzon (1997) generated investment cycles in a manner similar to the one employed to generate aggregate business cycles. Specifically, using the real capital formation series for each country over the period 1960–92, investment cycles were initially based on the conventional concept. This amounted to fitting the log of the investment series for each country to a time and time squared variable. The residuals from this regression would then represent cycles in investment.[10]

Then, after testing the stationarity of the data, an unconventional Beveridge–Nelson type procedure was used to generate the permanent and transitory components of the investment cycles.[11]

Table 12.3(A) shows the important role of investments in ASEAN business cycles. The results pointed to similar cycles (positive and highly statistically significant correlation coefficients) for Singapore, Malaysia and the Philippines for the entire sample period, as reported in Table 12.1(A). Indonesia and Thailand again appeared not to have much commonality in investment cycles with the former group of countries and among themselves. These results are not surprising, given that over the period of analysis Singapore, Malaysia and the Philippines have adopted an open door policy to foreign direct investment (FDI), which is a key component of capital formation in each country. Indonesia and Thailand, on the other hand, have been relatively less open to FDI and thus investment cycles in these two countries were not affected by FDI cycles as in Singapore, Malaysia and the Philippines.

Table 12.3(B) presents the results for the two sub-periods, 1960–79 and 1980–92. The extent of common movements in investment cycles was unambiguously stronger in the last decade compared to the 1960–79 period. This was due to the growing intra-ASEAN investment flows as alluded to earlier and the opening up of Indonesia and Thailand to greater amounts of FDI in the last decade, thus creating a common source of variation in capital formation across all five countries. Interestingly, comparing the results in Table 12.1 (business cycle correlations) with those in Table 12.3, it is clear that there was greater common variation in investment cycles than there was in business cycles.

Going back to Figures 12.1 and 12.2 which graphically depict the capital formation cycles for each country using both the conventional and nonconventional concepts, respectively, it is apparent that in all cases the cycles associated with capital formation series had greater amplitude and volatility than real output cycles.[12] To test the hypothesis that fluctuations in domestic capital formation is an important source of innovation in real output for the five ASEAN countries, a correlation analysis was made between business cycles and capital formation cycles for each country over the entire sample period, and for the decades of the 1970s and 1980s. Without exception investment cycles were the dominant source of business cycles, over the entire period of analysis for all countries, with the lowest correlation coefficient being 0.679.[13] The results further indicated that the importance of capital formation

Table 12.3 Correlation coefficients for cyclical components of real capital formation for five ASEAN countries (full sample)

(A)	Conventional approach					Nonconventional approach				
	S	M	I	T	P	S	M	I	T	P
S	1.00	0.760*	-0.027	-0.021	0.416**	1.00	0.796*	-0.462*	-0.049	0.473*
M		1.00	-0.380**	0.269	0.808*		1.00	-0.402**	0.103	0.810*
I			1.00	0.059	-0.430**			1.00	-0.109	-0.270
T				1.00	0.452*				1.00	0.121
P					1.00					1.00

(B)	Conventional approach					Nonconventional approach				
	S	M	I	T	P	S	M	I	T	P
S	1.00	0.947* **0.527****	0.014 **-0.019**	0.390 **-0.664****	0.877* **0.045**	1.00	0.963* **0.553***	-0.597** **0.714***	0.533 **-0.710***	0.901* **0.103**
M		1.00	-0.175 **-0.637**	0.415 **0.058**	0.933* **0.734***		1.00	-0.654** **0.257**	0.655** **-0.064**	0.912* **0.732***
I			1.00	0.567** **-0.089**	-0.193 **-0.532***			1.00	-0.171 **-0.438**	-0.466 **0.974***
T				1.00	0.584* **0.405**				1.00	0.792* **0.239**
P					1.00					1.00

Notes: S = Singapore, M = Malaysia, I = Indonesia, T = Thailand, P = Philippines. Bold-faced figures are for the 1960–79 period. * significant at 1% level. ** significant at 5% level.

Source: Taken from Mookerjee and Tongzon (1997).

Table 12.4 *Correlation coefficients between cyclical components of*
real output of the US and Japan vis-à-vis *five ASEAN*
countries (conventional approach)

	United States (full sample)	Japan (full sample)
Singapore	−0.732*	0.706*
Malaysia	−0.545*	0.566*
Indonesia	0.530*	−0.368**
Thailand	0.521*	0.056
Philippines	−0.506*	0.614*

	United States		Japan	
	1980–90	1960–79	1980–90	1960–79
Singapore	−0.761*	−0.718*	0.379	0.869*
Malaysia	−0.752*	−0.335	0.536	0.693*
Indonesia	0.457	0.618*	0.388	−0.544**
Thailand	0.472	0.568*	0.395	−0.208
Philippines	−0.535*	−0.443**	0.626**	0.775*

Notes: * significant at the 1% level. ** significant at the 5% level.

Source: Mookerjee and Tongzon (1997).

cycles in explaining business cycles across the sample of countries has
increased, as evidenced by the higher correlation coefficients.

12.3   Relationship between ASEAN, the US and Japan
Studies by Mookerjee and Tongzon (1997), and Nadal De Simone and
Tongzon (1997) have also confirmed a significant relationship between
ASEAN, the US and Japan in business and investment cycles. The trade-
oriented industrialization policies of ASEAN (together with continued
significant inflows of foreign investments from the US and Japan during
the period under consideration) are expected to make the ASEAN
economies sensitive to the business and investment cycles of the US
and Japan.[14]

12.3.1   Output cycles
Table 12.4 shows the correlation coefficients between the cyclical components of real output of the US and Japan *vis-à-vis* the five ASEAN
countries.

Based on the results for the entire sample period, it can be inferred
that the cyclical fluctuations of the real output of the US has a strong

correlation with the cyclical fluctuations of the ASEAN countries.[15] The negative signs associated with the correlation coefficients suggest that there could be some lagged relationships between the US and ASEAN output cycles. There is also a significant degree of synchronization between Japanese output cycles and the ASEAN countries' cycles, except for Thailand. This is not surprising since the US is a larger export market for Thailand than Japan.

For the decade of the 1980s the correlation coefficients between US output fluctuations and those of Indonesia and Thailand have actually declined, while those of Singapore, Malaysia and the Philippines increased, compared to the 1960–79 period. The trend in the case of Japan is more evident. The correlation between Japanese real output cycles and those of ASEAN have declined significantly in the past decade, except for Thailand which marginally increased.

12.3.2   Investment cycles

Previous discussion in section 12.2 and evidence presented in Chapter 2 have established the proposition that investment cycles have played a major role in determining business cycles across our sample of ASEAN countries. Moreover, significant common cycles in investment were detected for the three most open ASEAN economies, Singapore, Malaysia and the Philippines. This could be in large measure due to the relative openness of these three economies.

The results in Table 12.5 corroborate this observation across the whole period as well as by sub-periods. Specifically, the correlation structure of the investment cycles was similar to that of the output cycles. The negative correlation coefficients can be interpreted to suggest some lagged correlation between investment cycles in the US and those of Singapore, Malaysia and the Philippines. Thus, for the entire sample the US has a significant correlation with Singapore, Malaysia and the Philippines, but has no significant correlation with Indonesia and Thailand. This could be explained by examining the ratio of US investments in ASEAN to ASEAN total capital formation. Based on the latest available statistics, the inflow of US investment to Indonesia is very insignificant in relation to the country's total capital formation, accounting for less than 1 percent for the 1976–90 period, the lowest among the ASEAN countries.[16] Thailand has also one of the lowest foreign investment–capital formation ratios.

In the case of Japan, the results are similar across the entire period. Although Japan was Indonesia's largest foreign investor in the 1980s, Japanese foreign investment in Indonesia accounted for less than 1

Table 12.5 *Correlation coefficients between cyclical components of capital formation between five ASEAN countries, the US and Japan (conventional approach)*

	United States (full sample)		Japan (full sample)	
Singapore	−0.728*		0.412*	
Malaysia	−0.700*		0.535*	
Indonesia	0.122		−0.020	
Thailand	0.169		0.293	
Philippines	−0.595*		0.564*	
	United States		Japan	
	1960–79	1980–90	1960–79	1980–90
Singapore	−0.660*	−0.782*	0.450	0.517
Malaysia	−0.569*	−0.798*	0.673*	0.633**
Indonesia	0.057	0.423	−0.092	0.084
Thailand	0.325	0.059	0.110	0.727*
Philippines	−0.545**	−0.657**	0.644*	0.479

Notes: * significant at the 1% level. ** significant at the 5% level.

Source: Mookerjee and Tongzon (1997).

percent of the country's total fixed capital formation. A similar scenario applies to Thailand.

When the period is broken into two sub-periods to see any trend, the results are varied. There appears to be a significant strengthening in correlation of investment cycles between Japan and Singapore and Thailand in the 1980s, a marginal decline in the magnitude of the correlation coefficient *vis-à-vis* Indonesia and Malaysia, and a significant decline for the Philippines. The significant decline in the correlation coefficient with respect to the Philippines could be due partly to the political and economic uncertainty and the consequent collapse of investors' confidence in the 1980s. This result is consistent with a declining synchronization of Japanese business cycles with the Philippines and Thailand, but inconsistent with a significant decline in synchronization of business cycles with Singapore. One can say, however, that overall the trend observed in the output cycles is similar to the trend observed in the investment cycles.

12.3.3   Cointegration tests

To detect for the presence of long-run equilibrium relationships between cycles (business and investment) among the ASEAN countries and with respect to the US and Japan, Mookerjee and Tongzon (1997) used the technique of cointegration, as developed by Granger (1986), and Engle and Granger (1987).

The study found that innovations in US business cycles are highly cointegrated with ASEAN country cycles, but Japanese cycles are not cointegrated with any of the ASEAN country cycles, suggesting that divergences in cycles between the ASEAN countries and Japan will not be mitigated by equilibrium forces in the respective economies. Clearly then, over the long term the ASEAN countries appear to be fostering closer ties with the US economy than Japan, perhaps because of the relatively closed nature of the Japanese economy.

Innovations in US capital formation is cointegrated with all of the ASEAN countries. In the case of Japan, cointegration exists with Singapore, Indonesia and Thailand. An interesting finding of the cointegration analysis is that the US exhibits a strong long-run equilibrium relationship with both business and investment cycles in all of the ASEAN countries, but Japan does not.

12.4   Sources of commonality: common factors or transmission of domestic shocks?

One current controversy in the literature on business cycles is whether the strong association between outputs of countries is due to some common factor affecting all economies simultaneously or to the transmission of domestic disturbances abroad through both the current account and the capital account.[17] The empirical literature does not provide definitive answers on whether observed output coherences are due to common shocks or transmission.

To find out whether the observed commonality of business cycles in ASEAN is due to international factors or to transmission of domestic disturbances, two methodologies were used in the above-mentioned studies: correlation and multivariate latent variables techniques.

Table 12.1(B) presents the results of Mookerjee and Tongzon's (1997) correlation analysis. Comparing correlation coefficients in the two subperiods (1960–79 and 1980–92) allows one to test whether external shocks, such as the oil price increase of 1979 and the subsequent global recession, has enhanced interdependence among the ASEAN countries. In addition, structural shifts in intra-ASEAN relations due to political shocks such as the 1979 invasion of Cambodia by Vietnam may also be captured by such analysis.

One can perhaps infer from Table 12.1(B) that in general both the economic and political shocks of 1979 have enhanced the degree of common variation in ASEAN business cycles, as evidenced by the generally higher correlation coefficients in the latter period,[18] regardless of whether the conventional or nonconventional concept is used, with the exception of the Philippines, whose common variation with Singapore and Malaysia declined in the latter period. This finding cannot be conclusive since factors other than the oil and political shocks of 1979 could have been responsible. But the methodology used cannot identify these factors.

Ahmed and Tongzon (1997) attempted further to explain the commonality of ASEAN business cycles by determining the ordering of the transmission of business fluctuations within the ASEAN. This allows for an understanding of the extent to which policy coordination might be useful in mitigating the effects of business cycles within the ASEAN group of countries. To determine the lead-lag relationship in cycles among the ASEAN countries, and to generate insights into the transmission of shocks within the ASEAN countries, a vector autoregression (VAR) technique was employed, using quarterly real GDP data for the period 1975 to 1993.[19] While controversy still pervades the causality literature (Jacobs, Leamer and Ward, 1979), the direct test of Granger causality has been found to be the most efficient (Guilkey and Salemi, 1982).

A direct test of Granger causality is based on the following regression:

$$\Delta X_t = \alpha_0 + \sum_{i=0}^{n} \beta_{xi} \Delta X_{t-i} + \sum_{i=0}^{m} \beta_{yi} \Delta Y_{t-i} + \varepsilon_t \qquad (12.2)$$

where Δ is the first difference operator, and ΔX and ΔY are stationary series. The null hypothesis that Y does not Granger cause X is rejected if the coefficients of β_{yi} are jointly significant based on a standard F-test and vice versa. There are four possible outcomes: (a) unidirectional causality from X to Y; (b) unidirectional causality from Y to X; (c) bidirectional causality from X to Y; and (d) X and Y are causally independent.

The results showed that over the period of analysis only output in Indonesia, the largest economy in ASEAN, is not affected by output changes in any other ASEAN economy. Indonesia has a predictive power for Malaysia and the Philippines. The Philippines has Granger causal effects on Thailand and Singapore. On the other hand, Thailand Granger causes Malaysia. Malaysia and Singapore appear to be jointly determined, with output in each country having a predictive power for the other. These seem to indicate a direction of causation and transmission from Indonesia to the Philippines to Thailand to Malaysia while there is a two-way transmission between Malaysia and Singapore.

The factor analysis used in the Nadal De Simone and Tongzon study (1997) has confirmed the existence of international components in the commonality of the ASEAN business cycles, but could not determine whether the shocks are international affecting all countries simultaneously or are domestically-generated and transmitted.

To test for the presence of at least one international component, a maximum likelihood analysis was conducted on the five member countries of ASEAN plus the US and Japan. The results are presented in Table 12.6. The factor analysis pointed to the presence of three international factors, and the first common international factor has explained about 98.5 percent of the common variance of the series. The idiosyncratic factor was well below 1 per cent in all ASEAN countries, with the exception of the Philippines where it reached more than 14 percent. It was only 0.05 percent in the case of Singapore real GDP, about 1.1 percent in Japan and 2.3 percent in the US. The exclusion of Japanese and American real GDP from the latent variable analysis did not alter the results already obtained from the analysis of the international data set. This did not suggest the presence of regional factors playing a distinct separate role not accounted for already by the international ones. The ASEAN region seemed not to have additional factors of its own.

Although the study by Nadal De Simone and Tongzon (1997) pointed to the presence of an international/regional business cycle, it could not discriminate whether the commonality of ASEAN business cycles was due to common shocks affecting all countries simultaneously or due to quick transmissions of domestically-generated shocks.

12.5 Conclusion
The literature on ASEAN business cycles have provided conclusive evidence of the existence of a common ASEAN business cycle. The studies by Mookerjee and Tongzon (1997) and Nadal De Simone and Tongzon (1997) in particular have generally produced the same conclusion, although there were minor differences due to different approaches adopted.

The controversial issue of what causes the commonality of ASEAN business cycles still remains. But in a highly integrated world, as suggested by the high pairwise coherences across countries and the signs of the phase angles (Nadal De Simone and Tongzon, 1997), the distinction between common factors and transmission of country-specific shocks

Table 12.6 *Latent variable analysis of the business cycle frequency bands*

Country	International factors				Regional factors			
	Factor 1 loadings	Factor 2 loadings	Factor 3 loadings	Uniqueness	Factor 1 loadings	Factor 2 loadings	Factor 3 loadings	Uniqueness
Indonesia	1.0000	0.0000	0.0000	0.0000	1.0000	0.0000	0.0000	0.0000
Malaysia	0.9929	0.1175	-0.0060	0.0003	0.9929	0.1191	0.0000	0.0005
Philippines	0.8887	-0.1335	0.2225	0.1429	0.8887	0.1548	0.2037	0.1939
Singapore	0.9916	0.1278	0.0038	0.0005	0.9916	0.1259	0.0226	0.0004
Thailand	0.9912	0.1282	0.0125	0.0009	0.9912	0.1259	0.0264	0.0010
Japan	0.9920	0.0299	-0.0634	0.0111	NA	NA	NA	NA
USA	0.9712	0.0605	-0.1726	0.0234	NA	NA	NA	NA
Weighted variance explained (%)	98.47	1.49	0.04	NA	98.35	1.59	0.06	NA
Chi-square[a]	1932.84^b (38.92)	45.39^c (20.09)	8.80^d (11.34)		1411.19^b (23.21)	14.95^c (6.63)	0.26^d (.)[e]	
Schwarz–Bayesian criterion	88.84	67.66	58.76	NA	44.75	38.21	36.84	NA

Notes: [a] Values for the 99 per cent confidence level. Critical values are given in parentheses. [b] H_0: no common factor; H_1: at least one factor. [c] H_0: two factors sufficient; H_1: more factors needed. [d] H_0: three factors sufficient; H_1: more factors needed. [e] The degrees of freedom become negative with more than three factors, confirming that three factors are sufficient. NA means 'not applicable'.

Source: Taken from Nadal De Simone and Tongzon (1997).

may not be of practical relevance. It is likely that besides the presence of international common shocks, each country's output fluctuations are affected by economic conditions in other countries as not only markets but also policies become more interdependent.

These findings have an important policy implication for the ASEAN group of countries. It means that there is a need for policy coordination among the ASEAN countries to mitigate the impacts of output fluctuations. Growing economic interdependence points to the limitations of pursuing independent policy, especially exchange rate, fiscal and monetary policies. What is required is greater coordination in the policy arena if these countries are to exploit the advantages of greater interdependence.

Greater policy coordination is required as the ASEAN economies become more integrated with the reduction or removal of trade and investment barriers regionally (under ASEAN Free Trade Agreement) and across the globe (under the WTO-sponsored multilateral trade negotiations). Since most of the output fluctuations can be explained by international factors in a freer world trade beyond the control of national policymakers, there is no presumption that national monetary and fiscal policies can exert significant and lasting effects on cyclical output fluctuations.

Suggestions for further reading
For an excellent survey of concepts and measurements of international business cycles, see Gerlach (1988) and Camen (1990). For a discussion of the benefits of policy coordination, see Cooper (1985) and Fieleke (1988). For sources of macroeconomic fluctuations in small open economies, see Ahmed and Park (1994) and Ickes (1990).

Notes
1. Factors that have been identified to contribute to common cycles are capital flows, investment cycles, geographical proximity and weather, and external shocks (see Ickes, 1990).
2. For arguments in favour of policy coordination for economically interdependent countries, see Fieleke (1988) and Cooper (1985). If they are already economically interdependent, the establishment of AFTA will reinforce further their interdependence and thus the need for policy coordination.
3. For a review of this literature, see Zarnowitz (1985) and the references cited therein.
4. The magnitude of these correlation coefficients are typically much higher than those found by Cogley (1990) for a sample of European countries.
5. Squaring the correlation coefficient yields the R^2. In addition, a statistically significant correlation coefficient is tantamount to a finding of the slope coefficient being significantly different from zero.
6. Ickes (1990) found a significant drop in the magnitude of the correlation coefficient using the nonconventional approach for a sample of Soviet bloc countries.

7. In 1990 intra-ASEAN trade accounted for only 9.7 percent and 11.5 percent for the total trade of Indonesia and Thailand, respectively (Chambers, 1993, p. 62).
8. For a detailed discussion, see for instance Lucas (1977) and Baver (1978).
9. A number of studies have attributed business cycles largely to autonomous fluctuations in investments, for example, Faroque and Veloce (1991, p. 1190) and Beng (1992, pp. 759–69).
10. Good fits were obtained, as evidenced by the high adjusted R^2. Both the Durbin–Watson statistic and Ljung Box Q-statistic showed significantly autocorrelated residuals. All countries exhibited a significant trend rate of growth in investment. Interestingly, only Singapore and Indonesia exhibited a significant slowdown in capital formation over the period of analysis.
11. The forecast value of the real capital formation series is deemed the permanent component, and the difference between the forecast and actual value is the transitory component. The forecasting equation for Singapore is AR(1) while for the other ASEAN countries it is ARMA(1, 1).
12. We also computed the coefficient of variation in the growth rates of real output and capital formation. Typically, the coefficient of variation for the capital formation series was twice as large as the output series for all countries.
13. Since squaring the correlation coefficient obtains R^2, the results suggest that typically investment cycles explain anywhere from 55 percent to 86 percent of the variations in business cycles in our sample of ASEAN countries. Causality tests show causation from investment cycles to business cycles.
14. In 1991, the US and Japan were the largest importers of ASEAN goods, each country accounting for approximately 20 percent of ASEAN exports. The US and Japan together with the EC countries are the three largest sources of foreign direct investments in ASEAN (see Chambers, 1993). The study did not, however, provide conclusive evidence that the US and Japanese business cycles are the cause of the commonality of ASEAN business cycles.
15. The US–Philippines correlation might appear surprising, given that the Philippines is the most export dependent on the US in our sample of countries. This fact is not reflected in the magnitude of the correlation coefficient because the economy was seriously affected by political uncertainty and the resulting economic crisis in the mid-1980s. See Osada and Hiratsuka (1989).
16. Ramstetter (1993) estimated that the ratio of total inward flow of FDI to total fixed capital formation in Indonesia was 1.8 percent for this period.
17. These regularities have been reported in studies covering mostly industrial countries.
18. Ickes (1990) reported a similar finding for the former socialist countries of Eastern Europe.
19. The identification of leading and lagging relationships is accomplished through Granger (1969) causality tests.

13 Domestic capital development and the environment

Foreign direct investment has played a very important role in ASEAN economic development, as Chapters 2 and 9 show, as an important source of capital and technology. But the ASEAN economies and developing countries in general must develop their own local capital and home-grown technology to achieve a sustainable economic development. The importance of developing domestic capital and entrepreneurship has been emphasized on many occasions by the respective ASEAN governments.[1] This is because domestic capital can become a vanguard of economic development by fostering technology development, as demonstrated in the West. Further, it is a good way to reduce ASEAN's reliance on foreign capital and technology which is good for their long-term economic and political stability.

Another challenge confronting the rapidly industrializing ASEAN economies today is to ensure that economic success does not come at the expense of environmental degradation and lack of sustainability. Their depletable natural resources must be transformed into man-made resources while the rate of depreciation must not be more than the rate of growth of their renewable resources in the process of satisfying their economic needs. However, rising populations and expectations are likely to put more pressure on their natural resources including water, forests, coral reefs and other threatened natural resources.

Rapid growth and industrialization have constrained the capacity of the ASEAN countries' environment to provide suitable human habitats and ecological support systems. The negative side effects of industrial growth, which is centred around the capital cities, such as pollution, hazardous waste and congestion have caused so much concern that environmental considerations are now taken into account in their planning and policy decision making.[2] In this chapter a more detailed account of the rise of domestic capital in ASEAN is made with specific attention given to its major characteristics and accompanying problems. It will also provide an overview of the environmental issues in ASEAN and discuss the various measures that can be undertaken to deal with environmental problems.[3]

13.1 Rise of domestic capital

Political independence and economic nationalism were the main factors behind the rise of domestic capital in ASEAN. As pointed out in Chapter 2, all the ASEAN countries with the exception of Thailand were colonies of Western powers, either under the British, Dutch, French or Spanish rule, at one time or another, and understandably their economies during the colonial times relied on capital from their previous colonial masters. The ensuing achievement of political independence by these countries without sufficient local capital and entrepreneurial class has left an economic vacuum. This in most cases prompted their respective governments to take over certain enterprises left behind by their former colonialists and at the same time to stimulate development of indigenous enterprises. Economic nationalism was higher in countries where political independence was attained by force such as Indonesia and the Philippines.

13.2 Major characteristics of ASEAN domestic capital

One major characteristic that distinguishes ASEAN domestic capital from foreign capital is that the bulk of domestic capital is from family-owned firms where there is no separation between management and capital. They are highly concentrated in such sectors as property development, have substantial positions in banking, construction and light manufacturing but have minor interests in areas where sophisticated technology and large capital are required.

Another important characteristic is that these businesses are largely ethnic Chinese-owned in all sectors relative to private indigenous capital, especially in banking, trading and light manufacturing. Ethnic Chinese business in Southeast Asia has undergone a significant transformation from petty traders and emigrant workers in the early half of the 20th century to today's significant economic force. Over the last 20 years or so more than 70 large corporate conglomerates have emerged in the ASEAN countries, mostly owned or controlled by ethnic Chinese. For example, in Indonesia there was only one indigenous-controlled bank in 1988 among the top ten private banks and one among large manufacturing companies. It was reported that 30 percent of the Indonesian economy is owned by ten ethnic Chinese conglomerates (*The Straits Times*, 11 December 1993), and that 70 percent of the Indonesian economy is owned by the ethnic Chinese who account for only 3 percent of the 200 million Indonesian population (*Asiaweek*, 24 January 1997). It was also reported that Indonesia's wealthiest ethnic Chinese businessman has assets more than 12 times the asset value of the wealthiest indigenous businessman.

Table 13.1   Ethnic Chinese in ASEAN (1931 and 1981 in millions)

Countries	Chinese population		% of population (1981)
	1931	1981	
Indonesia	1.2	4.1	3.0
Malaysia	1.7	4.2	33.0
Philippines	0.1	0.7	1.5
Singapore	0.5	1.8	77.0
Thailand	0.5	6.0	13.0

Source: McVey (1992), Southeast Asian Capitalists, p. 163.

In Malaysia, despite the implementation of the New Economic Policy in 1971, Bumiputra investors still own a smaller portion of corporate equity. The ethnic Chinese still own 40–50 percent of corporate assets in Malaysia. In Thailand they own 90 percent of manufacturing and 50 percent of services (Yeung, 1997, p. 1). It is only in the Philippines that indigenous Filipinos own a more significant share than the ethnic Chinese. However, their economic presence is still significant as they control over a third of the 1000 largest corporations in the Philippines. Their economic strength is more appreciated if we consider their numbers, as Table 13.1 shows.

What accounts for the rise of Chinese capital over the indigenous capital? The literature on this issue cites a number of cultural and economic factors, but only the following major ones are highlighted:[4]

13.2.1   Personal and business networks
The Chinese in Southeast Asia are reported to have a penchant for networking which is a function of insecurity inherent in an immigrant community. Culturally, they rely on business networks to facilitate trans-actions and circumvent host country discrimination. The importance of networking in business (guanxi) cannot be overemphasized as it is not only a source of capital but also of know-how and operational flexibility.[5] In the pre-war Indonesia and Malaysia there was no bank to which they could turn to for capital, nor could the indigenous population get supplies on credit since it was the Chinese who controlled the distri-bution network and the latter did not trust indigenous traders. The indigenous population did not have enough exposure to business as most of their kin were probably farmers. Thus, they were usually barred from the Chinese networks.

The less organized indigenous traders, except in the Philippines, were unable to link with a foreign network. The Philippine situation was unique. The Chinese penetration into the economy was limited to only a few sectors due to the relatively small number of Chinese immigrants.[6] Second, the indigenous entrepreneurship in the Philippines was relatively strong. Third, the indigenous population in the Philippines included the *mestizos* who were more willing to exploit the commercial opportunities than the non-*mestizo* indigenous group and were helped by foreign contacts.

13.2.2 Institutional factors

It is often argued that the political–economic alliances developed by ethnic Chinese business firms have given them access to markets and resources. It was reported, for example, that in the case of the Salim Group, its rapid expansion and diversification in the past three decades was facilitated to a certain extent by the personal patronage of President Suharto (Yeung, 1997, p. 24).

Second, the ASEAN indigenous market economy before the sixteenth century was underdeveloped compared to the contemporary market economy of China. There is considerable evidence indicating that this was so, although there was no doubt an indigenous market.[7] This underdevelopment had prompted Thailand to introduce institutional measures such as the preferential tax treatment to Chinese immigrants to lure them to come to Thailand. On the other hand, the past requirement by the Thai government on the Thais to perform *corvee* labour had limited their ability to enter business (Yoshihara, 1988, p. 55).

13.2.3 Responsiveness to commercial opportunities

The Chinese are more responsive to commercial opportunities and more willing to work hard to exploit them for profits. This is largely due to the fact that the Chinese immigrants ventured for better economic opportunities and wanted eventually to return to China. They never, of course, returned, and learned to love their country of residence. The Chinese from the second generation onwards tended not to work hard for money, but the constant influx of new Chinese immigrants in the pre-war period kept alive their work ethic and commercial orientation. The inflow of Chinese stopped in the post-war years, but the need for survival in the midst of discrimination and uncertainty has kept their work ethic and commercial orientation alive.

13.2.4   Nature of the indigenous society

The indigenous societies' emphasis on leisure and adaptation of man to nature rather than on money and materialistic pursuits may explain why they are less hardworking than the Chinese. Also, historically life in Southeast Asia was not as hard as in South China where the population density was higher and which was often stricken by natural disasters (Yoshihara, 1988).

13.3   Areas requiring further improvements

13.3.1   Low level of technology

Although the role of domestic capital has grown significantly in importance over the years particularly in the downstream and less capital-intensive areas, its importance in technology and capital-intensive production is still marginal compared to foreign capital. The recent industrial transformation of the ASEAN countries, as described previously, has been driven mainly by foreign technology and capital. For example, MNCs are highly involved in the production of electrical and non-electrical machinery (the dominant item in their manufactured exports) in the ASEAN countries. The recent policy emphasis in the ASEAN countries on research and development to develop home-grown technology and on technology transfer is a clear indication of the low technological development in the ASEAN countries.

13.3.2   Quality of government intervention

We have already highlighted the importance of the quality of government intervention to a country's economic development in Chapter 5. On this count the ASEAN countries in general have fared much better than the other developing countries particularly in Latin America and Africa. However, there is still much scope for improvement in this area. Administrative and bureaucratic efficiency needs to be improved as they are facing greater competition in maintaining their international competitiveness.

13.3.3   Economic rationality

The economic ascendancy of the ethnic Chinese in all sectors has generated some resentment particularly in Malaysia and Indonesia. The prevalence of anti-Chinese feelings in these countries has resulted in certain affirmative policies in favour of the indigenous population. In Malaysia the racial riots of 1969 marked the beginning of an economic policy aimed at reducing the economic dominance of the Chinese by improving the share of the indigenous people in corporate equity and by granting them preferential access to Malaysia's institutions of higher learning. In Indonesia discriminatory measures against the Chinese started much earlier with its Benteng Programme of 1950 which gave preference to *pribumi* traders in the allocation of foreign exchange, similar to the Import Control Act of the Philippines. The Chinese discrimination, however, in Indonesia included all Chinese, even those with Indonesian citizenship. The other discriminatory measure was the government directive, called Regulation No. 10, barring Chinese traders from the rural areas. The government also nationalized a number of Chinese-owned enterprises and statized the economy. Discrimination in business stopped after Suharto came to power. During this time the Chinese did so well that anti-Chinese feelings heightened again among the *pribumi*. This, combined with other factors, led to the Malari Riot during the former Japanese Prime Minister Tanaka's visit in 1974. This incident forced the government to revise its economic policy and announced a *pribumi* policy as one of the remedial measures. Although this is in force today, the policy lacks clear-cut programmes like those of Malaysia's New Economic Policy.

This problem can only be resolved with economic rationality. So far there are indications that the ASEAN governments are acting so with economic rationality. The recent decision by the Philippine President Ramos to form a consortium comprising the six 'taipans' to invest in the infrastructural development of the Philippines is one example. The recent policy in Malaysia to forge greater cooperation and under-standing between religious sects in Malaysia and the most recent decision to allow the establishment of a Chinese school in Malaysia are examples of economic rationality. Its current policy of introducing English as a second language in schools and as a medium of instruction in certain technical courses suggests the government's flexibility. The long-term solution lies in the integration of the Chinese into the larger community.

13.4 Environmental issues

The overall quality of life in many ASEAN cities is deteriorating as a result of rapid industrialization and urbanization. The concentration of industrial activities in the capital cities and urbanization has caused pollution, congestion and hazardous waste. Thus, they have become victims of their own economic success.

13.4.1 Deforestation

Deforestation is one of the serious problems of environmental degradation in the region.[8] Clearing lands for farming and generating timber for exports have been the main sources of deforestation. Previous studies have shown that deforestation has resulted in such a substantial decline of ASEAN's forested area that it has evoked an international effort to campaign against deforestation, especially of tropical rain forests. About 25 percent of remaining tropical rain forests are located in Southeast Asia (Seda, 1993, p. 23).

This problem is most relevant to Indonesia and Malaysia who supply about 80 percent of the world's tropical timber trade and have higher average rates of deforestation. As Table 13.2 shows, the annual average rate of deforestation is 600,000 ha for Indonesia, 255,000 ha for Malaysia, 244,000 ha for Thailand, and 91,000 ha for the Philippines. More recently the Asian Development Bank estimated that between 1980 and 1990 Asia's total forest cover was reduced by 45 million ha or 9 percent (*The Straits Times*, 7 March 1995). It reported that the yearly average forest loss of 4.5 million ha was nearly double the replacement rate of 2.1 million ha. Among the six worst-affected nations during the period, four were in Southeast Asia with the following annual deforestation rates: Thailand (515,300 ha), Myanmar (400,500 ha), Malaysia (396,000), and the Philippines (316,100 ha).

13.4.2   Air pollution
This problem is quite serious in most ASEAN capital cities.

In Jakarta the annual cost of air pollution was estimated at about US$600 million and in Bangkok more like US$2 billion. Air pollution is largely generated from industries and transport. Motor vehicles, for example, are major generators of air pollutants such as carbon monoxide, nitrogen oxide and lead.[9] To keep air pollution within acceptable levels, the ASEAN countries have adopted a standard pollution index (SPI) and resolved to attain a PSI of below 100 by the year 2010.[10] ASEAN nations have prepared individual national programmes to achieve the target.

13.4.3   Traffic congestion
Traffic congestion has become increasingly a serious problem in all the ASEAN capital cities due to the proliferation of car ownership as more people can afford to buy cars.[11] Apart from the convenience they offer, cars are also considered a status symbol in the car-cultured ASEAN societies. In 1984 it was estimated that the Philippines had over 1 million vehicles. About 471,000 vehicles were reportedly operated in Metro Manila alone (Seda, 1993, p. 87). It is reported that currently about 1.5 million vehicles are operating in Metro Manila (*The Straits Times*, 1 August 1996). In Bangkok, it was reported that in 1982 there were

Table 13.2   Annual rates of tropical deforestation

Country	Forest and woodland (100 000 ha)	Annual average deforestation ('000 ha)	% of remaining forest area	% annual rate of deforestation
Indonesia	1215	600	1.4	0.5
Malaysia	198	255	3.1	1.2
Philippines	112	91	5.4	0.3
Thailand	148	244	8.4	2.4
Myanmar	322	102	3.3	0.3
Laos	131	100	1.5	1.2
Vietnam	131	60	5.8	0.6

Sources: Norman Myers (1988), 'Tropical Deforestation and Climatic Change', *Environmental Conservation* 15 (4): pp. 293–8; World Resources Institute (1990), *World Resources 1990–91*, New York: Basic Books.

about 600,000 vehicles. Between 1984 and 1988 the average annual growth in the number of motor vehicles reached 9 percent in Thailand, compared with about 2 percent in the US and 3 percent in the UK (Seda, 1993, p. 87).

Traffic congestion now costs the Philippines about 15 million pesos (S$850 million) a year in lost man-hours, bills for repair, maintenance and fuel (*The Straits Times*, 1 August 1996). The average speed around the centre of Makati, where big companies and MNCs are located, has slowed to 13 kmh. The average speed in the Thai capital is just 7 kmh (*The Straits Times*, 1 August 1996).

13.5   Alternative measures to deal with environmental problems

Economists argue that the inefficient use of natural resources and environmental degradation can be primarily attributed to market failure, that is, the market's inability to function efficiently due to the presence of external costs not borne by the producer and imposed on the public at large.[12]

Theoretically, there are a number of ways to deal with environmental problems caused by externality-induced market failure. Each of them has advantages and disadvantages, and the choice of which measures to use depends upon the objectives, criteria adopted and weights attached to the criteria. The following criteria are usually adopted: efficiency, acceptability and effectiveness, equity and flexibility.

13.5.1   Regulation

The most common form of regulation is the setting of environmental standards and penalties in relation to the use of the common resource. This could involve imposing certain limits on the extent and duration of deforestation, pollution emissions and other activities producing external costs. In ASEAN, for example, concern about the health and environmental effects of air pollution has prompted the introduction of emission standards such as the fitting of catalytic converters for motor vehicles. To control deforestation ASEAN countries have limited logging concessions to a certain number of years. To control traffic congestion in certain areas, they have adopted an area licensing scheme and in some instances resorted to virtual prohibition.[13]

Although this measure is theoretically effective and efficient provided the source of external costs can be easily traced, in practice it is difficult, if not impossible, to determine the optimal level of access and output. Under a market system the optimal output is determined without any government judgement. However, under regulation the regulators need to estimate the characteristics of the users' demand and producers' costs for the products of the common resource.

To illustrate the point, let us consider the regulation of air pollution,[14] as represented in Figure 13.1. The external costs of air pollution are manifested in the reduced welfare of others such as poor health, unsightly environment, lower property values, reduced productivity and income. There are also private costs to abating air pollution. The polluter may have to change his production method, or buy abatement equipment or reduce output. The external costs of pollution are represented by the MEC curve, and the private costs by MAC. MAC rises because it becomes increasingly costly to clean up air or water the stricter the standards, or the lower the level of contamination.[15]

To achieve the optimal level of pollution, the standards should be set at Q*. But to be able to know this optimal level, the regulator must know the external costs of pollution as a function of the levels of pollutants. This implies some method of finding the values placed by the affected individuals on environmental amenities such as clean air, water and soil. Survey and other methods are being developed but they are still experimental and beyond the scope of governments in many developing countries. There is also the problem of overstatement of the cost of abatement by firms so as to produce more output or avoid abatement costs.

In the absence of information on costs, regulators must and do set arbitrary standards based on previous studies on the impact of pollution on human health, animal survival and the like. Due to the uncertainty

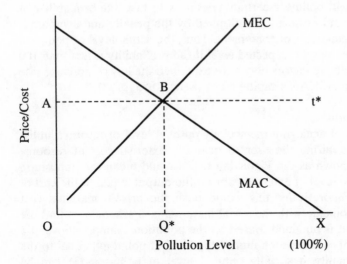

Source: Sathiendrakumar (1993)

Figure 13.1 Externality and government regulations

of these estimates and the conflicting objectives of environmental policy, setting standards becomes a political issue, subject to contention by interest groups. Policy struggles, the establishment of compliance staff and ensuing law suits all add significant costs to the imposition of standards and thus reduce the gains to society. In societies where rent-seeking is an important feature of legal and political systems, polluting industrialists are likely to use their financial and political muscle to influence the nature of environmental regulation.

Another source of inefficiency is that regulators are unlikely to know the various techniques of pollution abatement and have little incentive to find the most efficient way to reduce pollution. Their required method of achieving the optimal level of pollution is, therefore, likely to raise the MAC schedule above its minimum and so unnecessarily raise the cost to society. The costs of abatement, although they are directly borne by the polluters, are also costs to society because they entail less savings which might otherwise have been invested in other goods and services people want.

There is the problem of monitoring and prosecuting any violators of the regulations. The probability of catching a polluter is very low in areas where there are a large number of polluters, each contributing a small amount to the total level of pollution. Thus, to find out whether the polluter will pollute a certain amount is to take the probability of being caught and prosecuted multiplied by the penalty and compare it with the marginal cost of abatement. Thus, the actual level of pollution will be higher than the expected level if the probability is less than 100 percent. The above factors may have explained the low compliance rate of emission in ASEAN's capital cities (Seda, 1993, p. 88).

13.5.2 Taxation

Another way of achieving the socially optimal level of resource utilization is by requiring the user to bear the external cost of resource utilization. Known as the Pigouvian tax, it could mean the imposition of a tax on the level of externality or on the output, equal to the cost of externality. Theoretically, this would push the private marginal cost schedule to coincide with the social marginal cost schedule so that the optimal output is obtained. Based on the pollution example above, if a tax of t^* is imposed on each unit of the level of pollutant, equal to the cost of externality, a socially optimal level of pollution Q^* can be achieved. From a 100 percent level of pollution up to Q^* level of pollution, the cost of pollution control is cheaper than the per unit tax of t^*. Therefore, the firm will control pollution up to Q^*. Any control beyond Q^* (to the left) will make the cost of pollution control to exceed the per unit tax. Thus, the firm will pay the tax beyond Q^* level of pollution.

Apart from the inbuilt optimality property of taxation, it also has the advantage of allowing the firm to find the best way of reducing its production cost and of generating revenue for the government. There are, however, problems similar to the regulation measure. To obtain the optimal level of output or externality requires knowledge of the externality costs, producers' private costs and, if there are a few producers, the contribution of each firm to the total cost of externality.

There is also some uncertainty about the justice of the Pigouvian tax. Based on the standard producer pays (SPP) principle, the producer only bears the cost of optimal efficient control, which is equal to Q^*BX and not for the pollution damage done by the remaining optimal effluent, equal to area OBQ^*. According to the extended producer pays (EPP) principle, the producer must pay the cost of optimal effluent control as well as the pollution damage caused by the remaining optimal effluent. It is argued that industry might tolerate the SPP principle, but not the EPP principle. In the case of the Pigouvian tax, the producer is expected to pay, in addition to what the EPP prescribes, the cost, equal to ABO.

13.5.3 Assignment of property rights

Coase (1960) argued that the problem of externality was due to the lack of property rights. By establishing property rights, regardless of who has the property rights, an optimal level of resource utilization and level of externality will be achieved through the process of bargaining. With a clear definition of property rights, resources will be put to their highest value without the need for government intervention. There are, however, essential conditions for this approach to work. First, the transaction cost must be low enough for the bargaining process to occur. If the transaction costs become so high that the expected benefit from the bargaining process is lower than the transaction cost, then the bargaining process may not occur. In many party cases, it is clear that the transaction cost will be prohibitive in achieving an optimal bargaining solution. Second, the sources and victims of the externality must be identifiable. If there are many parties involved, the identification of how much each party contributes to the externality may be hard to find and thus the process may break down. Third, the preferences of the parties involved must be accurately represented. However, when many parties are involved, there will be an incentive for each party to engage in strategic misrepresentation of preferences to maximize their private benefits. Therefore, when the externality is a public 'bad', the conditions necessary for the Coase theorem to work will not be met. Further, the Coase theorem is based on the assumption that the willingness to pay and the willingness to accept are equal to one another. But empirical evidence shows the lack of equivalence between the willingness to pay and willingness to accept compensation, as people ascribe different values to gain as opposed to losses (Knetsch, 1990, p. 230). Fourth, to make violators pay requires effective policing, but effective policing requires an efficient property right structure. And an efficient property right structure has two important characteristics of exclusivity (that is, when all benefits and costs resulting from owning and using the resource accrues to the owner of the resource) and enforceability (that is, the property right is secure from involuntary seizure for encroachment by others). Thus, in the case of fund pollutants, market bargaining, as suggested by Coase, may be constrained by a large number of people that are affected and the inability to define clearly individual property rights to a clean environment.

13.5.4 Marketable permits

The regulatory authority decides on the allowable level of externality in a given area, and issues permits for this level of externality. These permits are transferable. Going back to our pollution example in Figure

13.1, if the authority seeks an optimal level of pollution, then it should issue OQ* number of permits and the optimal price for these permits is OA since the MAC is also the demand curve for pollution permits. At price OA, the producer will buy OQ* number of permits, as it is cheaper to abate pollution from X back to Q*. To the left of Q*, it is cheaper to buy permits than to abate pollution.

This approach has several advantages. In terms of efficiency, the regulator does not have to know the marginal cost of pollution control for each and every firm. This kind of information, as discussed earlier, is difficult, if not impossible, to obtain. But, even without this information, it can control the level of pollution in the most efficient way by letting the market do the rest. For example, let us suppose there are only two firms in an area, each emitting ten units of pollutants. The authority wants to limit the level of pollution to ten units, and thus sells ten permits to the industry where each permit is equal to one unit of pollutant. Suppose initially two firms purchased five units each at a price equal to P* (see Figure 13.2). Since the marginal cost of pollution control of firm B (MAC_B) is less than the marginal cost of pollution control of firm A (MAC_A), it is mutually profitable for firm A and firm B to trade. In this case there is an incentive for firm A to buy pollution permits from firm B at a price lower than its MAC. On the other hand, it is profitable for firm B to sell some of its permits to firm A, provided the selling price is higher than its MAC. A transfer of permits will take place until the price of the permit is equal to the marginal cost of pollution control of both firms. In the figure, this is achieved when firm A has seven units of permits and firm B has three units of permits. At this point the price of the permit is equal to P*. The permit system reinforces competition in the industry by allowing for new entrants. There is of course a unique scenario where the biggest and lowest cost firm may be able to buy all the permits. But this scenario could happen even without the introduction of marketable permits. An oligopolistic or monopolistic industry has to be regulated through other means so that their pricing policies do not harm the welfare of the consuming public.

The system also allows for the price of the marketable permits to reflect and adjust to macroeconomic conditions. Inflation erodes the effectiveness of the tax system unless the nominal value of the tax is adjusted accordingly. In the case of the permit system, the price of permits reflects the demand and supply conditions and thus it can be a factor in inflation. Since the firm only pays the cost of controlling pollution from X to Q*, and not from O to X, it is considered to be

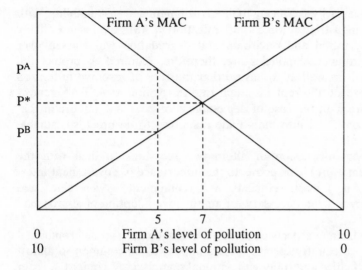

Source: Sathiendrakumar (1993).

Figure 13.2 Externality and marketable permits

fairer and more acceptable as it is consistent with the standard producer pays (SPP) principle.

There are many possible applications and versions of the marketable permit system. The Singapore government has been successful in avoiding traffic congestion and thus minimizing pollution from motor vehicles by adopting a system of certificates of entitlement (COE). The way it works is similar to the pollution permit system in that a certain number of permits (COEs) are determined and issued by the Singapore government every year for auction. The permits are also transferable.[16]

13.6 Conclusion

Although foreign direct investment has brought a number of benefits to the ASEAN countries, it cannot assure their long-term economic security. Thus, the importance of developing their own domestic capital, entrepreneurship and technology cannot be ignored and undoubtedly constitutes a major challenge facing the ASEAN countries. To promote domestic capital, entrepreneurship and technology, most of the ASEAN countries must find ways to deal with the prevalent resentment against the overseas Chinese capitalists who have been a significant source of domestic capital and potential source of technology.

Another challenge is how to maintain their robust economic growth without necessarily sacrificing their environment and sustainability. With increasing industrialization and urbanization in ASEAN it is most likely that deforestation and environmental degradation will worsen over time. Environmental policies are, therefore, required to protect the environment as well as to ensure that the rate of resource utilization does not exceed the replenishment rate in relation to ASEAN renewable resources. In the case of depletable resources, it is important that they are converted into man-made resources to ensure a sustainable development.

The above discussion of alternative measures to deal with the environmental problems points to the importance of government intervention. An honest, efficient and competent government and bureaucracy is again necessary for an effective adoption of appropriate policies.

Although some aspects of resource management and environmental problems are country-specific, others appear to be common to almost all ASEAN cities and transcend national boundaries.[17] Under the latter it is important to enhance ASEAN cooperation on the management of natural resources and on the control of external costs. The ASEAN countries are so far heading in the right direction. They have agreed to regard the entire region as one ecosystem and to enhance cooperation on the management of their natural resources. They have agreed to set up a regional early warning and response system to enhance their capacities to deal with natural disasters. They have also emphasized the need for increased consultation and cooperation with regard to issues raised at international conventions.

Suggestions for further reading
For studies on the development and role of local capitalists in the ASEAN economies, read McVey (ed.) (1992) and Yoshihara (1988). There is a vast and increasing literature on environment and development, but little attention has so far been paid to the links between economic sustainability and environmental concerns in ASEAN. To explore the different environmental concerns or issues and relevant environmental policies pursued by the ASEAN countries, Seda (ed.) (1993) is recommended. For a good economic evaluation of alternative policy options, read Gillis et al. (1996), Chapter 7 and Sathiendrakumar (1993).

Notes
1. Prime Minister Goh Chok Tong of Singapore has, for instance, made a strong call that Singapore must nurture a new breed of MNCs (*The Straits Times*, 25 March 1995).
2. Recently in Malaysia a plan to build a hydroelectric dam was suspended due to

environmental considerations. In the Philippines, a Taiwanese-led consortium's proposal to build a cement complex in the north of Manila was not given approval because of anticipated environmental damage.

3. Environmental problems may be classified into two categories: the 'population-basic needs' category and the 'natural cycles and processes' category. The former includes issues relating to the need for shelter, food, social services and amenities, work mobility and rural–urban migration. The latter includes the transformation and in many cases degradation of the biophysical environment as a result of human activities. This chapter will only discuss the major issues relating to the latter one.

4. The following discussion on ASEAN domestic capital will be mainly based on Yoshihara (1988).

5. Prime Minister Mahathir of Malaysia attributed the absence of the bumiputra in business to their lack of networks. See Mahathir (1970), p. 53.

6. The American Administration restricted Chinese immigration to prevent the Chinese from using the Philippines as a gateway to the United States. On the restriction of Chinese immigration in the Philippines, see Khin (1956).

7. This is based on the argument by Yoshihara (1988, p. 56).

8. See ASEAN Experts Group, *Environmental Programme III, 1988–1992* (1987), p. 21.

9. Air pollution in Thailand is frequently singled out as the worst among all countries in Asia. Carbon monoxide is reportedly 50 per cent above the WHO standard, while the level of lead, is double the standard. See 'Focus: Environment in Asia 1991', *Far Eastern Economic Review*, **153** (38), September 1991, pp. 37–57.

10. PSI ratings between zero and 50 indicate good air quality, between 50 and 100 moderate, and above 100 point to unhealthy or hazardous air.

11. Singapore and Brunei are exceptions. Singapore's policy of controlling car ownership through the allocation of entitlements due to its spatial constraints is mainly responsible for relatively smooth traffic flows. Brunei's small population and large space is the main factor.

12. Apart from market failure, policy failure has also been blamed for the inefficient use of natural resources in developing countries. For a detailed discussion of these issues, refer to Todaro (1997) and Gillis et al. (1996).

13. The Philippines, in dealing with its serious traffic congestion problem in Metro Manila, has recently adopted an odd–even system in which only cars with certain registration numbers are allowed in certain days.

14. This is one of the most common environmental problems faced by the ASEAN countries and the most commonly discussed environmental problem in the literature.
    Pollutants are classified into stock and fund pollutants, based on the absorptive capacity of the environment. Fund pollutants are those for which the environment has some absorptive capacity, whereas stock pollutants are those for which the environment has little or no absorptive capacity.

15. This approach to the economics of pollution abatement is based on the treatment by Pearce and Turner (1990), Chapters 4–7.

16. For a detailed discussion of Singapore's system of certificate of entitlement, see Phang Sock Yong (1993), pp. 329–36.

17. Occasional haze over Malaysia and Singapore as a result of forest fires in Indonesia is an example of pollution that transcends national boundaries.

APPENDIX   Estimation equations for trade creation and diversion

Equations for measuring trade creation and trade diversion effects under the aforementioned assumptions are as follows:

$$dQ_p = \%PX_p \, (1 + E_p) \, Q_p$$
$$dQ_f = \%PM_p \, (1 + E_f) \, Q_f \qquad \text{(A.1)}$$

The rate of change of PX_p is measured by:

$$\%PX_p = \frac{n_m + (1 - a) \, E_f \cdot RP}{aE_p \, (1 + RP) + n_m + (1 - a) \, E_f} \approx \frac{n_m + (1 - a) \, E_f}{aE_p + n_m + (1 - a) \, E_f} \cdot \frac{RP}{1 + RP} \qquad \text{(A.2)}$$

The rate of change of PM_p is:

$$\%PM_p = \frac{aE_p \cdot RP}{n_m + (1 - a) \, E_f \, (1 + RP) + aE_p} \approx \frac{aE_p}{n_m + (1 - a) \, E_f + aE_p} \cdot \frac{RP}{1 + RP} \qquad \text{(A.3)}$$

where

dQ_p = change in the volume/value of imports from the preference-receiving country;

dQ_f = change in the volume/value of imports from the nonpreferred countries;

$\%PX_p$ = proportional change in the preference-receiving country's export price;

$\%PM_p$ = proportional change in the importer's price;

Q_p, Q_f = original volume/value of imports from preferred and nonpreferred countries, respectively;

a = market share of the preference-receiving countries as a group;

RP = rate of preference, that is, preference margin as a proportion of c.i.f. value plus preferential tariff;

n_m = price elasticity of the preference-granting country's import demand;

E_p = price elasticity of the preference-receiving country's export supply to the preference-granting country;

E_f = price elasticity of nonpreferred country's export supply to the preference-granting country.

The above equation (A.2) is derived from Figure 3.1, drawn from Kojima (1969) as follows:

$$RP = (P_2 - P_4)/P_4 = AD/P_4 = AE + ED/P_4 \qquad (A.5)$$

$$RP = \frac{AE}{ED} \quad \frac{ED}{P_4} + \frac{ED}{P_4} \qquad (A.6)$$

But,

$$\frac{AE}{ED} = \frac{aE_p}{n_m + (1-a)\,E_f}\ (1 + RP) \qquad (A.7)$$

Substituting (A.7) into (A.6), and solving for ED/P_4, we have

$$RP = \frac{aE_p}{n_m + (1-a)\,E_f}\,(1+RP) \cdot \frac{ED}{P_4} + \frac{ED}{P_4} = \frac{ED}{P_4}\left[\frac{aE_p}{n_m + (1-a)\,E_f}(1+RP) + 1\right] (A.8)$$

$$ED/P_4 = \frac{RP/aE_p\,(1+RP) + n_m + (1-a)\,E_f}{n_m + (1-a)\,E_f} = \frac{[n_m + (1-a)\,E_f]\cdot RP}{aE_p\,(1+RP) + n_m + (1-a)\,E_f} \qquad (A.9)$$

The equation (A.3) is derived from the same diagram as follows:

$$RP = [P_2 - P_4]/P_2 = AD/P_4 = ED + AE/P_2 \qquad (A.10)$$

$$RP = \frac{ED}{AE} \cdot \frac{AE}{P_2} + \frac{AE}{P_2} \qquad (A.11)$$

But,

$$ED/AE = \frac{n_m + (1-a)\,E_f}{aE_p}\ (1 + RP) \qquad (A.12)$$

Substituting (A.12) into (A.11), and solving for AE/P_2, we have

$$RP = \frac{n_m + (1-a)\,E_f\,(1+RP)}{aE_p} \cdot \frac{AE}{P_2} + \frac{AE}{P_2} \qquad (A.13)$$

$$AE/P_2 = \frac{RP/n_m + (1 - a)\ E_f\ (1 + RP)}{aE_p} + 1 \qquad (A.14)$$

$$AE/P_2 = \frac{aE_p \cdot RP}{n_m + (1 - a)\ E_f\ (1 + RP) + aE_p} + 1 \qquad (A.15)$$

Bibliography

Books and articles

Abimanyu, Anggito (1995), 'Source of Indonesian Economic Growth and its Total Factor Productivity'. Presented at the 20th Federation of ASEAN Economic Association Conference, 7–8 December, Singapore.

Abonyi, George (1994), 'Challenges of Growth Triangles in SEA for Regional Institutions', paper presented during the 4th SEA Roundtable on Economic Development, Kuala Lumpur, June.

Ahmed, H. and J.L. Tongzon (1997), 'An Investigation of Economic Linkages among ASEAN Group of Countries', Department of Economics and Statistics, National University of Singapore (unpublished).

Ahmed, S. and J.H. Park (1994), 'Sources of Macroeconomic Fluctuations in Small Open Economies', *Journal of Macroeconomics*, **16** (Winter), 1–36.

Alburo, F.A., C.C. Bautista and M.S.H. Gochoco (1992), 'Pacific Direct Investment Flows into ASEAN', *ASEAN Economic Bulletin*, **8**(3), 284–320.

Alten, F. (1995), *The Role of Government in the Singapore Economy*, New York: P. Lang Press.

Amsden, Alice (1989), *Asia's Next Giant: South Korea and Late Industrialization*, London: Oxford University Press.

Anderson, K. and R. Blackhurst (eds) (1993), *Regional Integration and the Global Trading System*, New York: Harvester Wheatsheaf.

Ariff, Mohamed (1994a), 'APEC and ASEAN: Complementing or Competing?', in S.Y. China (ed.), *APEC: Challenges and Opportunities*, Singapore: Institute of Southeast Asian Studies, Chapter 7.

Ariff, Mohamed (1994b), 'Structural Change, Economic Development and the Role of the State: The Malaysian Experience', in Vu Than Anh (ed.), *The Role of the State in Economic Development: Experiences of the Asian Countries*, Hanoi: Social Science Publishing House.

Ariff, M. and L.H. Tan (eds) (1988), *ASEAN Trade Policy Options*, Singapore: Oxford University Press and ISEAS, pp. 1–37.

Arndt, H. (1993), 'Anatomy of Regionalism', *Journal of Asian Economics*, **4**(2), 271–82.

ASEAN Secretariat (1978), *Ten Years of ASEAN*, Jakarta.

ASEAN Secretariat (1995), *An Overview*, Jakarta.

Athukorala, Prema-Chandra and J. Menon (1996), 'Foreign Direct Investment in ASEAN: Can AFTA Make a Difference?', in Joseph Tan (ed.), *AFTA in the Changing International Economy*, Singapore: Institute of Southeast Asian Studies, pp. 76–92.

Austria, Myrna and Will Martin (1995), 'Macroeconomic Instability and Growth in the Philippines: A Dynamic Approach'. Presented at the 20th FAEA Conference, 7–8 December, Singapore.

Balassa, B. (1978), 'Exports and Economic Growth: Further Evidence', *Journal of Development Economics*, **5**, 181–9.

Balassa, B. (1985), *Adjustment to External Shocks in Developing Countries*, World Bank Staff Working Paper No. 472, Washington, DC.

Balassa, Bela (1991), *Economic Policies in the Pacific Area Developing Countries*, New York: New York University Press.

Balisacan, Arsenio M. (1989), 'Philippine Agricultural Development in Historical Perspective', in M.F. Montes and H. Sakai (eds), *Philippine Macroeconomic Perspective: Developments and Policies*, Tokyo: Institute of Developing Economies.

Balisacan, Arsenio M. (1996), 'Rural Poverty and Access to Land Resources in the Philippines', in M.G. Quibria (ed.), *Rural Poverty in Developing Asia*, Manila: Asian Development Bank, vol. 2, pp. 465–99.

Bautista, R.M. (1992), *Development Policy in East Asia: Economic Growth and Poverty Alleviation*, Singapore: Institute of Southeast Asian Studies, pp. 1–53.

Baver, T. (1978), 'Investment Cycles in Planned Economies', *Acta Oeconomica*, **21**, 153–9.

Baxter, M. and A. Stockman (1989), 'Business Cycles and the Exchange Rate Regime: Some International Evidence', *Journal of Monetary Economics*, **23**, 377–400.

Beason, Richard and David Weinstein (1993), *Growth, Economies of Scale and Targeting in Japan (1955–90)* Harvard Institute of Economic Research Discussion Paper 1644, October.

Beng, Gan Wee (1992), 'Private Investment, Relative Prices and Business Cycle in Malaysia', *Rivisita Internazionale di Scienze Economiche e Commerciali*, **39**(9), 753–69.

Bergsten, C. Fred (1996), 'A New Vision for the World Trading System', Paper presented at the World Trade Congress, 24 April, Singapore.

Beveridge, S. and C.R. Nelson (1981), 'A New Approach to Decomposition of Economic Time Series into Permanent and Transitory Components with Particular Attention to Measurement of the Business Cycle', *Journal of Monetary Economics*, **7**, 151–74.

Bhagwati, Jagdish (1968), 'Trade Liberalization among LDCs, Trade

Theory and GATT Rules', in J.N. Wolf (ed.), *Value, Capital and Growth: Papers in Honour of J.R. Hicks*, Oxford: Oxford University Press.

Bhagwati, Jagdish (1991), *The World Trading System at Risk*, Princeton: Princeton University and Harvester Wheatsheaf.

Bhagwati, Jagdish (1996), 'Preferential Trading Areas and Multilateralism: Strangers, Friends or Foes?', Paper presented at the Staff Seminar, 19 September, National University of Singapore.

Blackhurst, Richard et al. (1995), 'The Uruguay Round and Market Access: Opportunities and Challenges for Developing Countries,' in W. Martin and L. Winters (eds), *The Uruguay Round and the Developing Countries*, Washington, DC: The World Bank, pp. 97–115.

Brittan, Sir Leon (1996), 'Expanding World Trade: Challenges for the WTO', Paper presented at the World Trade Congress, 24 April, Singapore.

Cabanilla, L.S. (1988), 'ASEAN Cooperation in Food, Agriculture and Forestry: Past and Future Directions', in H. Esmara (ed.), *ASEAN Economic Cooperation: A New Perspective*, Singapore: Chopmen Publishers, pp. 55–68.

Camen, Ulrich (1990) 'Concepts and Measurements of World Business Cycles', in P. Artus, Y. Barroux and G. McKenzie (eds), *Policy Coordination and the International Transmission of Disturbances*, London: Macmillan.

Carling, R.G. (1995), 'Fiscal and Monetary Policies', in K. Bercuson (ed.), *Singapore: A Case Study in Rapid Development*, IMF Occasional Paper No. 119, Washington, DC.

Chambers, V. (1993), 'ASEAN–EC Relations: The Intersection of Two Regional Groupings or the Rise of Economic Rivals?', *Journal of Asian Business*, **9**, 55–76.

Chee Peng Lim (1987), 'ASEAN Cooperation in Industry: Looking Back and Looking Forward', in Sopiee Noordin et al. (eds), *ASEAN at the Crossroads*, Malaysia: Institute of Strategic and International Studies, pp. 91–138.

Chee Peng Lim and Jang-Won Suh (eds) (1988), *ASEAN Industrial Cooperation: Future Perspectives and an Alternative Scheme*, Kuala Lumpur: Asian and Pacific Development Centre.

Chee, S. and R.V. Navaratnam (1992), 'The Role of the Public Sector in Economic Growth', in H.Y. Teh and K.L. Goh (eds), *Malaysia's Economic Vision: Issues and Challenges*, Selangor: Pelanduk Publications.

Chenery, H. (1979), *Structural Change and Development Policy*, New York: Oxford University Press.

Chia, Siow Yue (1985), 'The Role of Foreign Trade and Investment in the Development of Singapore', in W. Galenson (ed.), *Trade, Foreign Investment and Economic Growth in the Newly Industrializing Countries*, Madison: University of Wisconsin Press.

Chia, Siow Yue (1986), 'Direct Foreign Investment and the Industrialization Process in Singapore', in Lim Chong-Yah and Peter Lloyd (eds), *Resources and Growth in Singapore*, Singapore: Oxford University Press.

Chia, Siow Yue (1992), 'China's Economic Relations with ASEAN Countries', in S.K. Sandhu et al. (eds), *The ASEAN Reader*, Singapore: Institute of Southeast Asian Studies, pp. 340–44.

Chia, Siow Yue (1993), 'Foreign Direct Investment in ASEAN Economies', *Asian Development Review*, **11**(1), 60–102.

Chia, Siow Yue (1995), 'Singapore and Regional Economic Groupings', Seminar on Singapore Economy in the Asia Pacific, National University of Singapore, 31 March, Singapore.

Chiew, Eddie (1987), 'ASEAN Cooperation in Food and Agriculture: Looking Back and Looking Forward', in S. Noordin et al. (eds), *ASEAN at the Crossroads*, Malaysia: Institute of Strategic and International Studies, pp. 303–322.

Chin, T.H. and H.G. Ng (eds) (1995), *Economic Management and Transition Towards a Market Economy: An Asian Perspective*, Singapore: World Scientific.

Chinwanno Chulacheeb and Somsak Tambunlertchai (1983), 'Japanese Investment in Thailand and its Prospects in the 1980s', in Sueo Sekiguchi (ed.), *ASEAN–Japan Investment Relations*, Singapore: Institute of Southeast Asian Studies.

Chng, Meng Kng (1985), 'ASEAN Economic Cooperation: The Current Status', *Southeast Asian Affairs*, Singapore: ISEAS.

Chng, Meng Kng (1991), 'A Comparative Study of the Industrialization Experience of ASEAN Countries', in Edward K.Y. Chen et al. (eds), *Industrial and Trade Development in Hong Kong*, Centre of Asian Studies, University of Hong Kong, 1991.

Chng, Meng Kng (1992), 'Institutional Structure for Enhanced Economic Cooperation', in *ASEAN Economic Cooperation for the 1990s*, A report prepared for the ASEAN Standing Committee, the Philippine Institute for Development Studies and ASEAN Secretariat, pp. 91–105.

Chng, Meng Kng and R. Hirono (1992) 'ASEAN–Japan Economic Cooperation', in K.S. Sandhu et al. (eds), *The ASEAN Reader*, Singapore: Institute of Southeast Asian Studies, pp. 329–34.

Coase, R. (1960), 'The Problem of Social Cost', *Journal of Law and Economics*, **3**, 1–44.

Cogley, T. (1990), 'International Evidence on the Size of the Random Walk in Output', *Journal of Political Economy*, **98**, 501–18.

Cooper, C.A. and B.F. Massell (1965), 'Towards a General Theory of Customs Union for Developing Countries', *Journal of Political Economy*, **73**(5), 461–76.

Cooper, R.N. (1985), 'Economic Interdependence and Coordination of Economic Policies', in *Handbook of International Economics*, vol. 2, R.W. Jones and P.B. Kenen (eds), New York: North Holland, pp. 1195–234.

Dellas, H. (1986), 'A Real Model of the World Business Cycle', *Journal of International Money and Finance*, **5**, 381–94.

Department of Labour and Employment (1995), *The Overseas Employment Programme*, Manila: DOLE.

Dollar, D. (1996), 'Economic Reform, Openness and Vietnam's Entry into ASEAN', *ASEAN Economic Bulletin* **13**(2), 169–84.

Economic and Social Commission for Asia and the Pacific (ESCAP) (1994), Steering Group of the Committee for Regional Economic Cooperation, Fifth Meeting, 29 August–1 September, Kunming, China.

Economic and Social Commission for Asia and the Pacific (ESCAP) (1995), *Trade Prospects for the Year 2000 and Beyond for the Asian and Pacific Region*, New York: United Nations.

Edwards, Sebastian (1992), 'Trade Orientation, Distortions and Growth in Developing Countries', *Journal of Development Economics*, **39**, July, 31–57.

Edwards, Sebastian (1993), 'Openness, Trade Liberalization and Growth in Developing Countries', *Journal of Economic Literature*, **31**, September, 1358–93.

Engle, R.F. and C.W. Granger (1987), 'Cointegration and error correction: Representation, estimation and testing', *Econometrica*, **55**, 251–76.

Esfahani, H.S. (1991), 'Exports, Imports and Economic Growth in Semi-Industrialized Countries', *Journal of Development Economics*, **35**, 93–116.

Esmara, H. (1988), *ASEAN Economic Cooperation: A New Perspective*, Singapore: Chopmen Publishers, Chapter 7.

Evers, Hans-Dieter (1995), *The Growth of an Industrial Labour Force and the Decline of Poverty in Indonesia*, Indonesia: Southeast Asian Affairs.

Faroque, A. and W. Veloce (1991), 'The Relative Importance of Direct

Investment and Policy Shocks for an Open Economy', *Applied Economics*, **23**, 1183–92.

Feder, G. (1983), 'On Exports and Economic Growth', *Journal of Development Economics*, **12**, 59–73.

Feder, G., R.E. Just and D. Zilberman (1985), 'Adoption of Agricultural Innovations in Developing Countries: A Survey', *Economic Development and Cultural Change*, **83**, 255–98.

Feder, G. et al. (1988), *Land Policies and Farm Productivity in Thailand*, Johns Hopkins Press for the World Bank.

Feldstein, M.S. (1986), *International Debt Service and Economic Growth: Some Simple Analytics*, NBER Working Paper No. 2138.

Fieleke, N.S. (1988), 'Economic Interdependence between Nations: Reason for Policy Coordination?', *New England Economic Review*, May/June, 21–38.

Gerlach, Stefan H.M. (1988), 'World Business Cycles under Fixed and Flexible Exchange Rates', *Journal of Money, Credit and Banking*, **20**(4), 621–32.

Ghaffar, F. (1996), 'The Southern Growth Triangle: A Recent Form of Malaysia–Singapore Economic Cooperation', Paper presented at the Sixth Malaysia–Singapore Forum, Petaling Jaya, 6–8 December.

Gillis, Malcolm et al. (1996), *Economics of Development*, New York: W.W. Norton & Company.

Godinez, Z.F. (1989), 'Privatization and Deregulation in the Philippines: An Option Package Worth Pursuing?', *ASEAN Economic Bulletin*, **5**(3), 259–89.

Goh Keng Swee (1977), 'Government Owned Enterprises', Speech given at the Income Annual General Meeting, 20 June, Singapore.

Gonzalez, Joaquin L. III (1995), 'The Philippines Labor Diaspora: Patterns and Trends', Paper presented at the 1995 ASEAN Inter-University Seminar on Social Development, Cebu, the Philippines.

Granger, C. (1969), 'Investigating Causal Relations by Econometric Models and Cross-Spectral Methods', *Econometrica*, **37**, 428–38.

Granger, C. (1986), 'Developments in the Study of Cointegrated Economic Variables', *Oxford Bulletin of Economics and Statistics*, **48**, 213–28.

Greenaway, D. (1993), 'Liberalizing Foreign Trade through Rose Tinted Glasses', *Economic Journal*, **103**, 208–23.

Greenaway, D. and D. Sapsford (1994), 'What does Liberalization do for Exports and Growth?', *Weltwirtschaftliches Archiv*, Band 130, 153–73.

Greenwood, J.G. (1993), 'Portfolio Investment in Asian and Pacific Economies: Trends and Prospects', *Asian Development Review*, **11**(1).

Guilkey, D.K. and M.K. Salemi (1982), 'Small Sample Properties of Three Tests for Granger Causal Ordering in a Bivariate Stochastic System', *Review of Economics and Statistics*, **64**, 668–80.

Habir, Ahmad D. (1990), 'State Enterprises: Reform and Policy Issues', in Hall Hill and Terry Hull (eds), *Indonesia Assessment 1990*, Political and Social Change Monograph 11, Canberra: Australian National University, pp. 91–107.

Han, Soo Kim and Ann Weston (1993), 'A North American Free Trade Agreement and East Asian Developing Countries', *ASEAN Economic Bulletin*, **9**(3), March.

Harris, Stuart and Brian Bridges (1983), *European Interest in ASEAN*, London: Royal Institute of International Affairs.

Hashim, Abd Amin Bin Haji (1996), *Foreign Direct Investment and Spillover Effects in Brunei Darussalam*, Masteral Thesis, Department of Economics and Statistics, National University of Singapore.

Hayami, Yujiro, M. Agnes, R. Quisumbing and L.S. Adriano (1990), *Towards an Alternative Land Reform Paradigm: A Philippine Perspective*, Manila: Ateneo de Manila University Press.

Herdt, R.W. and C. Capule (1983), *Adoption, Spread and Production Impact of Modern Rice Varieties in Asia*, Los Banos: International Rice Research Institute.

Hill, Hall (1988), *Foreign Investment and Industrialization in Indonesia*, Singapore: Oxford University Press.

Hill, H. (1990), 'Foreign Investment and East Asian Economic Development', *Asian–Pacific Economic Literature*, **4**(2), September.

Hill, H. (1992), 'Manufacturing Industry', in A. Booth (ed.), *The Oil Boom and After: Indonesian Economic Policy and Performance in the Soeharto Era*, Oxford: Oxford University Press.

Hill, H. (1994), 'ASEAN Economic Development: An Analytical Survey (The State of the Field)', *The Journal of Asian Studies*, **53**(3), August, 832–66.

Hooper, P. and C.L. Mann (1989), *The Emergence and Persistence of the US External Imbalance, 1980–87*, Princeton Studies in International Finance.

Huq, Ataul (1994), *Malaysia's Economic Success*, Malaysia: Pelanduk Publications.

Ickes, B. (1990), 'Do Socialist Countries Suffer a Common Business Cycle?', *Review of Economics and Statistics*, **72**, 397–405.

Idem (1974), 'Determinants of DFI', *Philippine Economic Journal*, Third Trimester.

Imada, P., M. Montes and S. Naya (1991), 'A Free Trade Area: Implications for ASEAN', *ISEAS Current Economic Affairs Series*,

ASEAN Economic Research Unit, Institute of Southeast Asian Studies, Singapore.

Ingavata, P. (1989), 'Privatization in Thailand: Slow Progress Amidst Much Opposition', *ASEAN Economic Bulletin*, **5**(3), 319–35.

Inkeles, A. and D.H. Smith (1974), *On Becoming Modern*, London: Heinemann.

Institute of Developing Economies (1988), *Business Cycles in Five ASEAN Countries, India and Korea*, Tokyo: Insatsu Co.

International Country Risk Guide (1996), **27**(5), May.

Jacobs, R., E. Leamer and M. Ward (1979), 'Difficulties with Testing for Causation', *Economic Inquiry*, **17**, pp. 401–13.

James, William E. (1983), 'Asian Agriculture in Transition: Key Policy Issues', *Asian Development Bank*, September.

James, W.E., S. Naya, and G.M. Meier (1989), *Asian Economic Development: Economic Success and Policy Lessons*, Madison, WI: University of Wisconsin Press, Chapter 1.

Johnson, B.F. and T.P. Tomich (1985), 'Agricultural Strategies and Agrarian Structure', *Asian Development Review*, **3**(2), 1–37.

Johnson, Chalmers (1982), *MITI and the Japanese Miracle*, Stanford University Press.

Johnson, Harry G. (1958), *International Trade and Economic Growth: Studies in Pure Theory*, London: Allen & Unwin.

Johnson, Harry G. (1965), 'An Economic Theory of Protectionism, Tariff Bargaining and the Formation of Customs Unions', *Journal of Political Economy*, **73** (June), 256–83.

Jomo, K.S. (1991), 'Whither Malaysia's New Economic Policy?', *Pacific Affairs*, **63**(4), 469–99.

Jomo, K.S. (1994), 'Privatization', in K.S. Jomo (ed.), *Malaysia's Economy in the Nineties*, Malaysia: Pelanduk Publications.

Jomo, K.S. and C. Edwards (1993), 'Malaysian Industrialization in Historical Perspective', in K.S. Jomo (ed.), *Industrializing Malaysia: Policy, Performance and Prospects*, London: Routledge.

Jung, W.S. and P.J. Marshall (1985), 'Exports, Growth and Causality in Developing Countries', *Journal of Development Economics*, **18**, 1–13.

Kavoussi, R. (1984), 'Export Expansion and Economic Growth: Further Empirical Evidence', *Journal of Development Economics*, **14**, 241–50.

Kawai, H. (1994), 'International Comparative Analysis of Economic Growth: Trade Liberalization and Productivity', *The Developing Economies*, **32**(4), 373–97.

Keefer, P. and S. Knack (1993), 'Why Don't Poor Countries Catch Up? A Cross-National Test of an Institutional Explanation', Center for

Institutional Reform and the Informal Sector, University of Maryland at College Park.

Kemp, M.C. (1962), 'The Gain from International Trade', *Economic Journal*, **72** (December), 803–19.

Khin Khin Myint Jensen (1956), 'The Chinese in the Philippines During the American Regime: 1896–1946', PhD Thesis, University of Wisconsin.

Knetsch, J.L. (1990), 'Environmental Policy Implications of Disparities between Willingness to Pay and Compensation Demanded Measures of Values', *Journal of Environmental Economics and Management*, **18**, 227–37.

Kojima, K. (1969), 'Trade Preferences for Developing Countries: A Japanese Assessment', *Hitotsubashi Journal of Economics*, **20**, February, 1–12.

Kreinin, M. and M. Plummer (1992), 'Effects of Economic Integration in Industrial Countries on ASEAN and the Asian NIEs', *World Development*, **20**(9), 1345–66.

Krishna, Pravin and Jagdish Bhagwati (1994), 'Necessarily Welfare-enhancing Customs Unions with Industrialization Constraints: A Proof of the Cooper–Massell–Johnson–Bhagwati Conjecture', Columbia University Working Papers, April.

Krongkaew, M. (1994), 'Income Distribution in East Asian Developing Countries: An Update', *Asian Pacific Economic Literature*, **8**(2), November, 58–70.

Kumar, Sree (1992), 'Assessing AFTA', in K.S. Sandhu et al. (eds), *The ASEAN Reader*, Singapore: Institute of Southeast Asian Studies, pp. 516–18.

Le, Vu Khanh (1995), 'Vietnam Opens up the Economy, Joins ASEAN and International Trade', Paper presented at the Seminar on Regional Economic Integration: AFTA and APEC Perspective – Implications for Vietnam, Hanoi (4–5 December) and Ho Chi Minh (7–8 December).

Ledesma, A.J. (1982), *Landless Workers and Rice Farmers: Peasant Subclasses under Agrarian Reform in Two Philippine Villages*, Los Banos: International Rice Research Institute.

Lee, Tsao Yuan (1990), 'An Overview of the ASEAN Economies', *Singapore Economic Review*, **35**(1), 16–37.

Lee, T.Y. (ed.) (1991), *Growth Triangle*, Singapore: Institute of Southeast Asian Studies.

Levine, Ross and David Renelt (1992), 'A Sensitivity Analysis of Cross-country Growth Regressions', *American Economic Review*, **82**, September, 942–63.

Lewis, W.A. (1955), *The Theory of Economic Growth*, London: Allen and Unwin.

Lim Chong Ya (1991), *Development and Underdevelopment*, Singapore: Longman Publications, pp. 197–214.

Lim Chong Yah and Associates (1988), *Policy Options for the Singapore Economy*, Singapore: McGraw-Hill.

Lim, D. (1996), *Explaining Economic Growth: A New Analytical Framework*, UK: Edward Elgar.

Limskul, Kitti (1995), 'Sources of Economic Growth and Development in Thailand', Paper presented at the 20th Federation of ASEAN Economic Associations Conference, 7–8 December, Singapore.

Lipsey, Richard (1957), 'The Theory of Customs Unions: Trade Diversion and Welfare', *Economica*, **24**, 40–46.

Lipsey, Richard (1960), 'The Theory of Customs Unions: A General Survey', *Economic Journal*, **70**, 498–513.

Low, L. (1991), *The Political Economy of Privatization in Singapore*, Singapore: McGraw-Hill.

Low, L. and M.H. Toh (1989), 'Economic Outlook: ASEAN 1993/94', in H. Osada and D. Hiratsuka (eds), *Business Cycles in Five ASEAN Countries, India and Korea*, Tokyo: Institute of Developing Economies.

Lucas, R.E. Jr. (1977), 'Understanding Business Cycles', in K. Brummer and A. Meltzer (eds), *Stabilization of the Domestic and International Economy* (Carnegie-Rochester Conference Series on Public Policy), Amsterdam: North-Holland.

MacKinnon, J. (1990), 'Critical Values For Cointegration Tests', Working paper, University of California, San Diego.

Maddison, A. (1970), *Economic Progress and Policy in Developing Countries*, London: Allen and Unwin.

Mahathir, Mohamad (1970), *The Malay Dilemma*, Kuala Lumpur: Federal Publications.

Mangahas, M. (1985), 'Rural Poverty and Operation Land Transfer in the Philippines', in R. Islam (ed.), *Strategies for Alleviating Poverty in Rural Asia*, Dhaka and Bangkok: Bangladesh Institute for Development Studies and International Labour Organization.

Martin, Will and L. Alan Winters (eds) (1995), *The Uruguay Round and the Developing Economies*, World Bank Discussion Papers, Washington, DC: The World Bank.

McClelland, D.C. (1961), *The Achieving Society*, New York: Van Nostrand.

McVey, Ruth (ed.) (1992), *Southeast Asian Capitalists*, New York: Southeast Asia Programme, Cornell University.

Meade, Edward James (1955), *The Theory of Customs Union*, Amsterdam: North-Holland.

Meade, Edward James (1956), *A Geometry of International Trade*, London: G. Allen & Unwin.

Menon, J. (1997), Lao PDR in the ASEAN Free Trade Area: Trade, Revenue and Investment Implications. Research Monograph No. 97–101. Melbourne: Centre for Policy Studies, Monash University.

Meyanathan, S. and I. Haron (1987), 'ASEAN Trade Cooperation: A Survey of the Issues', in Sopiee Noordin et al. (eds), *ASEAN at the Crossroads*, Malaysia: Institute of Strategic and International Studies, pp. 13–38.

Michaely, M. (1977), 'Exports and Growth: An Empirical Investigation', *Journal of Development Economics*, **4**, 49–53.

Michalopolous, C. and K. Jay (1973), *Growth of Exports and Income in the Developing World*, AID Discussion Paper 28, Washington, DC.

Min Tang and Myo Thant (1993), *Growth Triangles: Conceptual Issues and Operational Problems*, Paper presented at the Workshop on Growth Triangles in Asia, ADB, Manila, February 1993.

Mohamed, Rugayah (1994), 'Public Enterprises', in K.S. Jomo (ed.), *Malaysia's Economy in the Nineties*, Malaysia: Pelanduk Publications.

Mookerjee, R. and J. Tongzon (1997), 'Small Open Economies and Business Cycles: Evidence from the ASEAN Group of Countries', *Journal of Asia Pacific Economy*, **2**(1), 58–81.

Mya, Than (1992), 'ASEAN, IndoChina and Myanmar', in S.K. Sandhu et al. (eds), *The ASEAN Reader*, Singapore: Institute of Southeast Asian Studies, pp. 344–51.

Myo Thant and Min Tang (eds) (1996), *Indonesia–Malaysia–Thailand Growth Triangle: Theory to Practice*, Manila: Asia Development Bank.

Nadal De Simone, F. (1995), 'Macroeconomic Perspective of AFTA's Problems and Prospects', *Contemporary Economic Policy*, April, 49–62.

Nadal De Simone, F. and Jose Tongzon (1997), 'Is There a Business Cycle in Singapore? Is There a Singaporean Business Cycle?', *Atlantic Economic Journal*, **25**(1), forthcoming.

Naidu, G. (1988), 'ASEAN Cooperation in Transport', in H. Esmara (ed.), *ASEAN Economic Cooperation: A New Perspective*, Singapore: Chopmen Publishers, pp. 191–227.

Navaratnam, R.V. (1987), 'ASEAN Cooperation in Transportation: Looking Back and Looking Forward', in S. Noordin et al. (eds), *ASEAN at the Crossroads*, Malaysia: Institute of Strategic and International Studies, pp. 357–69.

Naya, Seiji (1987), 'Economic Performance and Growth Factors of the

ASEAN Countries', in Linda G. Martin (ed.), *ASEAN Success Story: Social, Economic and Political Dimensions*, Honolulu: East–West Centre, pp. 47–87.

Naya, S. and C. Barretto (1994), 'Future Prospects for the ASEAN Free Trade Area', Paper presented at the WEA International Conference, 8–13 January.

Naya, Seiji and P. Imada (1990), 'Trade and Investment Linkage in ASEAN Countries', in Soon Lee Ying (ed.), *Foreign Direct Investment in ASEAN*, Honolulu: East–West Centre.

Naya, Seiji and P. Imada (1992), 'Implementing AFTA', in K.S. Sandhu et al. (eds), *The ASEAN Reader*, Singapore: Institute of Southeast Asian Studies, pp. 513–15.

Naya, Seiji, K.S. Sandhu, M. Plummer and N. Akrasanee (1992), 'ASEAN–US Initiative', in K.S. Sandhu et al. (eds), *The ASEAN Reader*, Singapore: Institute of Southeast Asian Studies, pp. 321–8.

Nelson, C.R. and C.I. Plosser (1982), 'Trends and Random Walks in Macroeconomic Time Series', *Journal of Monetary Economics*, **10**, 139–62.

Ng, Chee Yuan and K.W. Toh (1992), 'Privatization in the Asian Pacific Region', *Asian Pacific Economic Literature*, **6**(2), 42–68.

Ng, Chee Yuan and Norbert Wagner (eds) (1991), *Marketization in ASEAN*, Singapore: Institute of Southeast Asian Studies.

Ng, Sai Cheong (1994/95), 'Vietnam as a Transitional Economy: Problems and Opportunities', Honours Thesis, Department of Economics and Statistics, National University of Singapore.

Nijathaworn, B. (1993), 'Managing Foreign Capital in a Rapidly Growing Economy: Thailand's Recent Experience and Issues', Paper presented at the International Conference on the Asia Pacific Economy, 25–28 August, Cairns, Australia, pp. 18–19.

Ooi Guat Tin (1987), 'ASEAN Preferential Trading Arrangements: An Assessment', in Sopiee Noordin et al. (eds), *ASEAN at the Crossroads*, Malaysia: Institute of Strategic and International Studies, pp. 55–61.

Osada, H. and D. Hiratsuka (eds) (1989), *Business Cycles in Five ASEAN Countries, India and Korea*, Tokyo: Institute of Developing Economies.

Oshima, H. (1993), *Strategic Processes in Monsoon Asia's Economic Development*, London: Johns Hopkins University Press.

Osman-Rani, H. (1985), 'New Directions in Industrialization: Some Strategic Issues', in K.S. Jomo (ed.), *Malaysia's New Economic Policies*, Kuala Lumpur: Malaysian Economic Association.

Otsuka, K. (1991), 'Determinants and Consequences of Land Reform

Implementation in the Philippines', *Journal of Development Economics*, **35**, 339–55.

Pangestu, Mari (1996), 'The Role of the State and Economic Development in Indonesia', in M. Pangestu (ed.), *Economic Reform, Deregulation and Privatization*, Jakarta: Centre for Strategic and International Studies, pp. 96–132.

Parsonage, James (1994), *The State and Globalisation: Singapore's Growth Triangle Strategy*, Working Paper No. 23, Asia Research Centre on Social, Political and Economic Change, Murdoch University, Western Australia, February, pp. 5–7.

Pearce, D. and R. Turner (1990), *Economics of Natural Resources and the Environment*, Baltimore: Johns Hopkins Press, Chapters 4–7.

Peebles, Gavin and Peter Wilson (1996), *The Singapore Economy*, UK: Edward Elgar, pp. 200–10.

Perkins, D.H. (1994), 'There are at Least Three Models of East Asian Development', *World Development*, **22**(4), 655–61.

Perry, M. and C. Grundy-Warr (1996), 'Growth Triangles, International Economic Integration and the Singapore–Indonesian Border Zone', in D. Rumley (ed.), *Global Geopolitical Change and the Asia Pacific: A Regional Perspective*, London: Avebury.

Phang Sock Yong (1993), 'Singapore's Motor Vehicle Policy: Review of Recent Changes and a Suggested Alternative', *Transportation Research* (A), July, pp. 329–36.

Piei, Mohd. Haflah and Noor Aini Khalifah (1996), 'Vietnam in ASEAN: Trade, Investment and other Economic Effects', *ASEAN Economic Bulletin*, **13**(2), 200–211.

Pomfret, Richard (1994), 'Strategic Trade and Industrial Policy as an Approach to Locational Competitiveness: What Lessons for Asia?', Paper presented at the 1994 Kiel Week Conference on Locational Competition in the World Economy, Institut für Weltwirtschaft, Kiel, Germany, 22–23 June.

Puntasen, Apichai (1988), 'ASEAN Cooperation in Tourism', in H. Esmara (ed.), *ASEAN Economic Cooperation: A New Perspective*, Singapore: Chopmen Publishers, pp. 205–27.

Pupphavesa, W. and M. Geeve (1994), 'AFTA and NAFTA: Complementing or Competing?', in S.Y. Chia (ed.), *APEC: Challenges and Opportunities*, Singapore: Institute of Southeast Asian Studies, Chapter 8.

Pussarangsri, B. and S. Chamnivickorn (1995), 'Trade Liberalization and FDI Policies of ASEAN Countries', Paper presented at the 20th Federation of ASEAN Economic Associations Conference, Singapore, 7–8 December.

Quibria, M.G. (ed.) (1996), *Rural Poverty in Developing Asia*, vol. 2, Manila: Asian Development Bank.

Ramstetter, E.D. (1993), 'Prospects for Foreign Firms in Developing Economies of the Asia and Pacific Region', *Asian Development Review*, **11**(1), 151–85.

Rao, B. and C. Lee (1995), 'Sources of Growth in the Singapore Economy and its manufacturing and Service Sectors', Paper presented at the 20th Federation of ASEAN Economic Associations Conference, Singapore, 7–8 December.

Riedel, James (1988), 'Economic Development in East Asia: Doing What Comes Naturally?' in Helen Hughes (ed.), *Achieving Industrialization in East Asia*, UK: Cambridge University Press, pp. 1–38.

Rieger, H.C. (1985), *ASEAN Cooperation and intra-ASEAN Trade*, Singapore: Institute of Southeast Asian Studies.

Rieger, Hans Christoph (1992), 'ASEAN–EC Economic Cooperation', in S.K. Sandhu et al. (eds), *The ASEAN Reader*, Singapore: Institute of Southeast Asian Studies, pp. 335–9.

Romer, Paul R. (1994), 'New Goods, Old Theory and the Welfare Costs of Trade Restrictions', *Journal of Development Economics*, **43**, 5–38.

Ronnas, P. (1992), *Employment Generation Through Private Entrepreneurship in Vietnam*, Asian Regional Team for Employment Promotion (ARTEP), International Labour Organization.

Rostow, W.W. (1952), *The Process of Economic Growth*, New York: Norton.

Saidi, N. and G. Huber (1983), 'Postwar Business Cycles and Exchange Rate Regimes', Unpublished working paper (mimeo).

Samuelson, P.A. (1939), 'The Gains from International Trade,' *Canadian Journal of Economics and Political Science*, **5** (May), 195–205.

Sandhu, K. et al. (eds) (1992), *The ASEAN Reader*, Singapore: ISEAS, pp. xvii–xxii; 3–49; 50–82; 242–253; 260–64.

Sathiendrakumar, R. (1993), 'Economic Evaluation of Alternative Policy Options Available to Control Fund Pollutants', Paper presented at the Staff Seminar, Department of Economics and Statistics, National University of Singapore, 28 January (mimeo).

Saw Swee-Hock (1980), 'ASEAN Economic Cooperation', in Saw Swee-Hock (ed.), *ASEAN Economies in Transition*, Singapore University Press, pp. 322–36.

Schultz, Siegfried (1996), 'Regionalism of World Trade: Dead End or Way out?' in M.P. Van Dijk and S. Sideri (eds), *Multilateralism versus Regionalism: Trade Issues After the Uruquay Round*, London: Frank Cass & Co. Ltd.

Schulze, David (1988), 'ASEAN Cooperation in Banking and Finance', in H. Esmara (ed.), *ASEAN Economic Cooperation: A New Perspective*, Singapore: Chopmen Publishers, pp. 157–89.

Seda, Maria (ed.) (1993), *Environmental Management in ASEAN: Perspectives on Critical Regional Issues*, Singapore: Institute of Southeast Asian Studies.

Shaikh, A.H. (1992), 'Malaysia's Public Enterprises: A Performance Evaluation', *ASEAN Economic Bulletin*, 9(2), 207–18.

Snodgrass, D.R. (1980), *Inequality and Economic Development in Malaysia*, Petaling Jaya: Oxford University Press.

Tambunlertchai, Somsak (1993), 'Manufacturing', in Peter Warr (ed.), *The Thai Economy in Transition*, Cambridge: Cambridge University Press.

Tan, Gerald (1987), 'ASEAN Preferential Trading Arrangements: An Overview', in Sopiee Noordin et al. (eds), *ASEAN at the Crossroads*, Malaysia: Institute of Strategic and International Studies, pp. 63–9.

Tan, Gerald (1996), *ASEAN Economic Development and Cooperation*, Singapore: Times Academic Press.

Tan Kong Yam, M.H. Toh and L. Low (1992), 'ASEAN and Pacific Economic Cooperation', in K.S. Sandhu et al. (eds), *The ASEAN Reader*, Singapore: Institute of Southeast Asian Studies, pp. 311–320.

Tham Siew Yean (1995), 'Productivity, Growth and Development in Malaysia', 20th Federation of ASEAN Economic Association (FAEA) Conference, Singapore, 7–8 December.

Thambipillai, Pushpa (1995), 'The East ASEAN Growth Area: Political and Economic Environment', Presented at the EAGA Forum in conjunction with the EAGA EXPO, Bandar Seri Begawan, 2–3 November.

Thee Kian Wie (1991), 'The Surge of Asian NIC Investment into Indonesia', *Bulletin of Indonesian Economic Studies*, 27(3), pp. 55–88.

Todaro, Michael P. (1997), *Economic Development*, Sixth edition, New York: Addison-Wesley Publishing Company, Chapter 10.

Toh Mun Heng and Linda Low (eds) (1993), *Regional Cooperation and Growth Triangles in ASEAN*, Singapore: Times Academic Press.

Toh Mun Heng and Linda Low (1994), 'Capital Stock, Latent Resource and Total Factor Productivity in Singapore', paper presented at the Workshop on Measuring Productivity and Technological Progress, Faculty of Business Administration, National University of Singapore, August.

Tongzon, Jose (1986), 'Australian Trade Preferences for Developing Countries: Are Quotas Necessary?', *Economic Papers*, 5(3), 53–64.

Tongzon, J.L. and S. Ganesalingam (1994), 'An Evaluation of ASEAN

Port Performance and Efficiency', *Asian Economic Journal*, **8**(3), pp. 317–330.

Tongzon, J.L. and T.K. Loh (1995), 'Trade Liberalizaton and Growth: The ASEAN4 Experience', Singapore (unpublished typescript).

Triandis, H.C. (1971), 'Some Psychological Dimensions of Modernization', Proceedings of the 17th International Congress of Applied Psychology, Brussels, **2**, 56–75.

Triandis, H.C. (1973), 'Subjected Culture and Economic Development', *International Journal of Psychology*, **8**, 163–80.

Tsao, Yuan (1986), 'Sources of Growth Accounting for the Singapore Economy', in Lim Chong-Yah and Peter Lloyd (eds), *Resources and Growth in Singapore*, Singapore: Oxford University Press.

Tyler, W. (1981), 'Growth and Export Expansion in Developing Countries: Some Empirical Evidence', *Journal of Development Economics*, **9**, 121–30.

United Nations Economic and Social Commission for Asia and the Pacific, *Review and Analysis of Intraregional Trade Flows in Asia and the Pacific*, Note by the Secretariat, Steering Group of the Committee for Regional Economic Cooperation, Fifth Meeting, 29 August–1 September 1994, Kunming, China.

Viner, Jacob (1950), *The Customs Union Issue*, New York: Carnegie Endowment for International Peace.

Vyas, V.S. (1983), 'Asian Agriculture: Achievements and Challenges', *Asian Development Review*, **1**(2), 27–44.

Wade, Robert (1990), *Governing the Market: Economic Theory and Taiwan's Industrial Policies*, New Jersey: Princeton University Press.

Weber, M. (1904), *The Protestant Ethic and the Spirit of Capitalism*, translated by T. Parsons, 1930, London: Allen and Unwin.

Wolfensohn, James D. (1996), 'Emerging Trends in East Asia: New Directions in the World Bank's Partnership', Paper delivered at a meeting organized by the Institute of Policy Studies, Singapore, 10 May 1996.

Wong, C.M. (1987), 'ASEAN Cooperation in Tourism: Looking Back and Looking Forward', in S. Noordin et al. (eds), *ASEAN at the Crossroads*, Malaysia: Institute of Strategic and International Studies, pp. 372–93.

Wong Fot-chyi and Gan Wee-beng (1994), 'Total Factor Productivity Growth in the Singapore Manufacturing Industries During the 1980s', *Journal of Asian Economics,* **5**(2), 180–81.

Wong, J. (1979), *ASEAN Economies in Perspective*, Singapore: The McMillan Press, Chapter 4.

World Bank (1992), *Vietnam Restructuring Public Finance and Public*

Enterprises: An Economic Report, 15 April, Country Operations Division, Country Department I, East Asia and Pacific Region.

World Bank (1993a), *Historically Planned Economies: A Guide to the Data*, Washington, DC.

World Bank (1993b), *The East Asian Miracle: Economic Growth and Public Policy*, New York: Oxford University Press, Chapter 1.

World Bank (1994), *Vietnam Public Sector Management and Private Sector Incentives: An Economic Report*, 26 September, Country Operations Division, Country Department I, East Asia Pacific Region.

Yeung, Wai-chung (1997), 'The Globalisation of Ethnic Chinese Business Firms from Southeast Asia: Strategies, Processes and Competitive Advantage', Paper presented at the Chinese Business in Southeast Asia Conference, Kuala Lumpur, 23–25 June.

Yoshihara, K. (1988), *The Rise of Ersatz Capitalism in Southeast Asia*, New York: Oxford University Press, pp. 1–31.

Young, Alwyn (1992), 'A Tale of Two Cities: Factor Accumulation and Technical Change in Hong Kong and Singapore', in NBER *Macroeconomics Annual 1992*, no. 7, Stanley Fischer and Olivier Blanchard, Cambridge: MIT Press.

Young, Alwyn (1994a), 'The Tyranny of Numbers: Confronting the Statistical Realities of the East Asian Growth Experience', National Bureau of Economic Research Working Paper No. 4680, March.

Young, Alwyn (1994b), 'Lessons from the East Asian NICs: A Contrarian View', *European Economic Review*, 38.

Zarnowitz, V. (1985), 'Recent Work on Business Cycles in Historical Perspective: A Review of Theories and Evidence', *Journal of Economic Literature*, **23**, pp. 523–80.

Magazines and newspapers

Asiaweek, 12 January 1996, 'Future in Review', pp. 46–7.

Asiaweek, 19 January 1996, 'Vital Signs', p. 60.

Asiaweek, 12 July 1996, 'Bottom Line', p. 53.

Asiaweek, 4 October 1996, 'No Pain, No Gain', pp. 25–7.

Asiaweek, 24 January 1997, 'Class Struggle', pp. 22–3.

The Business Times Shipping Times, 6 January 1997, 'Manila Sets Up 6 Direct Shipping Routes in EAGA', p. 1.

The Economist, 11–17 February 1995, 'Asia, at your Service', pp. 59–60.

Far Eastern Economic Review, **153**(38), September 1991, 'Focus: Environment in Asia 1991', pp. 37–57.

Far Eastern Economic Review, 16 June 1994, 'Rewards of Liberalisation', pp. 48–50.

Myan View, 'Will Myanmar benefit from joining ASEAN', July 1997, pp. 1–3.

The Straits Times, 20 October 1990, 'Razaleigh Hits Out at Federal Gov't Over GT Plan', p. 23.

The Straits Times, 27 August 1992, 'ASEAN Will Remain Attractive Despite NAFTA, Says Nomura', p. 36.

The Straits Times, 1 October 1992, 'Republic's Trade Likely to Face Threat From Mexico, Says UOB', p. 44.

The Straits Times, 4 November 1992, 'Regional Trade Groupings: Building or Stumbling Blocks'.

The Straits Times, 9 December 1993, 'ASEAN Adopts Index to Monitor Air Pollution', p. 22.

The Straits Times, 11 December 1993, 'Ethnic Chinese Conglomerates Own 30 per cent of Indonesian Economy', p. 12.

The Straits Times, 12 December 1993, 'GATT Fever', pp. 7–8.

The Straits Times, 9 August 1994, 'Crucial 12 months for ASEAN as it embarks on new phase of diplomacy', p. 23.

The Straits Times, 4 September 1994, 'Open regionalism: Framework for Asia–Pacific economic ties', p. 34.

The Straits Times, 23 October 1994, 'ASEAN Agreement on Environment Protection', p. 22.

The Straits Times, 7 March 1995, 'ADB Takes Steps to Preserve Region's Forests', p. 15.

The Straits Times, 25 March 1995, 'PM: Singapore Must Nurture New Breed of MNCs', p. 1.

The Straits Times, 4 August 1995, 'Growth Triangle Boosts Investments in Johor to S$8.5b', p. 21.

The Straits Times, 9 September 1995, 'ASEAN Ministers Give Pledge On Services' (Tan Kim Song), p. 1.

The Straits Times, 23 September 1995, 'Europe, Asia Can Become True Partners', p. 1.

The Straits Times, 5 March 1996, 'Jakarta announces package aimed at boosting exports'.

The Straits Times, 1 August 1996, 'The $850m Traffic Snarls', p. 10.

The Straits Times, 16 August 1996, 'TDB Office in KL will Provide New Push for Economic Ties', p. 46.

The Straits Times, 31 August 1996, 'Could Asian Economies Go the Way of Mexico?', p. 37.

The Straits Times, 12 September 1996, 'Philippine Economy Moving Towards Path of Sustainable Growth', p. 41.

The Straits Times, 5 October 1996, 'Vietnam Mulls Over Changes to Tax, Foreign Investment Laws', p. 45.

The Straits Times, 9 October 1996, 'New Balance in World Order with Maturing of East Asian Economies', p. 38.

The Straits Times, 7 January 1997, 'Indonesia Considers Tax Breaks for Strategic Industries', p. 38.

The Straits Times, 24 January 1997, 'Singapore is KL's Top Foreign Investor', p. 80.

The Straits Times, 18 March 1997, 'Karimun Launch Reaffirms Pledge to Work for Mutual Benefits', p. 20.

The Sunday Times, 23 August 1992, 'The Role of State-owned Enterprises', p. 6.

The Sunday Times, 17 September 1995, 'Spreading the Gains of Growth'.

The Sunday Times, 24 September 1995, 'The Role of Government in the East Asian Miracle', pp. 4–5.

The Sunday Times, 31 March 1996, 'How Fair Are the Country's Trade Practices: An Interview with Trade and Industry Minister Ariwibowo', p. 4.

The Sunday Times, 5 January 1997, 'Philippine Economy Likely to Continue Surge', p. 15.

Time, 17 January 1994, 'Growing by Leaps-Triangle', pp. 26–8.

Statistical sources

AFTA Reader, Jakarta: ASEAN Secretariat (various issues).

ASEAN Agricultural Development Planning Centre (1991), *ASEAN Statistical Yearbook on Food, Agriculture and Forestry: 1980–1990*, Bangkok, Thailand.

Asian Development Bank (ADB) (1995 and 1996), *Key Indicators of Developing Asian and Pacific Countries*.

Asian Development Bank (ADB), *Asian Development Outlook* (various issues).

Brunei Ministry of Finance (1993), *Brunei Darussalam Statistical Yearbook*.

Brunei Statistics Division, *Brunei Darussalam Key Indicators* (various issues).

ICEF–MIF Merger Congress, *World Industry Trends*, 22 November 1995, Washington, DC, USA.

International Monetary Fund, *Direction of Trade Statistics Yearbook* (various issues).

International Monetary Fund, *International Financial Statistics* (various issues).

Malaysian Ministry of International Trade and Industry, *International Trade and Industry Report* (1994).

Singapore Department of Statistics, *Economic Survey of Singapore* (various issues).

United Nations Conference on Trade and Development, *Handbook of International Trade and Development Statistics* (various issues).

United Nations Conference on Trade and Development, *World Investment Report* (various issues).

Vietnam Jewel of Asia (1993).

Vietnam's General Statistical Office, Statistical Yearbook (various issues).

World Bank, *World Development Report* (various issues).

World Economic Forum, *The World Competitiveness Report* (1992; 1994 and 1995).

World Trade Organization, Regionalism and The World Trading System (1995).

Index